Brief Strategic Family Therapy

Brief Strategic Family Therapy

José Szapocznik and Olga E. Hervis

AMERICAN PSYCHOLOGICAL ASSOCIATION
Washington, DC

Published by
American Psychological Association
750 First Street, NE
Washington, DC 20002
https://www.apa.org

Order Department
https://www.apa.org/pubs/books
order@apa.org

In the U.K., Europe, Africa, and the Middle East, copies may be ordered from Eurospan
https://www.eurospanbookstore.com/apa
info@eurospangroup.com

Typeset in Meridien and Ortodoxa by Circle Graphics, Inc., Reisterstown, MD

Printer: Sheridan Books, Chelsea, MI
Cover Designer: Gwen J. Grafft, Minneapolis, MN

Library of Congress Cataloging-in-Publication Data

Names: Szapocznik, José, author. | Hervis, Olga E., author.
Title: Brief strategic family therapy / José Szapocznik and Olga E. Hervis.
Description: Washington, DC : American Psychological Association, [2020] |
  Includes bibliographical references and index.
Identifiers: LCCN 2019033777 (print) | LCCN 2019033778 (ebook) |
  ISBN 9781433831706 (paperback) | ISBN 9781433831713 (ebook)
Subjects: LCSH: Family psychotherapy.
Classification: LCC RC488.5 .S982 2020 (print) | LCC RC488.5 (ebook) |
  DDC 616.89/156—dc23
LC record available at https://lccn.loc.gov/2019033777
LC ebook record available at https://lccn.loc.gov/2019033778

http://dx.doi.org/10.1037/0000169-000

Printed in the United States of America

10 9 8 7 6 5 4 3 2 1

Dedicated to our one true mentor,
Mercedes Arca Scopetta, PhD

CONTENTS

FOREWORD

I first met José Szapocznik and Olga Hervis when I was invited to consult with their team at the University of Miami in the early 1990s. Our common interest in, and commitment to, treating children, adolescents, and families who presented with behavioral problems and substance abuse led us to reach a similar conclusion: Family therapy was the most powerful approach to address the challenges faced by this population. In the course of our work together, we discovered that we also shared similar experiences early in our careers. In 1974, I did my internship in family therapy at the Philadelphia Child Guidance Clinic where I had the great fortune of being trained and mentored by two giants in our field, Salvador Minuchin in structural family therapy and Jay Haley in strategic family therapy. Szapocznik and Hervis had received training by them as well, and aspects of the work of these eminent scholars have been incorporated into the approach described in this book.

The trailblazing authors of this book are responsible for the development of Brief Strategic Family Therapy® (BSFT®), an evidence-based family therapy approach that was first used with Hispanic families. At the time I was invited to consult, they had already expanded their work to include African American and other ethnic minority youth and families. In recent years, research has continually demonstrated that BSFT is equally effective when treating families from a wide range of ethnic, racial, and socioeconomic backgrounds and geographic areas.

One aspect of BSFT that has remained consistent over the years has been its strength-based focus. The authors' pioneering approach was designed to access the strength and underlying love that exists within families who are in pain and struggling with real-world problems. In the preface, these authors make a statement that encapsulates this important premise of their approach: "Families change when the love that is trapped behind the anger is allowed to flourish." This positive focus often facilitates the engagement of families who might be wary of other treatment approaches. It is rare in the mental health field to find an evidence-based treatment that incorporates this emphasis on uncovering the underlying love in families so explicitly within its model. It is this special combination of clear family systems theory, solid evidence-based research, an emphasis on strengths, cultural competency and sensitivity, and the compassion that allows for the engagement of families that distinguishes BSFT from other treatment approaches.

Within the BSFT model, the authors provide clear descriptions of the techniques of joining and engagement and the process of overcoming the challenges of joining. They provide excellent examples of assessing family functioning, diagnosing the patterns of interactions, and the family process. Maintaining a viable therapeutic system, developing enactments, reframing, restructuring the family, and other BSFT interventions are discussed in detail. Two chapters, in particular, will be relevant and helpful to experienced clinicians as well as those starting careers in family therapy: identifying pitfalls to avoid when doing BSFT and how to engage reluctant families and family members in treatment.

Finally, this book discusses the various settings in which BSFT can be used, including health and mental health clinics, substance abuse treatment programs for youth, social service agencies, private practices, homes, schools, and churches. In addition, given the complexity of family structures in contemporary times, different family compositions, such as two-parent, single-parent, and blended families are discussed, as well as ways in which to access extended family support. One section that will be particularly valuable for all clinicians in every stage of their careers discusses families in which domestic violence and child sexual abuse are encountered and identifies three characteristics common to these families: (a) isolation, (b) poor boundaries within the family, and (c) family secrets.

This impressive book's comprehensive exploration of BSFT will make an important contribution to the field of family therapy and will be an essential resource for beginning clinicians as well as experienced family therapists. As a professor in a major university, teaching family therapy courses, this book will become a significant textbook in all my classes. In addition, I strongly recommend this book to all my colleagues who are teaching, training, and supervising the next generation of family therapists in all mental health fields, including marriage and family therapy, psychology, social work, and counseling programs.

—Nancy Boyd-Franklin, PhD
Distinguished Professor, Rutgers University
Graduate School of Applied and Professional Psychology
Piscataway, NJ

PREFACE

It is as if I were trapped with a stinking skunk in a room, and we are chained to each other, and we each have a part of the key that keeps us trapped. Our impulse is to pull away from each other, but when we pull away from each other, we move away from finding a solution to our captivity. We must change our relationship and come together to put the parts of the key together to release us both.

This story is a way of illustrating for the reader that systems are made of interdependent parts, and solutions to their problems are best developed when all the parts (family members) collaborate. We would like to tell you how we arrived at this conclusion.

We, the authors, and our mentor, Mercedes Arca Scopetta, come from the Hispanic culture that places families at the center of our world. We came together in 1974, at a time when the art of family therapy was exploding and many family therapy schools were emerging. When we opened our clinic in the Little Havana neighborhood of Miami, Florida, we recognized that a family focus was essential. We knew that in our Latin population, even when the child is going to have a tooth extracted, the whole family shows up. We then actively sought to identify among the various family therapy schools the one that was most congruent with our cultural values and customs. After visiting many masters in family therapy, we resonated with the work of Salvador Minuchin at the Philadelphia Child Guidance Clinic and that of his other Hispanic colleagues, also family therapy leaders, including Braulio Montalvo and Harry Aponte.

In structural family therapy, we found an approach that was consistent with what we had learned were the cultural characteristics of our population. First and foremost, families were the center of the world for our population. Our families came in crisis, were present oriented, and had an urgency for problem resolution. Our research also showed that they valued a directive therapist who could assume leadership in helping them solve their problems. In structural family therapy, we found an approach consistent with these values and expectations, with a therapist who takes charge, who works in the present to help families solve their "now" problems. Structural family therapy's focus on hierarchy was also most helpful in providing us with an understanding of the intergenerational and intercultural conflicts that occurred in acculturating families in which youth acculturated to individualist values more quickly than their parents. And most important, it provided us with a framework on which to build our Brief Strategic Family Therapy® (BSFT®) model. At the time when we were studying structural family therapy, Jay Hayley joined the staff of the Philadelphia Child Guidance Clinic. Hayley's contributions to the group's work helped us recognize that a strategic approach that was problem focused and brief was a great fit for our families who wanted quick solutions and did not have the orientation to stay in therapy long. They wanted their problems fixed quickly and to go on their way.

Even before we had developed BSFT, we began our program of research, initially studying the population and then looking at adaptations to our therapy that were needed to serve our families better (Szapocznik, Foote, Perez-Vidal, Hervis, & Kurtines, 1985; Szapocznik, Kurtines, Foote, Perez-Vidal, & Hervis, 1986; Szapocznik, Rio, et al., 1986; Szapocznik, Santisteban, et al., 1989; Szapocznik, Scopetta, Aranalde, & Kurtines, 1978; Szapocznik, Scopetta, & King, 1978; Szapocznik, Scopetta, Kurtines, & Aranalde, 1978). Shortly after developing our first version of BSFT, we began efficacy trials to evaluate outcomes. After many studies (e.g., Santisteban et al., 2003; Szapocznik, Rio, et al., 1989) that led to the refinement of BSFT and the development of additional modules such as BSFT Engagement (Coatsworth, Santisteban, McBride, & Szapocznik, 2001; Robbins, Feaster, Horigian, Rohrbaugh, et al., 2011; Santisteban et al., 1996; Szapocznik et al., 1988) and the inclusion of other racial and ethnic and cultural groups, we were ready for an effectiveness study. In the first decade of the 21st century, we conducted a national multisite study with a multiracial and ethnic population (Horigian et al., 2015; Robbins, Feaster, Horigian, Rohrbaugh, et al., 2011; Robbins et al., 2009).

TO OUR READERS

This book is written for clinicians who provide services to families of children between the ages of 6 and 18 who present with behavioral or emotional problems. This includes family therapists and their supervisors, those in private practice and in community service agencies. The book will also be of interest to persons responsible for making programmatic decisions for children and adolescent service programs, including family service agencies, mental health clinics, departments of welfare, juvenile justice diversion programs, school counseling departments, and substance use treatment clinics. BSFT can be delivered in various settings, including homes, office, schools, and other community settings. It has been used with youth in rural, urban, and suburban communities in a range of service settings such as psychiatric or substance abuse inpatient and outpatient settings, as well as welfare, juvenile justice, mental health, and children service systems.

Standing on the lessons we have learned over the past 40 years, we feel we have much to share with our readers. Above all, however, we want to share a bottom-line lesson: BSFT is a love therapy. Families change when the love that is trapped behind the anger is allowed to flourish. Our job as BSFT therapists is to transform family interactions from anger to love, from negative to positive, from conflictive to collaborative, and from habitual to proactive.

We offer in this book a level of instruction about BSFT that we think will help currently practicing clinicians as well as trainees looking to enter clinical fields that involve working with families. This manual represents over 40 years of work, funded mostly by the National Institutes of Health, including the National Institute on Drug Abuse, the National Institute on Alcohol Abuse and Alcoholism, and the National Institute of Mental Health. The work was also funded by the Substance Abuse and Mental Health Services Administration through the Center for Substance Abuse Treatment and the Center for Substance Abuse Prevention.

ACKNOWLEDGMENTS

The initial inspiration for the development of BSFT we owe to Mercedes Arca Scopetta, PhD. Although the model stands on the shoulders of many giants in the family therapy field, we owe our greatest debt to Salvador Minuchin, MD; Jay Haley, MA; and Marianne Walters, MSW. Over the years, many professionals have contributed their effort, imagination, and clinical skills to the development of the intervention and many others to its evaluation. We would like to thank especially Angel Perez-Vidal, PsyD; Daniel Santisteban, PhD; and Michael Robbins, PhD.

The largest debt of gratitude we owe is to the tens of thousands of families who participated in our development efforts, efficacy studies, and research-to-practice activities. The families were our ultimate teachers, and our outcomes in working with them were the ultimate judges of the usefulness of the work.

Brief Strategic Family Therapy

Introduction

Are you searching for an approach that will make you more effective in treating families of children and adolescents between the ages of 6 and 18 who present with behavioral and emotional problems? An approach that helps families regain their parental competence and leadership and that brings love, nurturance, and caring back to families who sorely need it? An approach that defines families functionally to respect the broad diversity of family cultures and compositions?

Forty-five years ago, we were looking for such an approach, and we spent the intervening 4 decades developing a model for clinicians working with such families. Our journey began in 1974 when parents came to our clinic not knowing how to help their teens who were out of control—teens who were delinquent, depressed, using drugs, constantly fighting with their parents, uninterested in school, and hanging out with other troubled teens. Their parents felt they had run out of options.

These families were in crisis and thus had a sense of urgency about getting a resolution to their troubles. Feeling they had no other options, they were looking for therapists who would take charge and give them relief. These parents had lost their ability to manage and guide their children. They were looking for a treatment that would eliminate the problems at home quickly and empower them to manage and guide their youth to become productive members of society. This is what the parents wanted. As for the teens, they simply wanted to "get their parents off their backs."

http://dx.doi.org/10.1037/0000169-001

Brief Strategic Family Therapy, by J. Szapocznik and O. E. Hervis

When we started our clinical work in 1974, we recognized the powerful influences of environment, and the family, in particular, on child and adolescent behavior. Much research has documented the role that families play as risk and protective factors for child and adolescent outcomes (Bögels & Brechman-Toussaint, 2006; Donovan, 2004; Hawkins, Catalano, & Miller, 1992; McComb & Sabiston, 2010; Morris, Silk, Steinberg, Myers, & Robinson, 2007; Pinquart, 2017; Repetti, Taylor, & Seeman, 2002; O. S. Schwartz, Sheeber, Dudgeon, & Allen, 2012; Wight, Williamson, & Henderson, 2006). Since then, a body of research in the field of epigenetics has revealed how environment "gets under the skin" of adolescents through the continuous interplay between biology and environment (National Academies of Sciences, Engineering, and Medicine, 2019). Although many laypersons believe that the impact of heredity is unchangeable, research into gene–environment interactions and epigenetics shows that the way heredity is expressed in behavior depends dramatically on environmental influences (Halfon, Larson, Lew, Tullis, & Russ, 2014), of which the family is the most impactful (Fraga, Ballestar, Paz, Ropero, & Setien, 2005). It follows that positive experiences in the family will produce flourishing child and adolescent development, whereas adverse experiences in the family lead to at-risk or poor development. According to the National Academies of Sciences, Engineering, and Medicine (2019) recent consensus report on adolescence, intervention in the present can remedy past adverse experiences. We thus propose that changing families' patterns of interaction from conflictive to collaborative and from angry to loving in the present will have a positive impact on the development of its children in the future.

WHAT IS BRIEF STRATEGIC FAMILY THERAPY?

To address this challenge, we decided to develop a flexible approach that can be adapted to a broad range of family situations in a variety of service settings (as mentioned in the Preface). We started by combining two important schools of family therapy: the structural, led by Salvador Minuchin, and the strategic, learned from Jay Haley. The therapy we developed by combining these two approaches, Brief Strategic Family Therapy® (BSFT®), is brief, problem focused, and practical. We incorporated the structural model because our families were overwhelmed with multiple problems, and one of the extraordinary features of structural family therapy is that it provided us with a formula for focusing not on each separate problem but on the ways that the family organizes itself in managing the lives of its members. Although problems are many, the interactional patterns that give rise to and maintain these problems are few. Among these few, to create a brief intervention, we focused on changing only those interactional patterns that were directly related to the youth's presenting symptoms. That made our work as therapists manageable. When we focused on family interactional patterns, we were clear on what we needed to change to correct the families' ways of managing their multiple problems. By changing the family's interactional patterns, we created self-sustaining changes in the lasting family environment of the child or adolescent. The "treatment environment" is thus built into the child's daily life.

BSFT builds on universal principles across cultures, such as the importance of the family and the focus on relational health (Kaslow, 1996; Walsh, 2012; Wynne, 1984) as reflected in patterns of interactions. In all cultures, the family's job is to be supportive and encouraging of each family member's well-being as well as to raise children to be productive members of their particular culture or society. However, cultures differ in the manner in which they accomplish these tasks. For example, regardless of culture, patterns of interactions occur in all families, although specific family patterns are more likely in some cultures than others (Herz & Gullone, 1999; Poasa, Mallinckrodt, & Suzuki, 2000; Shearman & Dumlao, 2008). BSFT's focus is to identify those patterns of interactions that are creating problems for the family, fully understanding the cultural tradition in which these patterns of interactions occur. The therapy itself is also conducted in a way that takes into consideration each family's cultural style and tradition. In this book, we use clinical vignettes to demonstrate the cross-cultural applicability of BSFT.

An Evidence-Based Intervention

BSFT is an evidence-based intervention that has been extensively evaluated for more than 45 years and is efficacious in the treatment of children and adolescents with internalizing and externalizing problems. With adolescents, much of the work has focused on acting-out behaviors that include alcohol or drug misuse, delinquency, associations with antisocial peers, and impaired family functioning.

BSFT is a brief intervention that can be implemented in approximately 12 to 16 sessions. The number of sessions depends on the severity of the presenting problem and the number of family members with problems that intersect with the youth's presenting complaint.

A Strengths-Based Approach

BSFT is the ultimate strengths based therapy. BSFT uses strengths to transform problematic family behaviors into constructive interactions. For example, when a family presents with pain, we help the family to uncover the concern, caring, and love that is behind the pain. When families fight, we talk about the strong connections among family members. When a mother is caring toward one child and not another, we help the mother to own her ability for caring and transfer it to her interactions with all her children. When a father is angry at his son, we redefine and relabel the anger as caring for the son's future and encourage the father to tell his son about his caring: "Your son knows you are angry, but tell him the other story about what is behind your anger because you care for him. Tell him the ways you care for him, the reasons you care for him, and the hopes you have for him." Thus, BSFT is an optimistic and strengths-based approach. In real time, we transform negative interactions into positive ones.

We are able to do this because we know that behind the negative interactions, there are bonds of love. We remind the reader of Nobel laureate Elie Wiesel's (1986) words: "The opposite of love is not hate, but indifference" (p. 68). As long as family members are fighting with each other, they are powerfully connected and far from indifferent. In BSFT, we give family members the opportunity to change their interactions in ways that free them to move toward happiness. We believe that all families have the potential to be caring, and all people have an inherent desire to be happy but may not know how to achieve happiness. In BSFT, we help families remove impediments to happiness and mental health such as fear, anger, insecurity, distrust, lack of self-efficacy, and inexperience, among others. In the upcoming chapters, we unpack the theory and research that supports our experience and deeply held beliefs about love and anger.

The James family came to therapy because the teenage granddaughter was disregarding curfew, failing her classes, and fighting with her grandmother. She was arrested and referred for therapy by her probation officer. When the session opened, Grandma immediately told her granddaughter that she was a disgrace who brought her nothing but sorrow. When the therapist asked the granddaughter to respond to her grandmother, the granddaughter said, "You don't even care that I lost my mother." It was clear to the therapist that no one was listening to her pain. The task of the therapist was to help Grandma attend to her granddaughter's pain.

For Grandma to be able to do this, the therapist had to help her view her granddaughter as someone in pain. Grandma had a long list of complaints about her granddaughter. With anger and disdain, she said to her granddaughter, "I am sick of you. You only bring me sorrow. I am too old to be saddled with raising you." The therapist told Grandma, "I hear your pain and frustration. You are two women in profound pain. You are both in great pain because you lost your daughter, and she lost her mom [cognition and affect]. Grandma, tell your granddaughter about what you are going through, how you miss your daughter [behavior]." After Grandma did so, the therapist was able to ask the granddaughter to speak about how much she missed her mom. The therapist highlighted the granddaughter's suffering and said to Grandma, "Grandma, you are more experienced [cognition]; you, unfortunately, have lost loved ones before [affect]. What can you tell your granddaughter to help her with her loss [behavior]?"

In this example, it is apparent that the therapy not only builds on strengths but also works in the here and now to change the way grandma and granddaughter interact and behave with each other in the moment. The focus of the therapy is to change how family members behave toward each other. In this case, we used cognitive restructuring (Beck, 2011) to change the way family members perceive each other, which changes the affect between them, thus facilitating a new way for them to interact. Ultimately, the job of BSFT is to rebond family members with each other in a loving and mutually caring relationship.

Another aspect of BSFT that reveals its strength-based foundation is our diagnostic approach. Whereas most diagnostic approaches in the health and mental health fields, such as the *International Statistical Classification of Diseases and Related Health Problems* (10th rev.; World Health Organization, 1992) and the *Diagnostic and Statistical Manual of Mental Disorders* (fifth ed.; American Psychiatric Association, 2013), focus on disorders, BSFT diagnoses both adaptive and maladaptive interactions. BSFT uses adaptive interactions or strengths to support the therapist's efforts to transform maladaptive interactions.

WHAT ARE THE GOALS OF BRIEF STRATEGIC FAMILY THERAPY?

BSFT has three major goals:

- to eliminate the presenting problem or to reduce it to where the behavior is no longer problematic for the family;

- to increase mastery and competence, where *mastery* is defined as the skill level family members need to competently manage family life; and

- to improve family functioning by correcting interactional patterns in ways that allow the family to reduce chronic negativity resulting from unresolved conflicts, increase the family members' sense of belonging and cohesion, and improve the family members' ability to cooperate in parenting and other aspects of family life.

Ultimately, the goal of BSFT is to transform interactions from conflictive to collaborative, from anger to love, from negative to positive, and from habitual to proactive. Families change because the love that is trapped behind the anger is allowed to flourish.

WHAT ARE SOME KEY COMPONENTS OF BRIEF STRATEGIC FAMILY THERAPY?

Several aspects that are key to understanding BSFT we explain in forthcoming chapters. Here, we review some key aspects of BSFT to give the reader a sample of the tools available to a BSFT therapist, including a focus on family interaction patterns; identifying who the family comprises; the systemic diagnostic approach; the role of strategy; congruency in changing affect, cognition, and behavior; and BSFT Engagement.

A Focus on Family Interactional Patterns

Perhaps the single most important lesson we would like our readers to take away from our work is to focus on how families interact and not on what they interact about. This is an important theoretical foundation of BSFT with many practical applications. A corollary of this lesson is that if the therapist focuses on the family's content and the many problems they enumerate, the therapist will be unable to help the family, just as the family is unable to help itself because it becomes overwhelmed by its many content issues. Whether the family talks about their kid's drug use or what they will have for lunch, the way family members interact with each other does not change.

For example, Dad says that he wants to have steak for lunch, and Mother says that she wants fish. The challenge is not in that they want different foods but in how they go about negotiating their differences (or fail) to come to an agreement. During the argument about what to eat, Mother may say to Father, "You never go along with me." What Mother has done with that statement is to change the topic of conversation from *what are we going to eat* to *what is our personal relationship*. When a family member changes the topic of conversation, the family is unable to come to an agreement on the original topic. Then, the family ends the discussion frustrated and angry and with no resolution to what to eat on which they can all agree.

This same pattern of how the parents interact repeats itself regardless of the topic of conversation, such as agreeing on a curfew for their drug-using youth. In BSFT, we let families resolve their own content problems, while we as therapists stay focused on helping them to improve how they go about solving their problems. The therapist's job in this example is to help the parents learn to resolve their differences of opinion by staying focused on the topic of discussion.

In BSFT, our job as therapists is to help family members interact (i.e., to behave with one another) in ways that are adaptive and result in symptom elimination. (We unpack these later in the book).

Identifying Who the Family Comprises

We consider the family to include all the individuals who are functioning in family roles that involve the identified patient (Pequegnat & Szapocznik, 2000). For this reason, we clarify that when we use terms such as *mom* and *dad* in BSFT, we are always referring to the persons who function in these roles. In 21st-century America, families come in many shapes and sizes. Many families are not made up of biological fathers, mothers, and children. Rather, families include a variety of persons who may function in specific roles, including stepparents, stepchildren, grandparents, aunts, cousins, and so forth. In some cultures, godparents can have an important relational role in the family as well. Among Latinxs, for example, the godmother is referred to as *comadre* or comother to the child's mother. In BSFT, we are always referring to the roles people play when we use terms such as *mom* and *dad*.

When we work with the families of children and adolescents, we define *family* as all the individuals who are significant contributors to the everyday life of the identified problem youth. These might include those persons who live under the same roof but excludes those who are transient—for example, an aunt or a friend who frequently "crashes" at the house. We include, however, other persons not living in the same household as the child who contribute to parenting and sibling functions—such as might occur with a remarried father and stepsiblings or a grandma who cares for the children until the single parent comes home from work. In our view, all these individuals who interact on an ongoing basis with the identified problem youth functionally compose the family and must be involved in therapy. All family members may not have to come to all the sessions, but we must bring them to the first session to enable us to diagnose how the family system functions with all the parts of the puzzle present. Thereafter, some may be excluded from some sessions, depending on the treatment plan.

Systemic Diagnosis

BSFT is a diagnostically driven therapy with a focus on interactional patterns. In BSFT, interactional patterns are what gets diagnosed and treated. This means that individuals are not diagnosed; rather, family interactional patterns are diagnosed. These are not static labels but dynamic descriptions of the repetitive patterns of interactions that occur among family members—that is, how family members behave with each other in interlinked sequences of behaviors that repeat over time. These patterns, unfortunately, are fairly rigid in families that make up our clinical population, and this is one of the reasons they are relatively easy to diagnose through any content that the family may bring up. In support of our therapeutic focus on interactional patterns, these diagnoses describe how the family interacts. The treatment, then, is simply to change the interactional patterns that have been identified and that are linked to the presenting problem. Our systemic diagnoses contribute to BSFT's brevity because treatment is fully guided by the diagnosis. The diagnosis provides a clear road map for the therapist to design specific treatment plans and allows the therapist to assess progress or the lack thereof. Moreover, because interactions are few (whereas contents are many), treatment has a small number of interactional targets.

When we diagnose family interactions, we choose to use the terms *adaptive* and *maladaptive* to connote that in BSFT, we view interactional patterns as malleable. That is, interactional patterns change as a function of therapy. We choose not to use terms such as *functional* or *healthy* and *dysfunctional* or *unhealthy* because these terms are often viewed more statically. A static view of interactional patterns is inconsistent with our philosophy and experience that family interactions can be changed, and in fact, changing them is the bread and butter of our work.

Strategy as a Theoretical Foundation

There are three major aspects to strategy in BSFT: It is planned, problem focused, and practical. The treatment plan that is designed to treat the maladaptive interactions diagnosed for each specific family is *planned*, which means that from session to session, therapy is planned to achieve the overall changes required to overcome each specific family's maladaptive interactions. Second, strategy also demands that plans are specifically designed to be *problem focused*, which means that we do not attempt to treat all maladaptive aspects of the family but only those that are directly related to the presenting symptom. In focusing on the problem or symptoms that bring the family into treatment, we typically have to treat a range of interactions that are linked to the presenting problem. For example, parents' ability to collaborate is required for them to parent effectively. This is intimately related to the couple's interactions, which have to be corrected to improve their collaborative parenting activities. The third aspect of strategy is that BSFT is *practical*, which means that for each specific family, treatment is planned to be most effective given that family's culture and idiosyncrasies. Practicality requires us to customize the therapy for each family. For example, if two families are both diagnosed as having an imbalance in the parental subsystem, and in one family, Dad has more power than Mom, we thus need to empower Mom, whereas in another family, Mom may have more power than Dad, and thus we need to empower Dad. In doing this, we have to carefully consider clinical, cultural, and other contextual realities of the family.

Congruency in Changing Affect, Cognition, and Behavior

In the years that we spent developing and refining BSFT, in addition to addressing behavior, we learned that achieving long-lasting change depends on a dance that includes cognition, affect, and behavior (Beck, 2011; Greenberg & Safran, 1987; Strümpfel & Goldman, 2002). For family members to behave differently, changes in cognitions and affect must always accompany behavior in a manner that makes the new behavior syntonic with the way family members are thinking and feeling at the time they behave in new and more adaptive ways.

Brief Strategic Family Therapy Engagement

All of this is well and fine when families come to therapy, but what if they do not? Early on, we learned that bringing families of troubled—and, in particular, acting-out—adolescents into treatment was hugely challenging. We also learned that many community agencies around the country had the same challenge. Thus, in the 1980s, we set out to understand what makes it so difficult to bring families into therapy, particularly when families members are in conflict with each other.

To address this challenge, we developed BSFT Engagement. Using what we had learned in building BSFT, we recognized that the kinds of family interactions that resulted in the presenting problem were identical to the interactions that resulted in the symptom of "resistance" to treatment. Families, in fact, are very consistent. Families have overlearned patterns of interactions that repeat themselves in all the content issues the family has to navigate in life. If family members have a set way in which they sit at the dinner table, which is inviolable, then other habits are similarly ingrained, and it is that consistency in the way family members behave with each other that becomes central to how we both diagnose and treat the family system. Hence, in BSFT Engagement, our first interaction with a family member who calls for help is directed at diagnosing whether the family's patterns of interactions will interfere with the family's ability to become involved in therapy as a whole family. We discuss BSFT Engagement in detail in Chapter 7.

Ms. Roura was referred by her son's probation officer to BSFT. When she called for an appointment, the therapist validated Ms. Roura's eagerness to help her son (this is part of what we describe later as *joining*), expressed the importance of the whole family coming to the first session, and explored and verified which members of the family are or should be involved in the son's life and whether she could foresee any impediments to any family member attending the first therapy session. The therapist emphasized the importance of each family member's participation and explained that the treatment can only be effective with everyone involved, and though it was possible that not everyone would have to come to every session, everyone did have to come to the first session: "Is it going to be OK with everyone to come to the first session?" Only with Ms. Roura's reassurance would the therapist go on to make the appointment, ending with an encouraging and motivational comment such as, "I am looking forward to working with you and your family. You will see that by working together, we will help your son."

If Ms. Roura indicated she expected that some family member(s) would be unlikely to want to or be unable to attend or that she did not want a specific family member to be involved or expressed hesitation in involving any family member, this is when the therapist would implement the BSFT Engagement model.

HOW DO FAMILIES TYPICALLY PRESENT FOR BRIEF STRATEGIC FAMILY THERAPY?

In our experience, a family typically brings a child or adolescent to treatment asking the agency "to fix him (or her)." If we look beyond the youngster, we readily see that the family is in turmoil. Emotions such as anger, guilt, pity, hopelessness, and despair are running rampant. Communication lines have collapsed. The family approaches the agency out of desperation and perhaps because it was ordered to do so by, for instance, the juvenile justice, welfare, or school system.

A family comes into the agency asking that changes be made because they are in pain. They typically demand that the youngster—the one the family views as responsible for inflicting all this pain—be cured. Having decided that this young person is the one with the problem, they ask the agency staff to "fix him, make him stop, or just send him somewhere for a long time and send him back when he is fixed."

Adolescents often present with more than one problem. Research has shown that many adolescent behavior problems co-occur (Donovan & Jessor, 1985; Donovan, Jessor, & Costa, 1988, 1991; Kazdin, 1992). Research has also suggested that families, in particular, play an important role in preventing, giving rise to, and maintaining the adolescent's problem behaviors (Coatsworth et al., 2002; Donovan, 2004; Hawkins et al., 1992; McComb & Sabiston, 2010; Pinquart, 2017; Stone, Becker, Huber, & Catalano, 2012; Szapocznik & Coatsworth, 1999; Wight et al., 2006). Some of the family interactional problems that have been identified as linked to adolescent acting out include

- parental under- or overinvolvement,
- parental over- or undercontrol,
- poor quality of parent–child communication,
- lack of clear rules and consequences,
- lack of consistency in the application of rules and consequences,
- inadequate supervision or monitoring of peer activities,
- poor parent–child bonding,
- poor family cohesiveness,
- lack of nurturance and guidance, and
- high negativity.

Many of these interactional patterns are also found in internalizing youth (Bögels & Brechman-Toussaint, 2006; Morris et al., 2007; Repetti et al., 2002; O. S. Schwartz et al., 2012). Because these family interactional problems are an integral part of the profile of internalizing and externalizing youth and because many of these family problems have been linked to the initiation and maintenance of youth symptoms, it is necessary to correct the family interactions to achieve a family context that discourages self-defeating symptoms and promotes the youth's positive development. BSFT targets all the family problems listed earlier.

THIS BOOK

This book introduces therapists to concepts needed to understand the family as an organism or system that may show symptoms in one of its members. The book describes strategies for gaining entry into families, assessing and diagnosing maladaptive patterns of family interactions, and changing patterns of family interactions from maladaptive into adaptive. The book also presents our strategies for engaging families whose members are reluctant to become involved in family therapy.

In Chapter 1, we discuss the basic theoretical concepts of BSFT. Chapter 2 explains how to join the family in such a way as to create an effective collaborative therapeutic system. Chapter 3 presents the BSFT systemic (relational) diagnostic approach, whereas Chapter 4 explains how to apply it clinically.

Chapters 1 and 2 each conclude with a section called Advice for Therapists, which gives practical pointers or indicates a key skill for prospective BSFT therapists to learn. From Chapter 3 to the end, all material is geared toward practical application; thus, our specific advice is incorporated within the body of the chapters.

Chapter 5 describes how to change the maladaptive patterns of family interactions that are associated with the youth's presenting problems. Through this process, maladaptive interactions are restructured into adaptive interactions. Chapter 6 discusses the kinds of pitfalls that prevent therapists from being successful in correcting maladaptive interactions. Chapter 7 provides a detailed discussion of how to engage families when some members are reluctant to become involved in family therapy. Chapter 8 discusses the application of BSFT to different practice settings, family compositions, and aggravating family circumstances. Finally, Chapter 9 presents an extended case vignette to provide an additional opportunity for readers to consolidate the lessons from the book and mentally rehearse how they might apply BSFT principles in their practice. In all case material we present in this book, we have taken steps to conceal individuals' identities and the details of their family situation to protect their privacy.

BSFT is manualized in this book with well-specified theory and intervention techniques. However, it requires the ability to use clinical judgment in its implementation. Clinical creativity and flexibility are needed to implement BSFT in an effective manner, so for readers who are trainees or early-career practitioners, we recommend undergoing a training program before offering BSFT in your practice.

1

Basic Concepts of Brief Strategic Family Therapy

In this chapter, we describe the basic principles and theoretical concepts that provide the foundation of Brief Strategic Family Therapy® (BSFT®). Before presenting these, we discuss our philosophy of human behavior and human behavioral change.

First and foremost, we believe that the family is the center of a child's world. Although we recognize that contextual social systems influence the child's well-being, we consider the family as the single most important influence in a child's life.

Second, we believe the definition of a family that functions adaptively is one that consistently provides the conditions needed for every person to be the best they can be while adjusting to changing circumstances. However, a family functions maladaptively when at least one of its members develops behavioral or affective symptoms as a way for the family system as a whole to remain unchanged. Obviously, there is a circularity embedded in this statement because the family maintains the symptom, and the symptom maintains the family system as is. This has been referred to by Minuchin and colleagues (1975) as the functionality of symptoms theory—that is, symptoms play a role in maintaining the family's maladaptive interactional patterns.

Third, we believe that symptoms are linked to maladaptive family patterns of interactions. Therefore, to get rid of the symptoms, the most effective approach is to change those families' maladaptive interactions linked to the symptom. The remainder of this chapter explains how our approach works and is organized

http://dx.doi.org/10.1037/0000169-002
Brief Strategic Family Therapy, by J. Szapocznik and O. E. Hervis

into five sections—the first two focusing on family systems and structure and the others on therapy strategy, context, and attending to family process versus content.

FAMILY SYSTEMS

Family systems theory (Bowen, 1974; Broderick, 1993; Galvin, Dickson, & Marrow, 2006; Titelman, 2014) holds that family members are interdependent. That is, family members are interconnected with action–reaction sequences in which the behavior of one sequentially triggers the behavior of another. Therefore, family systems theory views the youth's behaviors as related to what else is going on in the family.

A system is made up of components that are interdependent and inter-related. Families are systems that are made up of individuals (parts) who are responsive to each other's behaviors. Thinking about human problems from a systems orientation helps us understand the complex relationships and inter-dependence of family members. There are many examples, both in the physical and social world, that illustrate how systems work.

Think of your body's circulatory system. When the heart speeds up, your blood pressure goes up, your face flushes, and your breathing may accelerate. Why is this? Because the way systems operate is that when one part changes, it affects other parts of the system. When a balloon is blown up and its opening is tied into a knot so that the air stays inside, the balloon and the air (parts) become interdependent. If you squeeze a part of the balloon, the air moves from that side to the other side, thus overstretching that other side of the balloon by putting pressure on it. If too much of the balloon is squeezed, the air trapped inside will stretch the remainder of the balloon until it forces it to explode. The earth and the moon are in a gravitational system with each other. The earth keeps the moon in its orbit, and the moon makes the sea rise and ebb on earth. Systems are the way of the universe.

These examples make it easy to understand that systems are made up of parts that are in constant interaction with each other, and any change in one of the parts of the system triggers a change in the others. It is the same way with families.

Families are systems made up of people who are cognitively, emotionally, and behaviorally connected. If a child becomes severely ill, the family has to make accommodations so that a parent will be able to take the child to the doctor and care for the child. That means that the parent will have less time to do what she usually does for the family, such as cook and care for the house. The other children may feel neglected and overburdened by new chores they must take on for the family to continue to function effectively. When a parent feels unsupported and stressed by unfavorable environmental circumstances (e.g., poverty, job stress, discrimination, abandonment, immigration, infidelity), the most vulnerable members of the family—the children—will experience the stress and are most likely to develop symptoms.

The Family Is a Whole Organism

The important concept that systems theory teaches is that the family is one whole organism. That is, it is much more than merely the composite of the individuals it comprises. Over the many years that a family is together, the family system is formed as each of its members behaves in expected ways thousands of times. Hence, each member has become accustomed to act, react, respond, feel, and think in a specific manner in the context of the family. Each family member's actions elicit a specific set of reactions from the other family members, and this occurs over and over again over time. These sequences give the family its form and style. Individual members behave in unique ways that are predictable because they have been repeated and molded over time. Consequently, the whole organism (i.e., the family) grows out of the repeated behaviors of family members over the years in ways that each individual's behaviors fit with the rest of the family like a piece fits in a puzzle.

Consider an analogy. When we think about a book, say Mark Twain's *Adventures of Huckleberry Finn*, what makes the book (i.e., the whole organism) memorable is not just the characters but also how the characters interact to create a beloved story. In the same way, the family is a whole organism that comprises its members and the repeated sequences of behaviors that create the family's story.

Let us look at some examples. Whenever Mother and Stepfather argue, 5-year-old Jason gets nervous, so he begins to make a lot of noise and throws a fit. Mom and Stepdad then stop their argument and attend to Jason to calm him down. As this sequence repeats itself over time, Jason inadvertently learns that he can interrupt his parents fighting by calling their attention to his negative behavior. Soon, to avoid trouble arising between the parents, Jason learns to be the center of attention when his parents are together, and his distraction tactics have become a part of his way of behaving in systems, whether it be his family of origin, his school, or later on in life, his work or family of choice (Burkett, 1991; Halford, Sanders, & Behrens, 2000; Koerner & Fitzpatrick, 2002; B. E. Robinson & Post, 1995; Whitton et al., 2008). However, Jason's distracting behavior when Mom and Stepdad fight prevents the parents from resolving their conflicts. Over time, the parents grow apart; Mom spends a lot of time dealing with Jason's problems in school, and Stepdad gets busy with friends, work, and his carpentry hobby so he does not have to hear about them.

The patterns that develop in a family shape the behaviors and styles of each of its members. There are ways in which each family member has become accustomed to behaving in the family—behaviors that have occurred so many times they have shaped the members to fit together like pieces of a puzzle, a perfect, predictable fit. For this reason, when a therapist wants to help the family rid itself of a troublesome symptom, the therapist must understand how the family operates as a whole and the role that the member with the symptom plays in the whole of the family organism.

Every morning, Grandma goes to the kitchen to make breakfast, Mom wakes up the children, and Tommy, the eldest, takes the dog out for a walk. One morning, Mom wants to sleep late, and she asks Tommy to wake up the littler ones. Tommy complains that he hates to do that: "They don't do what I ask them." With that in mind, Grandma leaves the kitchen to get the little ones up and dressed. They want their mother, as usual, to do this job, and so they give Grandma a hard time. Grandma does not get to make breakfast in time, everyone is late for school, and the dog has an accident on the carpet.

The pattern has been disturbed. Tommy, Mom, and Grandma might figure out a better way to allow Mom to sleep in late that does not make every morning fall apart. Or they might not. It could be that the pieces of this puzzle (family members) are unable to adapt to a new situation in ways that achieve a successful resolution. Families are frequently confronted with new situations. Those families that are unable to adapt across novel situations as they emerge are the families that are most likely to develop symptoms and, thus, are most likely to need therapy.

The influence of the family on behavior is powerful. In part, this influence is so powerful because it has been reinforced hundreds and thousands of times in the past and because it continues to be reinforced. It is powerful enough to give shape to an individual's personality, to how a person sees herself and how she sees her place in the world. How a person has come to see her role in the family exerts a great deal of influence on how she sees her role in life altogether. A person who has always played the role of peacemaker in family arguments may go on to do that in other stations in life, such as at the office, among friends, or even as a career (she may decide to become a diplomat or a mediator). However, if a person's experience in the family was extremely unpleasant, she may become someone who appears insensitive and uncaring because she refuses to get involved in the problems other people have.

Complementarity

Given this tremendous influence and power that is exerted by the family system, it is not surprising that it is difficult for an individual who remains inside the sphere of their family to change in a lasting way unless the family changes along with the individual. This happens because change in one member requires change in other family members. If one piece of the puzzle changes its shape, some other pieces have to change their shape for the puzzle to continue to fit together.

Conversely, the family's power can be nearly irresistible when the family behaves in more adaptive ways that, in turn, elicit more adaptive or prosocial behaviors in the individual. After all, the influence that is effective in one direction (e.g., enabling) can be just as effective in the opposite direction too (e.g., setting limits). Typically, a family member, especially a child or adolescent, will readily respond to the family system's influence to behave adaptively. A youngster's behavior can drastically change when a parent or parents learn how to behave differently. This happens because family members who are linked emotionally are behaviorally responsive to each other's actions and reactions. This is the way *complementarity* operates (Minuchin & Fishman, 1981): For every action on the part of one family member, there is a complementary reaction on the part of the others. For this reason, family is a powerful change agent. However, when only the youth is in therapy, the family can unknowingly sabotage any changes that are brought about through individual therapy.

Complementarity teaches us that the behaviors of the family members are like the gears that make up the inner workings of a clock. For the clock to keep ticking and keeping time, all the gears must turn in a specific way. Similarly, for the family to continue to work in a certain way, whether it is adaptive or maladaptive, everyone's behavior must contribute to maintaining the family's particular pattern. The good news is that just as one member's actions can negatively influence another member, the opposite is also true. When one or more family members, especially parents because of their power and leadership role in the family, change their behaviors, this creates a new situation to which the youth has to respond, typically by either complying or pushing back. The parents' new behavior creates an opportunity for the youth to behave differently as well. As we discuss later in the book, the dance that occurs as changes take place in some family members creates opportunities for new behaviors in other members. Positive changes on the part of the parents will produce an opportunity for positive changes in the behavior of their youngsters. For example, often children may have learned to coerce parents into reinforcing negative behavior (e.g., throwing a temper tantrum and stopping only when the parent(s) give in; Patterson, 1982; Patterson, Reid, & Dishion, 1992). Only when the parent(s) change their behavior and stop complementing the child's negative behavior will the child change.

Homeostasis

Homeostasis (Anderson, Goolishian, & Winderman, 1986; Chrousos & Gold, 1992; Minuchin et al., 1975; Tononi & Cirelli, 2006; Wynn, Chawla, & Pollard, 2013) is the systemic force that operates to maintain the permanence of systems, thus preventing systems from changing. Homeostasis combines *homeo*, meaning same, with *stasis*, meaning status. To illustrate, gravity functions to keep us all grounded on Earth, and like gravity, homeostasis is a force that cannot be seen but is nevertheless operational in keeping systems from changing. For a person to overcome the pull of gravity, that person has to use exceptional force. In the same way, for therapy to overcome the pull of the family system attempts to stay the same, therapy has to overcome the pull of homeostasis. Homeostasis serves an important purpose for systems: It maintains them unchanged. However, when we are working to change the system, we fight against homeostasis to bring about change.

STRUCTURE: THE SCRIPT FOR THE FAMILY PLAY

As we noted previously, the family is a whole organism that includes its members and the wholeness that emerges as the family's repeated sequences of behaviors come together. *Structure* is the wholeness that emerges as a specific family's repeated sequences of behaviors come together in a way that is unique for each family. Individual patterns of interactions can be seen across different families (e.g., parents do not collaborate in parenting), but the way the various patterns of interactions come together is unique to each family and thus defines that family's particular structure. Structure (Minuchin, 1974; Szapocznik, Hervis, & Schwartz, 2003; Szapocznik & Kurtines, 1989) is the sum of all the repetitive interactional patterns that exist in a family and how they come together in a unique way for each family. In our discussion thus far, we have tended to identify one or another family interactional pattern, but in families, several interactional patterns co-occur, and the sum of the aggregation of all interactional patterns within a family is referred to as the family's structure. Likewise, in a play, the sum of all the interactions among the various characters constitutes the script. In dance, the sum of the sequence of steps and movements of all the dancers is referred to as the choreography. Structure explains how the family system has an impact on its members. Patterns of interactions are defined as the linked behaviors among family members that become habitual and repeat over time. It is a universal principle that occurs across eras and cultures, given that across eras and cultures, families are composed of members who interact with each other in some way. The role of the BSFT therapist is to identify those patterns of family interactions that are associated with the youth's problems and therefore have to be corrected.

Families and their members are interactive and interdependent. Thus, family patterns of interactions and individual family member's behaviors are interactive and interdependent. The family impacts, shapes, and determines the behavior of each of its members. Similarly, the individual family members impact, shape, and determine the family system.

Patterns of Interactions

When Maria and Lila meet, Maria acts in a certain way toward Lila. Lila, in turn, responds in a certain way toward Maria, who then responds to Lila's response. These linked behaviors of one person responding to another— either through actions or conversation—are called an *interACTION* (an interplay of interlinked actions) or, more precisely, a *series of interACTIONS*. In time, Lila and Maria's interactions become patterned and thus are referred to as *patterns of interactions*. Patterns of interaction are typically characterized by their repetitive nature. Two or more people who often have contact with each other (e.g., family members) form habits according to the way they interact with each other. As we mentioned in the Introduction, a simple type of repetitive pattern is found in how family members choose to sit in the same places at the dinner table every day. Where people sit may facilitate certain persons interacting with each other and not with others. Consequently, we would say that a repetitive pattern of interactions has emerged—a sitting pattern that may reflect an interaction pattern.

Patterns of interactions develop in any system—for example, among people who hang out together in school or the neighborhood. With older, more established systems such as families, the interactions that occur are overpracticed and thus become predictable. They are predictable in that, in a family, these interactions have occurred in just the same way thousands of times. They have become repetitive. Figure 1.1 shows, albeit in simplified form, that a family's patterns of interactions, or systems, shape the behaviors of its members and vice versa.

Every time Ron nagged his wife, Fran, for not taking adequate care of the home and children, Fran ignored him. The more he nagged, the more she ignored him; the more she ignored him, the more he nagged. Ron and Fran could be said to be stuck in a repetitive pattern of interactions in which they lost their ability to cooperate, and neither one of them feels satisfied.

In their family, father and daughter Nora became close and shared their unhappiness about Fran, Nora's stepmother. As Nora got a little older, Ron turned to her for emotional support instead of to Fran. Ron developed a close emotional tie to his daughter. Fran, in turn, remained distant from Nora because she sensed that her stepdaughter always sided with Ron. When Nora needed help with something, she instinctually knew she had to turn to her father, not her stepmother. This is another repetitive pattern of interactions—interwoven with the first—that developed in the family.

FIGURE 1.1. Patterns of Interactions in Family Systems

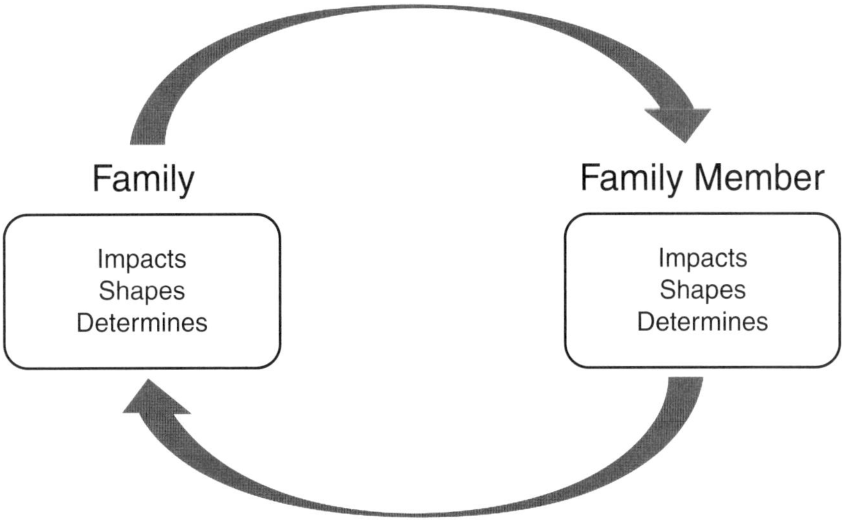

Family

Impacts
Shapes
Determines

Family Member

Impacts
Shapes
Determines

In this example, if Nora developed behavior problems when she became an adolescent, the family would be unable to manage her behavior effectively. Ron still turned to his daughter for emotional support. In doing so, the relationship between father and daughter was strengthened at the same time that the coalition between father and daughter against Fran was strengthened. This elevated the daughter in the family hierarchy to the level of her father. When Fran attempted to set limits on the daughter, her efforts were ineffective. Mother and father were unable to discuss, much less agree, on how to handle Nora's misbehavior. In families, we often see a linking of several patterns of repetitive interactions, where one pattern is likely to maintain and be maintained by another. As we discuss later in this book, the inability of parental figures to negotiate and agree on rules and consequences and to present a united and consistent front is perhaps one of the most frequent manifestations of a troubled family associated with disruptive problem behaviors in adolescents.

All families develop patterns of interactions that repeat over time and across topics. However, not all families develop symptoms because not all repetitive patterns of interactions are maladaptive. For example, a repetitive pattern of interactions that is nearly always adaptive is when father and mother collaborate about parenting issues. When a family has certain repetitive patterns of interactions that are unsuccessful in achieving the goals of the family or its members, these patterns of interactions are said to be at the root of the kinds of problems that are called symptoms that bring the families into treatment. Families that tend to have problems have them precisely because they continue to interact in fastidiously repetitive ways that are maladaptive. Families with problems tend to have less flexibility to adapt to new conditions and new circumstances. This lack of flexibility does not allow the family to solve problems effectively, thus explaining the family's inability to correct their maladaptive interactions or eliminate the symptoms that arise in its members.

For the BSFT therapist, that "something" that a family is doing that maintains the problem and that something that the family could do differently to eliminate the problem is always an interaction. In other words, what has to be changed is always a part of the family's structure (repetitive patterns of interactions) that does not work well and is maintaining the symptom(s).

Adaptive and Maladaptive Interactions

As noted earlier, we define the terms *adaptive* and *maladaptive* in reference to interactional patterns by whether these result in positive outcomes or symptoms. Hence, this definition has two important components: (a) the family's ability to adapt to changing conditions or circumstances and (b) that these changes result in positive outcomes for all members. In our definition of adaptive and maladaptive, we have thus been pragmatic, linking our definition of maladaptiveness to outcomes that families and society define as undesirable.

Through research and clinical experience with thousands of families, we have come to identify that certain patterns of interactions, particularly in families with children and adolescents, tend to result in negative or symptomatic outcomes (Szapocznik & Kurtines, 1989; Szapocznik et al., 1988, 2003). In this book, we discuss the role of culture, which is complex. Whether or not culture supports a certain pattern of interactions, if the result is negative outcomes for individual family members, we propose that these family interactional patterns have to be adjusted to improve a family member's individual well-being. However, this has to be done with the utmost respect and deference to culture.

An example of an interactional pattern that is always adaptive is family members collaborating in solving differences of opinion in such a way that the needs of all concerned are addressed. As long as these negotiations consider the age and circumstances of all concerned, these types of family interactional patterns are likely to be adaptive.

However, some interactions are adaptive at one point in the family's history and development but have to be adjusted over time and in response to new circumstances. A parent who was used to telling a young child what to do will not be as successful simply using this tactic when the child becomes a teenager because, at that age, the teenager is developing a sense of autonomy (McElhaney, Allen, Stephenson, & Hare, 2009; Noom, Deković, & Meeus, 1999). Parents are unable to "control" teenagers. Provided there is a good foundation for the relationship between the parent and teenager, negotiation is typically effective in managing a teenager (Gray & Steinberg, 1999; C. C. Robinson, Mandleco, Olsen, & Hart, 1995). If the parent is unable or unwilling to make a transition to negotiation, it is unlikely that the family will be able to reach a resolution that accommodates the goals of all family members involved.

Another example of an adaptive interaction that can become maladaptive over time occurs when the family composition changes. The mother who passed away had more time to spend in guidance and nurturance than the mother who was the primary breadwinner and thus spent long hours outside the home. How does the system adapt to this loss while still providing the amount of nurturance and guidance the children need? The breadwinner now has to make time to care for her children and possibly involve extended family members to support her in this role because she must continue to work. If reassignment of the roles that the deceased mother played does not happen, the children may feel and/or be neglected.

Some interactional patterns are never adaptive. A typical example of a maladaptive interaction that is frequently seen in families of acting-out teens is a triangulated relationship (Dallos & Smart, 2011; Dallos & Vetere, 2012; Franck & Buehler, 2007). A triangle is formed when two people are in conflict and a third one is brought in or brings himself into the conflict. When this happens, the triangulated person finds himself involved in a conflict between two other persons. In the case of adolescents, this pattern often starts in early childhood. This interaction usually involves the youngster in ongoing conflicts between two parental figures, (e.g., mother and grandmother) who are involved in parenting the child. It may have started as follows.

The mother takes a drink, and the grandmother (the second parental figure) admonishes her that she is going to kill herself with so much alcohol. The 6-year-old begins to cry and interrupts the argument. The mother is angry because she has been scolded by her own mother and takes her anger out on the child by spanking him and yelling at him to "shut up." The grandmother is then even more angry with her daughter, and the fight escalates as she calls her daughter an unfit mother. Mother claims that Grandmother spoils the child. Grandmother defends herself by assuring her daughter that the child is not spoiled and that she is not one to spoil a child. The child has now unfairly become the center of the parental fight—a fight that initially had nothing to do with the child. Meanwhile, the conflict has shifted from focusing on the mother's drinking to focusing on how to raise the child, which conveniently leaves the mother off the hook about her drinking.

As the child grows, the triangle evolves to the grandmother and child forming a coalition (supporting each other) against the drinking mother. Typically, this leads to the mother losing power in her parental role, with the child acquiring additional power through his coalition with Grandma. As this pattern repeats itself over the same and different parenting arguments, the child will grow up to learn that (a) he does not have to listen to his mother, (b) his grandmother will defend him no matter what he does, and (c) he has become more powerful than his mother. As this pattern repeats over time, it becomes responsible for the maintenance of symptoms such as alcohol use in the mother and drug abuse in the youth. When the family comes into therapy because of the youth's drug use, these maladaptive patterns of interactions must be a target of BSFT treatment.

In sum, the concept of family systems teaches that family members are interdependent. The interplay of behaviors among family members is defined as an interaction. Structure (i.e., the aggregation of the sum of the family's repetitive patterns of interactions) teaches that the patterns of interactions are repetitive and thus predictable. It also teaches that, in some instances, the repetitive patterns of family interactions do not result in desired cognitive, emotional, and behavioral outcomes for all its members. Instead, these patterns of interactions succeed only in frustrating the family members and in eliciting or allowing problematic behavior that becomes the symptom of the family's inability to solve its interactional problems.

STRATEGY

The third foundational concept of BSFT is strategy (Haley, 1963, 1971; Madanes, 1991; Nardone & Watzlawick, 2005; Rabkin, 1977; Zeig, 1980). Strategic therapy designs for each family the best method to achieve treatment goals. There are two concepts of strategy that we use in BSFT. One (with a capital S) refers to the nature of the overall approach to treatment that is diagnostically driven and is unique to each family. We present our systemic diagnostic schema in Chapter 3. The overall Strategy for the direction of therapy with a specific family is driven by the unique diagnosis of the adaptive and maladaptive interactional patterns that characterize it. In this case, *Strategy* refers to the overall direction of changing the specific maladaptive patterns of interactions that are linked to the presenting problem. Such a Strategy is used from the first to the last session and drives the treatment plan throughout the full therapy process. The Strategy is also used to plan the specific changes that will be pursued across all sessions that will transform the targeted patterns of maladaptive interactions linked to the presenting symptoms. For this reason, every session always looks to the bigger plan of Strategy for the interactional patterns that have to be changed. Figure 1.2 illustrates this idea.

Practical

The other aspect of strategy (with lower case *s*) in BSFT refers to the practical approach to selecting those particular tactics or interventions that are best suited to a family's idiosyncrasies (of organization, values, language usage, culture, content, etc.), with the ultimate goal of successfully pursuing the overall Strategy. In Chapter 5 of this volume, we explain the considerations involved in selecting the specific tactics and interventions targeted at each family at each moment.

To be practical in BSFT means that the therapist may use any technique, approach, or tactic that will help her achieve the objective of changing specific

FIGURE 1.2. Strategy Across and Within Sessions

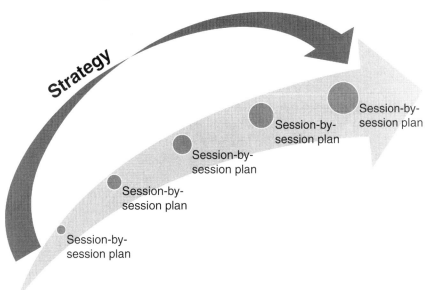

maladaptive interactions that are contributing or maintaining the symptom(s) and thus eliminate the symptom(s). The tactic is the particular method used for a specific family to achieve the desired interactional change. In BSFT, practicality is based on the belief that more importance should be placed on the achievement of interactional change rather than on the use of any particular approach or tactic. Thus, the BSFT therapist uses the tactics or approaches that are most likely to achieve the desired changes in interactional patterns with maximum speed, effectiveness, and permanence. An example of the practical aspect of BSFT is found in the use of reframing (also explained in more depth in Chapter 5): Rather than portray the entire reality of a situation, reframing emphasizes only a particular aspect of reality, the one that will best serve to move the family from a maladaptive interactional pattern to a more adaptive set of interactions.

In the case of a father who is berating his son for skipping school, the therapist may choose to either focus on Dad's concern for the future well-being of his son as a way of building a positive affective bridge between father and son or to point out that the son appears to be depressed, which may be the reason the son is not going to school. Each of these frames is intended to elicit from the father a more nurturant response, which in turn moves the family from negativity from father toward the son to more positive, nurturant, and constructive interactions. The practical aspect of BSFT in this instance will inform the decision of which one to use. This will depend on the clinician's assessment of which has the best likelihood of being accepted by the father and the son and thus to be successful in transforming the quality of the interaction.

Problem Focused

A problem focus is characteristic of strategic family therapies (Nardone & Watzlawick, 2005). BSFT, like other strategic approaches, emphasizes changing those family interactions that are most directly related to the youth's presenting problem. The BSFT strategic plan aims to bring about change only to those family interactional patterns that give rise to or maintain the youth's problems. In all families, there will be other problems that the therapist will observe, but if they are not directly impacting the youth's presenting problems, these other family problems do not become the target of BSFT treatment. It is not that BSFT cannot handle these other problems; rather, we are making choices about what problems to handle first as part of a time-limited intervention that prioritizes eliminating the most urgent symptoms.

However, there might be necessary changes that appear to be outside of the presenting problem but are not. These changes are undertaken only to the extent that they are necessary for a resolution of the focal problem. For example, it may be determined that the youth's parents are not setting and enforcing clear limits on the youngster's behavior. In trying to get them to decide on a plan for discipline management, it becomes obvious that the parents are not able to work together as a team because of underlying marital issues that keep them angry and distrustful of each other. In this case, the marital problem has to be addressed to the extent that it is necessary to get them to cooperate in managing their child's behavior. The parental couple can be helped to successfully handle their parenting functions, although not all their marital problems might have been solved.

Several aspects of being problem focused deserve more attention. One of these is that families do indeed come to therapy presenting with many different problems. Frequently, therapists complain, "This family has so many problems that I don't know where to start." One aspect of problem focus is that the attention of the therapy is in interactional patterns linked to the presenting symptoms. However, the pattern of interactions that may underlie the presenting symptoms are most likely the same interactional patterns that underlie other presenting problems.

Planned

As we noted, there is an overall Strategy that provides the direction for the treatment plan and is based on the systemic diagnosis—that is, what interactional patterns linked to the presenting problem have to be changed. The larger Strategy defines the overall treatment plan. However, each session is planned so that all sessions in the aggregate take us from where we are to where we want to go. For this reason, for each session, the therapist makes deliberate plans that move the family toward accomplishing the overall Strategy or treatment plan. Before each session, then, the therapist knows exactly what she is going to do (i.e., what interactions to change, such as creating a parental alliance with the goal of improving parental collaboration, leadership, and practices) and how she is going to do it. Therefore, BSFT sessions are purposeful in transforming interactional patterns from maladaptive to adaptive. The BSFT approach is a dance between "strategy with a small *s*," which is practical by capitalizing on the emerging process while intervening in a deliberate fashion to pursue the "Strategy with a large *S*." Hence, the therapist must flow and yet be able to move from a diagnosis—point A—to a planned outcome—point B.

As will be evident in later chapters, BSFT is like using a river current to get to a specific target: It is fastest and most effective to take advantage of its flow. However, the therapist always knows where she wants to arrive.

CONTEXT

Context is the circumstances that envelop us. We are enveloped by our past and present circumstances. Our circumstances define who we are and what we think, feel, believe, and do. For a person, our context ranges from our biology to our family to our society and our political and physical environment. We think of context as a series of circles of influence on our behavior (e.g., family, friends, school or work, support systems, neighborhood, and macrosocial influences such as culture, economics, and policy; see Figure 1.3).

In our work, we focus primarily on the family, a person's most immediate and influential context (Bronfenbrenner, 1996, 2005).

Bronfenbrenner (1996, 2005) recognized the enormous influence of the family, suggesting that the family is the primary context for the child for learning and development. Much research since Bronfenbrenner's early work has supported his contention that the family is the primary context for the socialization of children and adolescents (Laible, Thompson, & Froimson, 2015; Perrino, González-Soldevilla, Pantin, & Szapocznik, 2000; Szapocznik & Coatsworth, 1999). Beyond the family context, a broad range of contextual influences operates on the family and individual. A contemporary understanding of the role of social context reveals that social influences on the

FIGURE 1.3. Relationship Among Ecological Systems

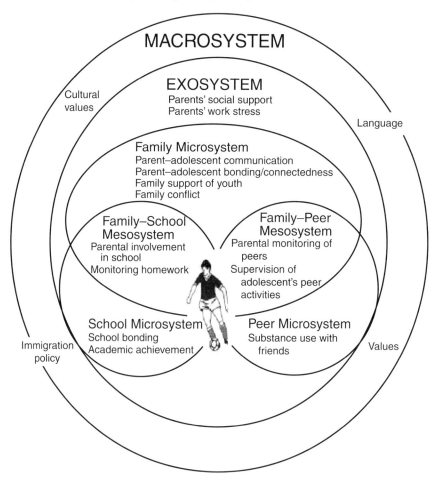

From "Preventing Substance Abuse in Hispanic Immigrant Adolescents: An Ecodevelopmental, Parent-Centered Approach," by H. Pantin, S. J. Schwartz, S. Sullivan, J. D. Coatsworth, and J. Szapocznik, 2003, *Hispanic Journal of Behavioral Sciences*, *25*, p. 477. Copyright 2003 by Sage Publishing. Adapted with permission.

individual have an important impact on her behavior (Espelage, Bosworth, & Simon, 2000; Sallis, Owen, & Fisher, 2008; Szapocznik & Coatsworth, 1999). Such influences are particularly powerful during childhood and adolescence because childhood and adolescence represent developmental periods when children are critically dependent on their social context, particularly their family (Steinberg & Morris, 2001).

Our work with youth includes individuals and families from a broad spectrum of cultural and historical backgrounds. Research on culture and the family has been extensive, demonstrating that the family and the child are influenced by their cultural contexts (Boyd-Franklin, 2003; Chen, Fu, & Zhao, 2015; Kagitçibaşi, 1996; Szapocznik & Kurtines, 1993). We have examined the role of cultural context in influencing families' values and behaviors and how these, in turn, influence the relationship between parents and children in ways that affect adolescents' development toward or away from problem behaviors (Cano et al., 2015; S. J. Schwartz et al., 2015, 2016; Sullivan et al., 2007).

What does this mean for the therapists working with troubled youth? Most important, it means that the clinician will not be able to understand the behavior of the child and his family without understanding the context to which a family is exposed. In this case, by *context*, we are referring both to the social and the cultural context. Behavior does not happen in a vacuum but instead exists within an environmental reality that shapes the rules, values, and behaviors of the youth and her family and defines the universe of options that are available to a family and its members. Therapists who ignore these contextual factors in developing an understanding of the youth's problems and the challenges facing her parents will be handicapped in their ability to help these families. An example of a contextual issue is found in a family living in a dangerous neighborhood where stray bullets have killed children playing on the sidewalk. The family comprises a mother, grandmother, and three children, ages 10, 13, and 15. The mother does not allow the children to leave their apartment when they come home from school, for good reason. However, the context is preventing children from developing neighborhood friends, playing team sports in the neighborhood, and getting to know the families of their friends. The parents' unusually high protectiveness is a direct function of their context.

Another aspect of context is therapy itself, where the culture of the client, the therapist, the agency, and the funding source can all affect the nature of therapy. For example, an agency's perspective could be that a family in which members are constantly screaming and cursing each other may not be appropriate for family therapy and that the youth should be in treatment by himself. From a family therapist's perspective, however, the best families with which to work are those families in which there is a strong connection, even if that connection is manifested in negative ways. In our experience, an angry family is easier to work with than a family in which there is not much interaction because the negativity can often be easily transformed into positive interactions. Negativity is a form of caring, odd as that may sound. As we cited earlier, in the words of noted Nobel laureate Elie Wiesel, the opposite of love is not hate, it is indifference.

PROCESS VERSUS CONTENT: A CRITICAL DISTINCTION

The distinction between process and content is vital to BSFT (B. L. Duncan, Parks, & Rusk, 1990; Held, 1986; Prochaska & Norcross, 2014; Szapocznik et al., 2003). As noted earlier, *content* refers to the topic of the family's interactions, whereas *process* refers to the interactions that emerge when the topic is brought up. Content is what are we going to eat for dinner today, and process is how the family goes about deciding (or failing to decide) what to eat. It is not which movie they selected but how they went about selecting the movie and who was going to go to see the movie. Content is the obvious aspect of what we observe when we hear families talk. It is what people are actually saying when they are interacting. Content refers to the specific or concrete facts used in communication. Content includes the reasons families give for a particular interaction (e.g., I was late because I missed the bus).

The approach proposed here for understanding families is based strictly on an understanding of the patterns of interactions (process) that occur among family members. To identify these repetitive patterns of interactions, it is essential for the BSFT therapist to understand the difference between the process and the content of the family—because patterns of interactions, the target of BSFT, is always process. Process is like the software that operates your email. Content is the subject and text of each email. The process never changes, but the content can change all the time, although some of us will prefer to email about relationships and others about sports. When the spelling checker of your email is set for French, and you write in English, it will miscorrect words and thus prevent you from communicating effectively. In this regard, it does not matter what the content of any one email is. Rather, what had to be corrected was the spelling checker settings to allow the family to communicate effectively. BSFT helps the family system select a more adaptive process to improve the family communication—like switching from a French to English spelling checker to write in English.

Process is the how, and content is the what. Process is how family members relate to each other. What is the form that their interaction takes? When one person does something, how does the other person respond? It is also the "what happens when" in an interaction. What does John do when Michele does this thing? What does Michele say when John says this? Process describes the flow of actions and reactions between family members. The how of the flow of actions and reactions between and among family members typically repeats for a particular family, even as the content varies.

Process is what happens when we respond automatically according to long-established patterns of interactions. All families behave in ways that are overlearned and have happened thousands of times. Amazingly then, process typically is stable and predictable, whereas content changes all the time. When Mother says, "Let's pick up our clothes," Mother's sister may say, "Oh, let them watch TV a little longer," thus undermining Mother's leadership in the family. Two days later, Mother says to the children, "Pick up your plates," to which Aunt responds, "They are too tired from school; leave them alone. I will pick them up." Those are the kind of interactional patterns (Aunt undermining Mother) that will be overlearned, stable, and predictable. However, what Aunt undermines Mother about, the content, changes all the time across situations and time (see Table 1.1 for examples).

In Conversation 2 in Table 1.1, regardless of whether the content is taking out the garbage or what to have for lunch today, the process is going to be the same. That is, when a disagreement occurs, the couple will fail to resolve the disagreement because the partners will conspire to change the focus from the particular topic being discussed by using a personal attack (i.e., diffusion—see Chapter 3).

Process Can Be Nonverbal

Sometimes the process occurs in a nonverbal fashion. This is because the process is how people relate to each other. A nonverbal process might be a certain look, gesture, or intonation. Some of the most important processes that show up in family interactions are nonverbal—for example, people hugging each other as a demonstration of affection and closeness or a smirk from an adolescent to show disrespect when a parent speaks. Nonverbal messages always

TABLE 1.1. Distinction in Communication Between Process and Content

Communication	Process	Content
Conversation 1—nonconflictual		
John to Michele: "Let's go to the movies."	John and Michele doing something together	Going to the movies
Michele: "OK, that sounds good."		
Michele: "What would you like to see?"		
John: "How about the new Star Wars movie?"		
Michele: "Great, I hear it is a lot of fun."	John and Michele agreeing on what to do	Star Wars movie
They go to the movies and have a good time.	John and Michele sharing a pleasant time	It does not matter what the content was
Conversation 2—conflictual		
Wife to husband: "Take out the garbage."		
Husband: "No way, housework is women's work."	Disagreement	Taking out the garbage
Wife: "You are just a low life." Husband: "You are always nagging."	Negativity (name calling, criticizing) and diffusion (changing topic of conversation)	She calls him "low life," and he blames her for nagging.

fall under the category of process communication. We suggest, however, that body language be corroborated before making assumptions.

Process and content can, at times, be at odds with each other. They can send contradictory messages. Although the words may be, "Sure Mom, I'll come home early," the daughter's sarcastic gesture and intonation indicate, "When hell freezes over." In this case, the words are the content, and the process is how it is said. Which one do you think is more reliable? Which one does the better job of letting a therapist know just exactly what is going on and what the daughter intends to do? More important, which one more clearly describes the nature of the relationship between the mother and daughter?

If a father and son have a conflictual relationship, they may fight on Monday about school, on Tuesday about chores, and on Friday about coming home late. The BSFT therapist must focus on the process—that they fight—and not the content—what they fight about. The strategies that are designed for change are those that can alter the fighting between the father and son, such as reframing that dad is concerned about his child, and guiding them to negotiate and collaborate in resolving their differences.

The family is focused on the content, whereas the BSFT therapist is always interested in the process—that is, the interactional sequences of behavior that occur as a content is being discussed. The content is the concern of the family, whereas the BSFT therapist is only concerned with identifying and changing those processes that are maladaptive and create symptoms for the family.

Separating Process From Content in Therapy

The focus of BSFT is to change the nature of those interactions that constitute the family's maladaptive processes. The family comes to therapy because it needs help in developing the skills it requires to manage effectively the multiple contents that emerge daily. The therapist who attends to content and loses sight of the process will be unable to bring about the kinds of process changes that the family needs to manage effectively the multiple contents that emerge on a daily basis. In BSFT, these process changes are always in the form of changes in patterns of interactions that are linked to the family's symptoms.

One useful tip may be helpful to the therapist in separating process from content. Frequently, a family member will want to tell the therapist a story about something that happened with another family member. Whenever the therapist is being told a story about another person, the therapist is allowing the family to trap him in content. For example, Mom says to the therapist, "Let me tell you what my son did yesterday. He came in at two in the morning . . ."

If the therapist wants to refocus the session from content to process, when Mom says, "Let me tell you what my son did," the therapist would say, "Please tell your son directly so that I can hear you now and help you with this." When Mom talks to her son directly, how they talk with each other is process. In observing what happens when Mom talks to her son directly, the therapist can identify the interaction that happens between them.

For example, Mom could say, "You came home at two last night, and that is not allowed, and as we had agreed, when you break your curfew, the consequence is that you will not be allowed to go out the rest of this week." That would be a healthy and direct communication that clarifies the rules and their relationship to the consequences. However, when the therapist asks Mom to talk to her son, the interaction could be very different. For example, Mom may be unwilling to talk to her son; instead, she turns to Dad and says, "How can I tell him to come home on time if I know that he doesn't want to be home because you are drunk?" The process observed will be the triangle of mother, father, and son.

Another aspect of this process is that mother protected the misbehavior of the child by giving a justification for the child's lateness (of course, the youth did not want to come home—his father is drunk). Thus, a single interaction can reflect more than one maladaptive interactional process. As we can see, our diagnostic approach is rich because so much can be learned about the family process even from a short interaction. This is one of the reasons BSFT is brief: because the diagnosis of the problem interactions can be done quickly.

Because diagnosis is critical to knowing what should be changed in a family, it is essential for the therapist to choreograph the opportunity for the family to interact. This is so that the therapist can observe how the family interacts because the root of the problem is how the family interacts. It has been said that one picture (seeing a single interaction) is worth a thousand words (stories). That was never truer than in family therapy. In BSFT, one interaction among family members is more useful to the therapist than a thousand stories. Stories may not truly explain what goes on in the family, whereas directly observing interactions never lies.

It should be clear from this chapter that in BSFT, complete attention is devoted to understanding family process—the interplay of behaviors between family members that we call *interactions*. Content plays a minimal role in BSFT. Although content is important to the family because it represents the issues the family has to manage, what is important to the therapist is how the family interacts regarding these issues. The therapist's job is to help the family learn more effective and competent ways to manage their issues to allow the family to resolve their content issues, both during and beyond therapy. This reminds us of the Chinese proverb "Give a poor man a fish, and you feed him for a day; teach him to fish, and you give him an occupation that will feed him for a lifetime." In BSFT, we teach families how to effectively resolve their problems so that they can resolve their many content issues using the new skills we have helped them develop—for a lifetime. One of the features that makes BSFT brief is that rather than having to help the families with their multiple content problems, in BSFT we focus on correcting just a few interactional patterns (often less than a handful). This empowers the family to solve its many content problems in the present and the future.

As will be seen in the chapters that follow, the interventions recommended are oriented entirely toward changing the family's process. Content will be used in these interventions as the vehicle by which interactions are changed. This allows us to be responsive to the family's content while using that content to transform interactional patterns. From the therapist's perspective, it does not matter which content is used. Rather, any content can be used to help families develop and practice new ways of interacting.

ADVICE TO THERAPISTS

If you want to waste your time as well as the family's, let family members tell you stories. If, however, you want to know what the family's interactions are (process) instead of allowing family members to tell you stories, encourage them to talk with each other. When you see how the family interacts, you see the family's process, which is the bread and butter of BSFT—what you will diagnose and what you will change. Of course, the therapist sometimes allows a story as a way of establishing rapport with a family member. However, listening to a story should be brief (i.e., less than 5 minutes) as a matter of strategy to provide the therapist with sufficient rapport to permit him or her to move the conversation back where it belongs: among family members.

As discussed in Chapters 3 through 5, the BSFT therapist has a decentralized role in both diagnosis and restructuring. To diagnose, we allow the family to behave as it usually would when the therapist is not present. In restructuring, the focus is on changing the patterns of interactions within the family, which means that the therapist is a choreographer, not a dancer. The therapist guides the family, but the interactions, old and new, occur among family members.

KEY TAKEAWAYS

- Family members are interconnected with action–reaction sequences in which the behavior of one sequentially triggers the behavior of another.

- The BSFT approach is a method of empowering families to adapt to new situations in ways that achieve successful outcomes for the family.

- There is a constant tension between family homeostasis and therapy. Homeostasis is about staying unchanged, whereas therapy is about change.

- The family's structure is the script for the family play.

- Strategy (with a capital *S*) refers to a diagnostically driven therapy that sets the overall course for treatment.

- Rather than portray the entire reality of a situation, the BSFT therapist emphasizes the particular aspect of reality that will best serve to move the family from a maladaptive interactional pattern to a more adaptive set of interactions.

- Content plays no role in the diagnostic process, nor in treatment; if you want to waste time, let the family members tell you stories.

2

Joining

Preparing the Terrain

Every farmer knows that the ground has to be prepared before it can be planted; every baker knows that the dough has to be kneaded before it is baked. Likewise, every therapist must know that the family has to be "prepared" before change interventions are attempted (Szapocznik & Kurtines, 1989). This chapter presents several important aspects of joining, including how to join, the intended result (building an effective therapeutic system), specific techniques, and challenging joining examples.

CREATING THE THERAPEUTIC SYSTEM

In our work, the purpose of joining is to establish an effective therapeutic system. Families are systems, and all systems have their rules. One important rule that all systems have in common is that they must preserve themselves, and even more important, they must preserve themselves in the same way that they have always been. It is an interesting dilemma: The therapist establishes a collaborative relationship with a family, in large part by initially accepting the family as it is, to change the family. The therapeutic system is that collaborative relationship in which the therapist is accepted as its leader to change the family.

In this section, we discuss how families have to be approached in such a way that the therapy goals of changing their interactions can be achieved. Much research has been conducted on the impact of the therapeutic alliance on

http://dx.doi.org/10.1037/0000169-003
Brief Strategic Family Therapy, by J. Szapocznik and O. E. Hervis

treatment outcome (Flückiger, Del Re, Wampold, & Horvath, 2018; Flückiger, Del Re, Wampold, Symonds, & Horvath, 2012; Karver, De Nadai, Monahan, & Shirk, 2018; Martin, Garske, & Davis, 2000; Murphy & Hutton, 2018; Shirk & Karver, 2003). Consistently, studies show that the quality of the relationship between the therapist and the client, whether the client is an individual (e.g., Barber et al., 2001; Campbell, Guydish, Le, Wells, & McCarty, 2015; Krupnick et al., 1996) or a family (Friedlander, Escudero, Welmers-van de Poll, & Heatherington, 2018; Welmers-van de Poll et al., 2018), is a strong predictor of retention and outcome.

All therapies have a prescription for what the therapeutic relationship should be and how to achieve it. Most writings on the therapeutic relationship or alliance refer to individual therapies (Muran & Barber, 2010). Since the early 1970s, with the work of Salvador Minuchin, the term *joining* as a method for establishing a therapeutic relationship with a family (Minuchin, 1974; Minuchin & Fishman, 1981) has been widely adopted into the family therapy field's lexicon (Sexton & Lebow, 2016) and has contributed to our thinking. The Brief Strategic Family Therapy® (BSFT®) approach takes the notion of joining one step further by discussing the intent of joining as the establishment of an effective new system, which we refer to as the *therapeutic system*. This new system is composed of the family and the therapist, with the therapist as its leader. The most important function of this therapeutic system is to create the context that supports the therapist's work as she leads the family through change-producing interventions.

Because BSFT is based on a systems orientation, all relationships are conceived as systemic. As such, the therapeutic system, like all systems, is composed of members who are interdependent and whose behaviors trigger responses from each other. Inside an effective therapeutic system, when the therapist behaves, families are likely to respond, and when families behave, the therapist is likely to respond. One of the great challenges to the therapist is to respond in a way that is neither personal nor automatic but rather strategic, in keeping with the treatment plan. This point will be covered in more detail in Chapter 5.

In establishing a therapeutic system, the challenge for the BSFT therapist is to develop a therapeutic alliance with several individuals who are related to each other and who frequently come into therapy in conflict with one another. For example, it is quite usual that adolescents come into treatment in conflict with their parent(s) or guardian(s). Both parties approach therapy wanting to find out whom the therapist will support. The job of the therapist is to find ways of supporting all members of the family without initially taking sides. For example, as a way of joining the adolescent, the therapist might validate the adolescent's concerns by saying, "I am here to make sure your parents can hear you so that you can explain what is important to you." Similarly, the therapist might join the parents by validating their concerns, saying, "I am here to help you help your son get rid of his problems."

The desired qualities of the therapeutic relationship are respect, empathy, and commitment to working toward achieving the content goals of the family (e.g., have the son stop using drugs). There are several ways to maintain a strong therapeutic relationship in family therapy. Strategies include validating or supporting family members, attending to the family members' goals, and being responsive to each family member's experience. Besides affording each family member a personal experience of the therapist's regard and commitment to her or his well-being, it is of crucial importance that the family perceive the therapist as the leader of the therapeutic system. Families come for help with problems that they have not been able to resolve by themselves. They expect, need, and are entitled to a therapist who will lead them in a new and more effective direction.

Becoming the Leader

The therapist becomes the leader of the therapeutic system by accepting, respecting, and earning the trust of the family. To earn a position of leadership, one must show respect and validate each family member. This means that the therapist must not label, criticize, or dismiss any family member and must initially seek the participation and opinion of all family members. The most difficult individuals to join are those who are powerful and/or angry, those who are reluctant, or at times, those the therapist may find least likable. Powerful members are those in positions of control and leadership in a family. This does not mean that the powerful family member offers positive leadership but simply that the family does or accepts (often without awareness, sometimes against their better judgment) whatever the powerful member wants. Some family members acquire power through leadership or nurturance. Others acquire power through their anger. Angry members are usually perceived as powerful by the family—and are sometimes feared. Reluctant members are those who are less interested in participating in therapy. They, most likely, have the most to lose by participating. That is, they are reluctant to lose the benefits they perceive they have under the current family arrangement.

> The purpose of joining is to create an effective therapeutic system. Joining is the art and ability to create a truly human connection. An important component of a therapeutic system is establishing a governing coalition. This is achieved when the family allows the therapist to take a leadership role, and in exchange, the therapist agrees to pursue a course of treatment that will give each family member something that she wants.

By offering family members something each would like to achieve, the therapist is able to establish a therapeutic alliance with the family—a governing coalition—in which they are, at best, willing to participate in family therapy, most hoping that negative conditions will improve, while also hoping that their behavior will not have to change. A governing coalition is achieved when the family allows the therapist to take a leadership role, and the therapist, in exchange, agrees to pursue a course of treatment that will give individual family members something that each wants. Thus, the therapist weaves together a coalition of family members who pursue both individual and common goals by committing to therapy.

The Clinical Aspects of Joining

Joining is not just a set of techniques; rather, it is the art and the ability to create a truly human connection between people, one of which happens to be the therapist and the others which happen to be each member of the family. This is an amazingly tall order, particularly in a fast-moving therapy in which this human connection has to be established in the first session and strengthened throughout therapy.

In therapy, we ask the family to change old overlearned patterns of behaviors, thoughts, and feelings. Therefore, they have to feel safe and trust the therapist completely. How is it possible in such a short time, within the first session, to achieve such bonding between therapist and family members? Every utterance, behavior, look, phrase, and intervention has to communicate empathy, concern, and professional commitment to the family members' well-being. In joining, the therapist must value each person's feelings, thoughts, needs, and experiences and let them know that he does. The therapist must also refrain from ever judging, criticizing, or labeling a family member.

What happens when you, the therapist, do not feel empathy, concern, and professional commitment for one or more family members? You must connect to something in each person that you can care about and validate. What happens when the welfare department refers to you a family because the father had hit his child?[1] Your job is to prevent it from happening again. What if you feel that this father's behavior is despicable? Look for the pain, for the child inside that father. What is behind the ugly mask? Maybe a horrific upbringing? How does it happen that this person acts the way he does? And what are the current experiences and interactions in which the father is embedded that are linked to the father's unacceptable behavior toward his son?

Therapist Maturity

It should go without saying that to be a BSFT therapist (and possibly most other kinds of therapists), the therapist must be an adult in their own life who brings that maturity into the therapy session. The role of the adult is to listen, understand the family and family members, see family members' pain well beyond the surface of a person's defensive behaviors, never take things personally, and never make therapeutic decisions based on personal feelings. Rather, decisions are made on the basis of strategy; that is, the intervention

---

[1]We distinguish between the person who is sociopathic and does not feel remorse for abusing and the person who in the context of his circumstances resorts to abusive behavior.

that is most effective in helping the family. The therapy is not about the therapist and much less the therapist's needs. Rather, the therapy is about the family. This sounds simple, but it is rather difficult to have the emotional maturity to go beyond one's wants, needs, and preferences and instead focus on those of the family and its members. Although we bring this up in this chapter on joining, it is true throughout all aspects of BSFT.

Who takes care of the therapist's needs and wants? The therapist must have her needs, wants, and preferences met in her personal life or in her own therapy. Clinical supervisors, although empathic, cannot effectively attend to a supervisee's personal needs. In fact, clinical supervisors should not be placed in the position, nor should they place themselves in the position, to attempt to meet a therapist's needs and wants. Rather, the role of the clinical supervisor is to help the therapist identify when the line between the therapist and the family gets blurred and explore whether that boundary is blurred because the therapist is attempting to get her needs met by her client and families. In an ideal world, if our concern were only the growth of the therapist, the clinical supervisor would suggest that the therapist consider seeking therapy. We recognize that this might not be possible in all legal and human resources contexts.

For all of us, there are individuals and families who "push our buttons." When the family pushes the therapist's buttons, and the therapist is unable to maintain a proper boundary, the result is that the therapist's emotions get in the way of his expertise as a therapist. In this case, the therapist may best serve the family by transferring the family to another therapist. In determining whether a case has to be transferred to another therapist, there are some questions a supervisor can ask to assess whether the therapist has become engulfed in the family process. Is the therapist blaming the family or a family member for lack of progress, usually by using terms such as *resistant, low functioning*, or *unmotivated*? Is the therapist taking the side of some family members against another family member? Is the therapist enabling the family when it blames all of its problems on outside systems?

When the therapist blames a family, a family member, or outside systems for the lack of progress, the therapist has lost her systemic perspective, and she is no longer able to help this particular family. These are sure signs that the therapist has lost sight of the circularity of systems in which the therapist plays a part. Because the therapeutic relationship is a component of a system in which the therapist plays a part, a mature therapist always takes responsibility for the lack of change. The mature therapist must ask himself, "What is my role in the lack of progress? And what can I do differently?"

JOINING TECHNIQUES

The purpose of the artful use of joining techniques is to achieve an effective therapeutic system. To do so, the therapist must have a systemic perspective that guides the process of joining (e.g., be the leader, join all family members, do not take sides). The joining intervention techniques (cf. Minuchin, 1974; Minuchin & Fishman, 1981) we review in this chapter are maintenance, mimesis, and tracking. We also review how enactment springboards from tracking.

Maintenance

Maintenance is the stress-free first minutes of all therapy sessions. It starts with simple talk, introductions, greeting each family member, and allowing the family to talk about what they want to talk about, as we usually do in social situations when we start a conversation by asking, "How is the weather?" We might say, "Did you find our place without problems?" This is the unstructured chitchat that establishes an initial rapport. In the first session, it is an opportunity for the family to "smell out" the therapist and realize that the therapist does not have horns, that he appears to be a regular person like anyone else. It is an opportunity for the family to become comfortable in the presence of the therapist, with all of them sitting in a room (which can be an office or a room in the family's home).

The therapist's agenda for these first few minutes is to make everyone feel comfortable and to get to know who is who in the family. This includes the family coming into the room and the therapist inviting the family to seat themselves. If the family asks questions about where to sit, the therapist can say, "Sit wherever you like" to help the family feel comfortable. The therapist might introduce herself and ask, "Who would like to introduce the rest of the family to me?" (the therapist might have had contact with only one person, but that might not be the person who takes the lead in introducing the family to the therapist). During this time, the family begins to reveal who leads, which family members sit next to each other, who fights over a chair, and so forth. The therapist takes mental notes about the emerging patterns in the family. This initial impression will be helpful for planning the best strategy to join and diagnose the family.

Shifting from the initial chitchat to actual work can be challenging for several reasons—for example,

- A family member tells a long story, and the therapist is uncomfortable in stopping it. However, it is always possible to empathize with some aspect of the story, which moves the chitchat into therapeutic work.

- The therapist is uncomfortable in leading and being directive (e.g., he finds it hard to say to the family member with the long story, "Tell that directly to your son").

- The therapist gets seduced by the content of the story.

BSFT is not for the faint of heart. It requires courage. It requires that a therapist have the abilities and the chutzpah to be a leader who takes charge of the therapy session and does not get drawn in by content.

Maintenance in the first session might take up to 10 minutes and in subsequent sessions, about 3 minutes. The therapist then gives the "work" signal by asking a question that will launch the therapy. In the first session, the question might be, "Who would like to tell me what brings you here?" In subsequent sessions, the therapist work signal could be, "What would you like to work on today?"

Mimesis

When in Rome, do as the Romans do. Or as in nature, we could say be a chameleon. *Mimesis* is the act of imitating the family to blend in, to avoid being rejected. The therapist can mimic by speaking in ways that are similar to that of the family, using the tone or volume of the family, or using the affect (funny, serious) of the family, the rate of speech, or anything else that can help the therapist be more like the family in their style. Note that we emphasize the term *imitate* and not *adopt* because this is a temporary tool to better blend with the family as part of joining. However, mimesis is effective when it looks like appropriate behavior on the part of the therapist but not when it looks ridiculous. For example, it would not seem natural for a mature therapist to imitate a teenager by saying, "Hey dude, wassup?" In other words, mimesis has to be done tastefully and with judgment, and it must appear genuine.

> An effective therapist is a leader who knows how to blend but does not allow herself to be engulfed by the family.

Mimesis is used in everyday social situations—for example, in trying to know how others will dress so as to dress appropriately for an event, people seek to blend in and be appropriate to a situation. People mimic mood so that, for example, at a funeral they act like others do—sad or thoughtful—whereas, at a celebration, they act joyful. By imitating, an individual blends in with the group and shows the group that its style is respected and accepted.

Mimesis in Behavior

Just as we do in social situations, in family therapy, we can strategically imitate behaviors as a way of blending with a family, such as being serious with a serious family or making jokes with a jovial family. Moreover, if it is important to establish rapport with a particular family member, the therapist may mimic the member's behavior and/or style. For example, if a grandmother has a young child on her lap, when she puts the child down, the therapist might ask the family whether she can pick up the child, and if the family agrees, the therapist will place the child on her lap.

Mimesis in Language

Each family has their own vocabulary; each person has her own world. If a man is a carpenter, it is helpful to speak in terms of tools, explaining that he has been using a hammer with his son when perhaps he needed to have polished a surface, suggesting that the use of the right tool for the right project will get the job done. If a woman is an accountant, it is helpful to speak in terms of assets and liabilities. If a family is musically inclined, the therapist might refer to each person as a note and the family as a symphony. A person's world should be referenced in the language used to communicate with them. The therapist does not talk to a family using vocabulary that is found in this book—words such as *interactions, restructuring, family systems*, or even *therapy* or *therapy sessions*. No psychobabble! Instead, the BSFT therapist uses the "pots and pans" language that the family uses in their everyday life. As one example, it may be more comfortable for a family if therapy sessions are referred to as *meetings* rather than *sessions*. For therapy, the family might be more comfortable if the therapist uses the term *the family's work*, and so on.

Tracking and Enactment

We use the technique of *tracking* for encouraging enactments. When tracking, a therapist encourages family members to talk with each other directly. Often, an effective way to do this is to turn content into process. Tracking occurs when the therapist uses what a family member says or does regarding another family member to connect these two members by encouraging them to speak with each other, rather than with the therapist, thereby eliciting an enactment. This can be done in one of two ways: The therapist can say to the father, "Please tell your son what you are saying to me," or she can ask the son to respond to what his father just said. Tracking thus uses verbal and nonverbal cues to springboard from one family member to another.

Tracking is a technique to develop enactments. *Enactments* allow us to observe how the family interacts in their usual ways, its overlearned pathways. For example, when Farah tells the therapist that her big brother bugs her (content), the therapist asks Farah to tell her big brother directly. Farah will probably say, as most family members do before they get to know how BSFT works, "But I have told him a hundred times," and the therapist will reply, "I wasn't there when you told him before. I want you to do it now so that I can help you with it." This conversation between the therapist and the family that encourages family members to speak directly with each other is repeated multiple times as family members are directed to speak with each other rather than with the therapist. Farah says to her brother, "I hate you." Brother, in turn, says, "I hate you too." The process between them shows negativity and vagueness of communication. In this interaction, the tracking was the process of moving from content to encouraging an interaction about the content. The enactment of this interaction revealed the process (i.e., hostility and negativity). Another way to handle this example is for the therapist to track by asking the brother to respond to Farah about her complaint.

There are two aspects to the term *tracking*. One of these refers to the work of the clever hunter who finds the tracks left by an animal and knows how to follow these tracks to his goal—finding the animal. Hence, tracking involves the skill of following the signs left by the animal not only to learn where the animal went but also the ways of the animal. In a family, tracking means to follow—that is, to attend to—how the family interacts. It is to do more than passively follow; the therapist encourages the family to interact in front of her to observe its patterns of interactions.

The second origin of the term *tracking* is responsible for its great power in bringing about changes smoothly and quickly. This meaning is best explained in terms of the tracks of a train system. A person wanting to travel from New Orleans to Miami by train would have to know about the train routes. That person could not possibly attempt to travel from New Orleans to Miami in a straight line, or she would find the train traveling in the waters in the Gulf of Mexico, and the train would sink. There is a prescribed way in which a train can travel, according to how the tracks and train routes have been laid out. It makes equal sense, therefore, that if the therapist wants to take a family from point A to point B, he should travel along the routes that the family has established. In the case, for example, in which a father is domineering, the son becoming more autonomous will require permission from the father. In the case of a mother who is central to all child-rearing issues, the therapist would track this family by asking the mother to discuss with other family members the problems that the family is having with a youth's behavior. If the therapist wants to be accepted by a family, she must travel on the family's pathway, which is identified by following the family's behavior and encouraging the family members to behave in their usual way.

When family members interact with one another, they do so in their over-learned ways, which when displayed, constitute an enactment of the family process. For an enactment to take place, the therapist has to let the family members interact with each other without restraints from the therapist. During the enactment, the therapist has to step back to let the enactment evolve without therapist interference, at least long enough for the enactment to complete itself (which could be seconds or a few minutes). Some therapists may not be used to the kind of boisterous interactions that may happen, particularly when family members are angry with each other, which is typical in families that present with acting-out problems. Typically, acting-out problems grow from an inability to address the anger between family members effectively. Hence, when they speak with each about what bothers them about the other, what comes out can be explosive. High negative affect (i.e., angry yelling, cursing) is to be expected during sessions in families who have acting-out problems. This is the bread and butter for experienced therapists. But for a new therapist, high negative affect can be scary. In that case, the therapist may feel compelled to put a stop to the interactions. If the negativity gets physical, it must be stopped immediately, hopefully before injuries happen, which is extremely rare. In our experience, it happens in less than one session out of 240 families in therapy (Robbins, Feaster, Horigian, Rohrbaugh, et al., 2011).

With verbal altercations, there is a delicate balance between allowing sufficient time for the enactment to occur before intervening and intervening
early enough to transform the interaction, before it disrupts the therapy (e.g.,
erodes the role of the therapist as a leader), into something more constructive
(described in Chapter 5).

Verbal fights are conflicts between family members that BSFT therapists
can diagnose in seconds. Why let the enactment continue? Because we want
to see how the whole family reacts. A family can react by not responding, but
most likely, someone will take sides. That alliance between two individuals
who support each other is important to diagnose. The response of a family
member may also be to attempt to stop the verbal fight. In that case, it is
important for the therapist to determine whether that person's intervention
is effective in stopping the fight. If the person is a parent figure and that person
is ineffective, it is important diagnostic information that we will have to correct
during therapy because parents have to be effective executives of their families. However, as in the case of the Lewis family, grandmother often embarked
on a ranting rampage against the identified patient (IP), the family member
with "the problem" who has to be "fixed." The rant repeated itself for as long
as the therapist allowed it to continue and resulted in the IP leaving the room.
In such instances, it is important, once the therapist has determined that this
is a repetitive process, that he intervene early enough to avoid the repetition
of unproductive negative interactions.

> One of the most important factors that makes BSFT brief, effective, and effi-
> cient is that we encourage enactments that permit us to diagnose the family
> interactions quickly, and we use the diagnosis to determine what has to be
> corrected in the family.

Clinicians might wonder whether enactment truly displays how the families behave when the therapist is not present. Typically, the behaviors the
family display when allowed to interact freely with each other in the therapist's presence are the same overlearned ways family members use in their
daily life. When family members talk with each other, they cannot help but
do it in the ways they have practiced thousands of times. If you have any
question about whether this is the genuine overlearned family repetitive patterns of interactions, you will see these patterns repeat in each and every
enactment, until the therapist corrects them. In fact, individuals can put on
an act for outsiders, but they are unable to do so in interactions with each
other. If one individual attempts to behave differently in front of the therapist, other family members will quickly call him out. If one family member
usually puts down another, it is likely that in their interaction in the therapy

they will do just that. Why? Because it is what they have practiced thousands of times.

The interaction among family members in the therapy is called an *enactment* because it enacts what the family typically does every day at home. As we noted in Chapter 1, families' ways of behaving with one another are deeply scripted. Families come to therapy, in fact, because their script, their over-learned behaviors, are getting them into trouble. Our job in diagnosing repetitive patterns of interactions is to identify the interactions among family members, recognize that they are repetitive, and identify those that are linked to the problem behaviors and thus are not serving the family well, as well as those that are adaptive and should be reinforced. Once repetitive patterns of interactions that are maladaptive are recognized (Chapters 3 and 4), they can be changed (Chapter 5).

Although some enactments are elicited by the therapist, some enactments occur spontaneously. Spontaneous enactments occur anytime the family members interact with each other without the therapist prompting. When an enactment occurs spontaneously during the diagnostic process, the therapist should allow it to happen. If it occurs spontaneously during restructuring, it should be used as an opportunity to transform interactions. It should be noted that clinical families often have crises. A form of a spontaneous enactment is a family crisis. They are particularly opportune types of enactments because they are highly charged, family members are emotionally available to try new frames and new behavior, and consequently, there is great motivation for change. Crises are opportunities that must be seized quickly.

Specific and Targeted Joining

The therapist's job is to use joining techniques to avoid threatening the family's homeostasis until a viable therapeutic system has been established. However, joining takes place at the beginning of therapy and also repeatedly and contin-uously throughout therapy, with instances that require focused, intense, and targeted joining, such as in the case of family members who are particularly reluctant to join therapy or reluctant to become engaged in a therapeutic inter-vention. There are also family members who from experience we have learned require an extra dose of joining on the part of the therapist—for example, indi-viduals who are angry, critical, targets of criticism, or silent family members and anyone whom the therapist is about to ask to behave in a way that is new for that person. An example of the latter is a person who is critical and the thera-pist reframes as concerned for his family. To join with this person, who may not view himself as loving, the therapist reframes criticism as a loving trait he, in fact, possesses, before asking the individual to discuss her feeling of concern and love for the person who is being criticized. Also, whenever restructuring takes place, it must be preceded by intense targeted joining. When a family member loses power in a relationship, the loss of power has to be balanced with an increase in joining.

In another example, a single-mother family was referred for treatment. She had three older sons and a 14-year-old daughter who had attempted suicide. When the girl told her mother, "You never listen to me. You always take my brothers' side. You have no idea what I am feeling," she was asking for recognition of her feelings, validation, love, and care of her mother. Mother responded by looking at the ceiling and cleaning her nails, with her stance suggesting a complete lack of interest in what the girl was saying. Mother followed up her nonverbal communication by saying, "Stop bugging me. You are always so demanding and needy. I have a life too, you know?" Of course, the therapist's heart went out to the young girl and was resentful toward a mother who could be so cold and uncaring. But what was happening with the mother? What was the mother feeling when her daughter spoke? The therapist had first to validate the daughter to let her know she was heard before addressing the mom. The therapist also gave the daughter an explanation of why he wanted to reach out to the mother. To the daughter, the therapist said,

> It sounds to me that you feel lonely in this family and that you really need your mother, which is normal for a 14-year-old teen. But for me to get the whole picture and be in a better place to help you, you also have to hear from your mother and learn where she is at and how she feels.

The therapist then asked the mother to tell her daughter, "What are you feeling? This is a place for you to say anything you want." The therapist, by reaching out, by showing interest, by not coming across as judgmental, is giving the message that the mother's experience and feelings are also important and should be heard.

An effective BSFT therapist has to understand that everybody in the family has to be valued for their feelings, thoughts, and needs. In the example, the therapist was able to empathize with the mother's emotional void and, by her response, communicate to the mother that she was understood and not judged. To create the conditions under which the mother can be nurturant and be able to communicate it to her daughter, the therapist must have a joined position with the mother to elicit nurturance from the mother to the daughter. It would have been easy to criticize or judge the mother as uncaring or negligent or, even worse, narcissistic. However, this would result in a damaging rupture in the therapist–mother relationship, and consequently, the therapist would lose her role of leadership and ability to create change.

Use of Self: A Caveat

As we can see from these examples, joining ultimately requires the use of the self by the therapist to empathize with even the most apparently dislikable family members. By the term *use of the self*, we are not necessarily advocating for self-disclosure because in BSFT self-disclosure can be used only when it furthers the therapeutic relationship and treatment plan, and even then, it should be quite limited, short, and brief. Please also note that we use *dislikable* to describe a behavior or stance in a moment in time but do not ascribe the term to the person. We recognize that once we come to know a person better, we see their behavior in the context of their humanity. It is true in nearly all therapies, that there is an important difference between expressing our "self" in the service of therapy (e.g., connecting with the family members) and losing the "self" in therapy (e.g., becoming a part of the family; D'Aniello & Nguyen, 2017; Knox & Hill, 2003; Roberts, 2005). In the latter, the boundary between the "self" and the client or family fades. Salvador Minuchin (personal communication, January 19, 1977) used to speak about the dance of the therapist being in and out of the family. That is, the therapist can connect and care and yet never truly get lost in the family's process or become overly involved with any one family member. The therapist never becomes a member of the family, and the therapist never does the family's work.

> Never function in the role of a family member.

Joining is directed by strategy. It is the people whose behaviors are most objectionable whose involvement in the therapy may be most critical to engage because they have the most to change and the most to lose by changing, and it is their change that might have the greatest impact in transforming family interactions.

ADVICE TO THERAPISTS

In joining, the family therapist must join all family members and not just those who show up or with whom she happens to agree. In fact, the person with whom it is most critical to establish an alliance or bond is frequently the one the therapist is most likely to find dislikable. Inexperienced family therapists are experts at taking the side of one family member against another because one is "right," and the other is obviously "wrong." Being right or wrong usually has to do with the content of the argument and not the process of the family's interactions. When joining, the BSFT therapist does not take one family member's side against another; he is on the side of all family members and respects each individual's position and point of view. The focus is not on who is right or wrong in terms of the content of an argument. Rather, the focus is on defining the interactions that have to be changed and on how the family can be helped to change them.

As discussed in Chapter 5, a therapist may take the side of one family member against another for a short period. However, when this is done, it is used as a strategy—strictly to create an imbalance that brings about a change in family interactions. We cannot say it enough: The strategic BSFT therapist does not take sides about who is right or wrong on the basis of content issues.

Typically, the therapist's heart tells him to support the underdog. However, in giving support to the weaker person at the beginning of therapy, the therapist is supporting a family member without power. The unfortunate outcome of this error is to have entered into a coalition with the powerless family member against the powerful family member. This, in turn, makes the therapist powerless within the family. In almost every case, when the intuition of the therapist suggests supporting a particular family member, it would be the wrong strategic move. Because the powerful member of the family is the one with the ability to bring the family to therapy as well as to take the family out of therapy, an alliance with the powerless member as an initial move will cost the therapist her job as the therapist for this family. In other words, she will lose the family by not being willing to enter their family system according to their established rules. The BSFT therapist has to join the "boss" of the family if the therapist is to attain and maintain the leadership needed to change the way the family operates. There will be plenty of time to help and support the underdog. The therapist can only help the powerless person if she joins the powerful member of the family and gets her or his cooperation. Otherwise, she will not be given the opportunity to be this family's therapist.

One of the most useful strategies in joining is supporting the existing family structure. The BSFT therapist supports those who are in power by demonstrating respect for them—even when disagreeing with them—because they are the ones with the power to accept the therapist into the family; they have the power to place the therapist in a leadership role, and they have the power to take the family out of therapy.

To establish a viable therapeutic system and gain a position of leadership in the family requires considerable skill and initiative from the therapist. From a systems perspective, the therapist takes full responsibility for behaving in ways that will be acceptable to the family, blending with and respecting their ways. Although the emphasis in this area, as in most of the therapist's work, is in attending to the family's process and interactions, blending with the family may require using the family's content while never getting lost in or buying into the family's content. Thus, by using their language (content) and by accepting the validity and importance of some of their content concerns (such as the presenting symptom), the therapist is better able to communicate her acceptance of the family and thereby is more likely to be accepted.

KEY TAKEAWAYS

- The therapeutic system is a collaborative relationship between family and therapist in which the therapist is accepted as its leader in order to change the family.

- The process of creating and maintaining this therapeutic system is referred to as *joining*. In BSFT, joining occurs continuously from beginning to end of treatment, including before and after each intervention.

- Joining is the art and science of establishing a truly human connection.

- The therapist becomes the leader of the therapeutic system by accepting, respecting, and earning the trust of all family members and by accepting and respecting the family system organization initially.

- Each family member allows the therapist to become the leader of the therapeutic system when the therapist agrees to pursue the interest of that member. Hence, the therapist must agree to pursue the interest of each member to establish a governing coalition.

- There are three techniques to promote joining: maintenance, mimesis, and tracking.

- Tracking is used to elicit enactments. Enactments are interactions among family members during the session.

3

Diagnosing Family Systems Patterns of Interactions

Understanding how families interact is of crucial importance to Brief Strategic Family Therapy® (BSFT®) therapists because BSFT's central function is to allow the strengths of the family to replace those interactions that are not working well for the family. Doing this work effectively and efficiently requires identifying how families interact (which we refer to as *family process*) and then, more specifically, identifying which patterns of repetitive interactions are related to the presenting problem and have to be replaced with strength-based interactions.

The strategic character of BSFT emerges clearly during systemic diagnosis. This is because BSFT diagnoses are made to identify both adaptive and maladaptive patterns of interactions so that a practical, strategically efficient treatment plan can be developed. This chapter describes the BSFT approach to systemic diagnosis and illustrates how to use this systemic diagnostic approach to create a treatment plan. Rather than diagnosing individuals, BSFT therapists apply systemic diagnoses to how the family system interacts. As discussed in Chapter 2 of this volume, the first step is to observe how the family members interact among themselves. Thus, the therapist must encourage a family enactment. This may seem obvious, but it is quite challenging to teach therapists that they must observe families interact (process) rather than hear stories (content) from the family. Interactions are behaviors that are available for observation in the here and now. As such, we can have confidence that what we are observing is objective. However, stories and content are, by definition, subjective. To observe the family interacting, the therapist allows or

http://dx.doi.org/10.1037/0000169-004
Brief Strategic Family Therapy, by J. Szapocznik and O. E. Hervis

encourages the family to interact within the family session. The interaction is elicited when the therapist directs a family member to speak directly to another member. When the family members interact with each other, they "enact" their overlearned interactional patterns. Enactment, thus, is accomplished by the therapist redirecting the family to interact with each other rather than with the therapist. In the diagnostic process, the BSFT therapist must place herself in the position of observer and never in the position of participant or actor. The therapist is the choreographer or director of the play, but the therapist never takes the role of a family member.

The diagnostic process has two components. One is to identify the family's processes, and the second is to link the family's process to the presenting symptoms. In a problem-focused strategic approach such as BSFT, we prioritize (a) correcting those interactional patterns that are linked to the presenting problems and (b) strengthening adaptive processes. Hence, other maladaptive interactional patterns not directly related to the existence of a symptom can be identified but must have a lower priority of being addressed, if at all.

A family comes to the first session, and Mom tells the therapist that they are seeking help because George, the 14-year-old, is refusing to go to school. When Mom tells the therapist that George refuses to go to school, the therapist asks Mom to talk with George about what is going on that he is refusing to go to school. Mom: "You are just like your grandfather: You have no drive; you will never amount to anything." In response, George looks away and does not respond. The therapist observes that when Mother's communication with George is accusatory, George ignores her. The result of these behaviors is that the conflict between them is not resolved, and the hostility between Mom and George will continue to build up. This is an example of what we have referred to as *maladaptive interaction*. Neither Mom nor George is likely to be satisfied with their interaction. More important, this interaction does not help correct George's chronic truancy.

To assist therapists in maintaining a systemic focus to diagnosis and to enable the therapist to quickly review the family interactions that should be identified during diagnosis, we provide at the end of this chapter Exhibit 3.1 (pp. 76–77), the Family Systems Diagnostic Checklist. Although we do not have this checklist with us during the session, immediately after the first session, we complete the checklist to more formally formulate our diagnosis. We also modify the checklist as we notice new interactional patterns that we missed in the first session.

As it is obvious from this example, a critical skill we teach in this chapter is the BSFT therapist's ability to observe the process—the interactions—and not get distracted by the content, whether the content (problem) is about not going to school or about doing chores or coming home past curfew. The therapist observes the interaction between Mother and George, an interaction that will repeat across all contents, until the BSFT therapist helps the family to change its interactions.

In this example, we have illustrated how the BSFT approach to systemic diagnosis differs drastically from conventional approaches. In conventional approaches to family assessment, the therapist is likely to take a family history and ask questions about the nature of the symptoms, such as their onset and duration. This type of assessment is considered to be content oriented, and as such, it is essentially irrelevant to the BSFT model. Another important distinction between conventional and BSFT approaches to diagnosis is that, in conventional approaches, the youth who has been identified by the family as a "symptom-carrying youth" and one parent figure are typically present for the assessment and diagnosis, whereas in BSFT, we require all individuals that function as family members to be present for the systemic diagnosis. Unless all persons who are involved in the family on a routine basis are present, the assessment of interactional patterns will be inaccurate. All individuals who live under one roof and are not transient are included, as are any other individuals who are involved in parenting functions. This is easier said than done. Let us say that George lives with his mother and her other children but visits overnight one day per week with his biological father and his dad's new family. Initially, the diagnoses may require bringing George, his mother and mother-related siblings, and biological father to therapy. However, as the therapy moves along, it may become clear that rules in his mother's and father's homes are quite different. In that case, it is necessary to bring his father, stepmother, and potentially stepsiblings into a session with George, his mother, and her children living at home. Again, this is easier said than done, but it is doable, and we do it because we know that we cannot build a puzzle when pieces are missing.

Once the BSFT therapist has observed an enactment and identified what patterns of interactions emerge, there is now the opportunity to categorize interactions using a common language. This language reflects the five major categories of patterns within the family that we find useful to classify our observations. In addition, in this section, we also discuss the relationship of the family to the life context. In the rest of this chapter, we explain these dimensions that, in our experience, therapists find useful in their daily work. A formal approach to measuring these dimensions is found in Szapocznik et al. (1991; see also Minuchin, Rosman, & Baker, 1978; Rosman, 1978; Szapocznik, Hervis, & Schwartz, 2003). The five dimensions of family patterns of interactions are organization, resonance, developmental stages, identified patienthood, and conflict resolution.

ORGANIZATION

As repetitive patterns of interactions in a family occur over time, they reveal three aspects of how a family organizes itself:

- leadership,
- subsystem organization, and
- communication flow.

For systems to function well, they must have a functional organization. Let us take the example of a company. The company must have clearly defined leadership, clearly defined divisions that attend to various aspects of the work of the organization, and good communication among the leadership, the division leaders, and their employees. Families, like companies, are systems. The family system needs defined leadership, clearly defined groupings that attend to various aspects of the work of the organization, and good communication between the parent figures, the parents and the children, among the children, and when relevant, the extended family.

Leadership

Leadership is defined as the distribution of authority and responsibility within the family. In functional two-parent families, leadership is in the hands of the parents. In modern societies, both parents usually share authority and decision making. Frequently, in one-parent families, the parent shares some of the leadership with an older child. In the case of a single parent living within an extended family framework, leadership may be shared with an uncle, aunt, or grandparent (Bengtson, 2001).

In assessing whether leadership is adaptive, BSFT therapists look first at the family hierarchy. Who is in charge of directing the family? Who are the family members in positions of authority? Is this leadership in the appropriate hands? Is it shared between (or among) the appropriate people? Is hierarchy assigned appropriately with respect to age, role, and function within the family? Leadership should be assumed by the parental figures. Some leadership can be delegated to older children as long as such delegation is not overly burdensome, is age appropriate, and is delegated and not usurped.

Closely related to hierarchy is behavior control. Behavior control is one of the greatest challenges a family may face. *Behavior control* refers to establishing and maintaining discipline, in most cases, among the children. Discipline, in general, refers to the dos and don'ts of what is acceptable and needed for family members to engage in behaviors that succeed in the context of the cultural streams and circumstances that influence their family. We specifically look at the following: Who keeps order in the family, if anyone? Who carries out and enforces discipline? Are attempts to discipline and keep order successful, or are they undermined or ignored?

In general, parents should exercise effective behavior control with their children. However, there are times when one parent may find herself in the position of having to establish the dos and don'ts of what is expected because the other parent behaves like a child, such as when a parent comes home drunk or watches TV all day and does not help in the home. There is much we could write about what constitutes appropriate dos and don'ts. Our job as therapists, however, is to help parents establish appropriate rules for their family, taking into consideration the children's age, the social and cultural contexts, the family composition, and the idiosyncratic realities of any one family.

The next aspect of leadership a therapist observes is nurturance and guidance. We have combined nurturance and guidance because, in practice, guidance does not work in the absence of a nurturant bond between parent and child. A nurturant bond is established when the parents show interest in the children's world, help them when they need it, and let them know they are loved by saying it often and showing it. How do parents "show" nurturance toward their children? By hugging them, kissing them, spending time doing what the children like to do, complimenting them while reprimanding them, and so forth.

We do not expect parents' guiding behaviors to be successful unless they are accompanied by nurturance. Exceptions to this statement are found in the research literature on parenting and child development (Henneberger, Durkee, Truong, Atkins, & Tolan, 2013; Roche, Ensminger, & Cherlin, 2007). When assessing guidance, look for the following: Are parents nurturant? Do parents provide guidance in the family? Are parents appropriate role models?

Subsystem Organization

If the family is the "corporation," subsystems are the "divisions" within the company. Families have both formal subsystems (e.g., spouses, siblings, grandparents) and informal subsystems (e.g., the women, the people who manage the money, those who do the housekeeping, those who play chess). Each of these subsystems must have a certain degree of privacy and independence (i.e., boundaries).

BSFT therapists are concerned with issues such as the adequacy or appropriateness of the subsystems that exist in a family. BSFT therapists also assess the nature of the coalitions that give rise to these subsystems. To assess the family's functioning within this category, the BSFT therapist is concerned with subsystem membership, alliances, and triangulation.

Subsystem Membership

The therapist wants to determine that the appropriate subsystems are in place with the appropriate membership, that there is an executive subsystem composed of the persons in charge, and that, if there is a couple, a couple subsystem exists both for parenting and marital activities. How are subsystems identified? Subsystems comprise those family members who are in agreement and supportive and who work in cooperation with each other. Alliances are reflected in these kinds of cooperative and supportive relationships.

Subsystems also need permeable boundaries. By *boundaries*, we mean the psychological separation of the subsystem from the rest of the family. By *permeable*, we mean that communication and activities can occur across subsystems. Boundaries and permeability represent the pull and push of having a border while allowing transactions to occur across that border. For example, a boundary can be like the wall of a room, whereas permeability suggests that the wall has windows and doors that can be opened and closed to improve the effective functioning of the family. A therapist might look for the following when assessing subsystems: Which are the subsystems in the family? Are the subsystems appropriate given the family composition? Who is a member of which subsystem (e.g., parental, older sibling, extended family, younger children)? Are subsystems formed by the appropriate members in terms of age and function? Are the boundaries between subsystems clearly defined while remaining permeable?

Alliances

We discuss four types of alliances in this section. The first type and the most common are *parental alliances* between two partners, where the primary alliance must be between the couple. The support partners give each other is process. Content, such as who does what chore when, is the context in which support occurs. If the process of mutual support is faulty, it is unlikely that the couple will be able to cooperate with each other in the content of parenting. If the parents are separated or divorced and still involved in coparenting children they have together, it may be that the parents do not agree on many topics, but they must work together and present a united front to their children.

In the case of a single parent, where an extended family member is part of the authority or parental subsystem, as in a marital couple, the authority figures must be allied with each other and not with one child against the other authority figure.

In families in which there is more than one child, attention must be given to the nature of the sibling alliances. The quality of relationships among siblings is important to the BSFT approach because siblings are in a position to enhance or impede each other's well-being. Siblings are most likely to be the longest-lasting relationships for each other, and thus, to ensure a supportive future, we attend to the strength of the sibling relationship during childhood and adolescence. To assess the sibling relationship, we ask the following: Is there collaboration or conflict and hostility among the siblings? Is the identified patient—the family member with "the problem" who has to be "fixed"—marginalized? Is there competition for preferred status among siblings?

The second type of alliance, cross-generational, is often problematic (e.g., between a parent figure and a child). These alliances often spell trouble because such alliances blur hierarchical lines and undermine a parent's ability to control behavior, particularly the behavior of the child in the cross-generational alliance. For this reason, cross-generational alliances become damaging to family functioning when the child gains more power than the parent through this alliance. They are frequently seen in families of acting-out youth, where the youth has gained so much power through her participation in a cross-generational alliance that she dares to challenge authority and get away with it. This power to be rebellious, disobedient, and "out of control" is achieved by having gained the support of one parent figure who, to disqualify the other parent figure, enables the adolescent's inappropriate behavior. This maladaptive pattern of interactions is referred to as *triangulation*.

Triangulation

There is a type of subsystem formation that occurs when two people are in conflict with each other, and a third member of the family either is drawn into the conflict or immerses herself in the conflict. For example, Mother and Grandmother are fighting, and Grandma calls out to Lizzy, "Lizzy, don't you agree with me?" If Lizzy says yes, she has unwittingly become triangulated. Triangulation is a form of cross-generation alliance because the child becomes allied with a parent figure. Mother is left out of the Grandma–Lizzy alliance. In our experience, triangulation invariably has a negative impact on the child who will express internalizing or externalizing symptoms. Typically, to keep Mom and Grandma from fighting, Lizzy might develop maladaptive behaviors to distract them when they fight. Here we see the circularity in the system in which Lizzy was brought into the triangle to side with Grandma against Mother but eventually takes the role of disrupting fights between Mother and Grandma.

> Triangles always spell trouble because they prevent the resolution of a conflict between two authority figures. Typically, the triangulated third party, usually a child or adolescent, experiences stress and develops a symptom. Conflict can only be solved when the discussion occurs directly between the two conflicting parties.

There are two unfortunate outcomes from triangulation. One is that the conflict between the two adults is avoided, and thus, it does not get resolved. The second is that when the triangulated child interrupts the conflict, the anger is redirected toward the child, and consequently, the child often becomes symptomatic. These symptoms may range from depression and suicidal behavior to severe and aggressive conduct and behavioral disorders.

Ultimately, two people can resolve their differences of opinion only by discussing, arguing, or fighting about their respective positions directly with each other. When, instead of keeping the discussion or argument limited to the two of them, they bring in a child (or allow a child to come in and "save" them from their fight), the authority figures prevent themselves from confronting their differences and reaching a resolution. This unresolved conflict becomes an ongoing source of frustration, irritation, and anger for all involved family members.

Although we have presented the negative aspect of triangulation, there are two instances that are adaptive: (a) when two small children are fighting, it is appropriate and necessary for a parent to get involved to stop the fight; and (b) if a parent is fighting with a child, it is appropriate for the other parent to become involved in support of the first parent.

Communication Flow

The final category of organization is the nature of communication. In functional families, communication flow is characterized by the extent to which it is direct and dyadic and by its level of specificity. Good communication flow is the ability of every two family members to communicate directly and be specific in their expression of what they want from each other. For example, a declaration such as, "I don't like it when you yell at me" is a sign of good communication because it is dyadic, specific, and direct.

Indirect communications indicate problems. Take, for example, a father who says to his son, "You tell your mother that she better get here right away" or the mother who tells the father, "You better do something about Juanito because he won't listen to me." In these two examples, the communication is conducted through a third person. In these cases, communication through a third party is neither dyadic nor direct.

Nonspecific (i.e., vague) communications are also troublesome, as in the case of the father who tells his son, "You are always trouble." The communication would be clearer if the father referred specifically to what trouble he wants to communicate about to his son—for example, "You broke our rules by coming home late."

In summary, effective communications must occur directly between two family members without interference from others, and they must have the kind of specificity that allows the parties to understand what is being communicated.

RESONANCE

Resonance defines the emotional and psychological distance between family members. *Resonance* is the extent to which what happens to one person is also experienced by another and is defined as the reactivity of family members to one another (Minuchin, 1974; Szapocznik et al., 2003; Szapocznik & Kurtines, 1989). A raincoat may help illustrate the meaning of resonance. A raincoat protects us from the weather. To the extent that the raincoat is impermeable, the person wearing it will not feel the rain or cold. However, to the extent that the raincoat is permeable, both rain and cold will get through, so that the person wearing the raincoat will soon feel the weather. If resonance were applied to this example, *high resonance* would imply that whatever happens with the weather is clearly experienced by our protagonist, and thus it could be said that too much of the weather gets through. However, if the raincoat is impenetrable, and thus neither rain nor cold can get through, the protagonist will not experience any of the weather. This second case would be called *low resonance* because too little of the weather is experienced by our protagonist.

A 6-year-old son who hangs onto his mother's skirt at his birthday party may be said to be overly close to her. A mother who cries when the daughter fights with her boyfriend is emotionally too close to her daughter. These are cases of high resonance/enmeshment. On the other hand, a father who does not care that his son is in trouble with the law may be described as psychologically and emotionally distant. This is a case of low resonance/disengagement.

There are two ways in which the level of resonance can become problematic for the family: when the interpersonal boundaries are too rigid or impermeable (referred to as *disengagement*) or when the interpersonal boundaries are practically nonexistent or too permeable (referred to as *enmeshment*). Therefore, to understand resonance, we must first discuss interpersonal boundaries.

An *interpersonal boundary*, just as the term implies, indicates from a psychological perspective where one person or group of persons ends and the next begins. People set their boundaries when they let others know which behaviors that intrude on their world they will allow and which they will not allow. The following are some examples of boundaries:

- a permeable boundary: The sign at the door reads, "Knock before you enter!";
- an impermeable boundary: The sign at the door reads "Do not enter!" or "No trespassing"; and
- a minimal boundary: an open door.

In systems such as families, boundaries develop as a function of the interactions that occur in the family over time. Sometimes boundaries are discussed ("You never tell me how you are doing in school" or "I want to know everything he said to you") or never discussed, but everyone understands them (big brother never participates in any family activity). These boundaries determine how family members psychologically (emotionally and behaviorally) respond to one another.

Enmeshment and Disengagement

Enmeshment refers to family members who are overinvolved with each other and overreact to each other. They lack psychological and emotional distance from each other as if, in the extreme, their two selves blend into one. Mary says, "I want to eat sushi," and Jane says, "No, you don't. You prefer Mexican." At another time, Mary cries because she has gained weight, and Jane cries along with her. At the other extreme of involvement are members who are underinvolved with one another and underreact to each other. These are said to be *disengaged*. These are family members who are indifferent to each other, and there is little or no interaction, and few or no feelings are expressed about or to each other. Somewhere in the middle of the resonance range are members with the proper degree of involvement—that is, family members who react to one another while still maintaining their separate individuality. Enmeshment (excessive closeness) and disengagement (excessive distance) can often occur at the same time within a single family. This frequently happens in families of drug-abusing youths, where one parent is protective and closely allied to the youth (i.e., enabling), whereas the other parent is marginalized from the enmeshed dyad and may appear disinterested and uninvolved.

How do we assess the emotional and psychological distance between and among family members? Put another way, how can we observe over- and underinvolvement between or among family members? As indicated, there is an ideal midpoint where families function properly. This midpoint makes interactions and communication possible at appropriate times, while members continue to retain their separateness and individual differences. This midpoint permits cooperation with individuation.

All behaviors indicative of enmeshment have in common that these behaviors compromise the separateness of individual family members. That is, enmeshed behaviors reflect a lack of individuality and separateness of the persons involved. Enmeshment is distinguished from closeness or intimacy in that in intimate relationships, persons know each other, whereas in enmeshed relationships, there is a lack of clarity about the other person because they see each other as an extension of the self. For example, when my face is half an inch away from your face, I cannot see your face. I cannot tell what you look like. I have to move out to 18 inches before I can see the contour of your face and the fullness of you. Hence, for two persons to know each other, they have to have sufficient closeness to care and sufficient distance to have clarity on who the other person is.

Behaviors That Reflect Enmeshment or Disengagement

Some of the observable behaviors that reflect enmeshment or overinvolvement are described next.

Mind Reading
Mind reading is said to occur when one family member speaks for another, stating what the other wants, thinks, believes, and likes without the latter having said anything. For example, when grandfather Lolo asks granddaughter Susie about what she wants to do for the holidays, her mother—without having discussed with Susie—answers, "She wants to stay home." An extreme example of mind reading also happens when a family member overrides what another member has said about his or her beliefs, feelings, wants, and so forth. For example, Ileana says, "I want to go to the beach," and her husband says, "No, you don't. You hate the sand, the sun, and the saltwater."

Mediated Response
A special case of mind reading occurs when one family member acts as a pathway or mediator of a conversation between two other members. For example, Mary and Dad are having a heated discussion. Reacting to the tension, Mother rushes in to interpret for Mary what she thinks Dad means and interpret for Dad what she thinks Mary means. This kind of communication is not only evidence of enmeshment but also indicates the presence of a triangulated structure, thus reflecting interlinked maladaptive patterns of interactions.

Simultaneous Speech

Simultaneous speech occurs when two or more family members speak at the same time for more than a few seconds. This is sometimes typical of cultures in which persons are emotionally close to each other. One person speaks over the other and is thus unable to understand fully what the other is saying. It prevents them both from fully being heard. A special case of simultaneous talking is interruptions. This occurs when one person speaks over another, and the first speaker stops talking. An example of simultaneous speech occurs when Pilar and Jane are speaking to their friend Joe—at the same time over each other—about the movie they saw. Pilar says, "Superman was so cute. I cannot imagine what it must be like to be his girlfriend," while Jane is telling Joe, as if not caring whether Pilar is speaking or not, "I hated when they threw kryptonite at him. He was so vulnerable." However, an interruption occurs when Pilar is talking about Superman being cute, and Jane stops her, "Wait, Pilar, stop. I want to tell Joe about the kryptonite."

Continuations

Continuations occur when one member breaks into another's speech to complete the first speaker's thought. For example, José said, "I think that family is . . .," and Olga finished the sentence, saying, "Enmeshed." A continuation could be a form of mind reading, with Olga trying to communicate what she thinks José wants to say. However, a continuation can be an effort to take the conversation in a different direction. In both cases, the psychological separateness of the two individuals is compromised.

Personal Control

Sometimes one family member indicates that he has "special" knowledge or control over another member. There is a sense of power, control, or authority of one member of the family over another for purposes of influencing or directing the other's decisions and behaviors. For, example, a mother exerting personal control over her partner would say to the daughter, "I know what I am going to tell your father so that he will let you go out with your boyfriend tonight."

Physical Loss of Distance

Interpersonal distance is a developmental process. An infant needs a lot of closeness and can be controlled, nurtured, and managed physically only because he cannot yet understand verbal communication. We are diagnostically concerned with loss of distance when it is not developmentally appropriate, such as when the child grows up or in the relationship among adults. *Loss of distance* refers to a family member's use of physical behavior to control, silence, intimidate, or influence each other (e.g., Brother begins to tell Mom what Sister was saying on the phone, and Sister hits him and/or puts her hand over his mouth).

Joint Affective Reactions

Joint affective reactions are evidenced by inappropriate behaviors such as crying together, laughing or giggling simultaneously, or some other nonverbal emotional expression by two or more members at the same time. This must happen in the absence of an appropriate "trigger," or it must be exaggerated (e.g., laughing when no jokes have been told). This behavior is frequently seen as a way of replacing more appropriate and direct verbal communication.

Undifferentiated Response

In the case of *undifferentiated responses*, family members are lumped together into one (e.g., "We like picnics," "We never fight"). When the "we" reflects a family's inability to see each member as an individual or to permit individual separate behaviors, it becomes diagnostically important as a possible sign of enmeshment. Often a young person in this type of family has to exhibit extremes of behavior if she wants to "break free."

Behaviors indicative of disengagement can be obvious—for example, when one or more family members indicate that they do not do anything together (e.g., eating dinner, watching television, going to a movie) or when one or more family members express the desire to be apart or away from other members or the family as whole—though this excludes normal adolescent wishes to be on their own—or when one or more family members use the pervasive "whatever" in response to family concerns.

Disengagement can also be more subtle and may include lack of any support or alliances between one or more family members or situations when one or more family members are not spoken about or spoken to or when one or more family members are not speaking—that is, not getting involved in the family conversation.

In evaluating resonance, the BSFT therapist must not be fooled by a conflictive relationship into thinking that it is disengaged. An intense and conflictive relationship is a sign of overinvolvement or enmeshment. The key is to attend to the emotional intensity of the interaction. Intense interactions, regardless of whether the quality is negative or positive, reflect too much closeness. These families can be helped by a reduction of closeness.

It should be noted that in any family, any one of these behaviors might occur without there being family members who are enmeshed or disengaged. However, when groups of these behaviors occur, there is mounting evidence that a family may have members who are either enmeshed or disengaged.

Distance Between the Family and the Outside World

The notion of emotional and psychological distance applies not only to the relationship between and among family members but also to the relationship between a family and their outside world (the social context). Sometimes families are so isolated from their social context and, at other times, they are so involved in the outside world that this over-closeness or over-distance between the family and the outside world can interfere with the healthy development and functioning of its members. In our experience, new immigrants run the risk of remaining underinvolved with the relevant context, which deprives them of the community resources and support they need to adjust successfully to their new home. Overinvolvement sometimes is observed in wealthy families in which the parents are involved in their business and community activities. Meanwhile, because the parents are busy, they do not notice their daughter falling in love with a gang member and beginning to spend nights out.

As in the case of a family's internal family resonance described earlier, the relationship between a family and its social context can be overinvolved, underinvolved, or involved in ways that are adaptive for all family members. However, that is a somewhat simplistic view because one family member may be involved with his outside world and underinvolved with his family. For example, a child may be having problems with school, but the adults have no interactions with relevant school personnel. In another example, a youth may be so involved with peers that she becomes underinvolved with her family, and in turn, the adults in the family may have multiple jobs and do not have sufficient time to spend with the youth.

Culture and Developmental Considerations in Assessing Resonance

Resonance has to be assessed with some knowledge of culture. This is important because some cultures encourage family members to be close to each other, whereas other cultures encourage greater distance. Caribbean Latinxs, for example, are more likely to prefer greater involvement or closeness within their families compared with indigenous populations of Latin America (McEachern & Kenny, 2002). Consistent with a traditional Chinese culture where the eldest male son is responsible for the care of his mother (Das Gupta et al., 2003), a Chinese mother may be overly close to her oldest male son compared with her daughters, who are likely to live with the family of their husbands.

However, whether or not the culture or rules of a cultural group dictate the distance between family members, it is important for therapists to question whether a particular interactional style is linked to problems for the family. In other words, even if an interaction is typical of a culture, when it is linked to symptoms, it has to be changed. Such a situation must be handled with great knowledge and sensitivity to demonstrate respect for the culture and to allow a family to risk a change that is countercultural.

In BSFT, we distinguish between closeness that is nurturing and closeness that may be linked to presenting symptoms. Closeness is desirable when children are young. For example, when the family has a baby, the parents have to be able to sense the child's needs, so they pay tremendous attention to the child's behavior. Thus, it is appropriate that the parent becomes anguished when the baby appears to be in distress. However, as children grow up and can communicate their needs verbally, the level of closeness has to be adjusted to allow for this. Closeness is again adjusted during the teen years to allow for normal individuation. In cases when the adults are unable to adjust by allowing the youth more psychological and emotional distance than they allowed that child when she was younger, the teen may rebel. We explain this to contextualize psychological and emotional closeness. The context may be traditional culture or the developmental moment of a teen, each of which may prescribe diametrically opposed levels of closeness. *Adaptive*, in this case, means that all family members can grow and develop without being inhibited while feeling close enough to feel nurtured.

FAMILY DEVELOPMENTAL STAGE

In the prior sections, we discussed how the family is organized and the closeness or distance among family members. In this section, we discuss the developmental stage of the family and its members. As noted earlier, individuals go through a series of developmental stages from infancy to childhood, adolescence to young adulthood, and middle age to old age. It is known that certain conditions, roles, and responsibilities may typically occur at each stage. It is not always realized, however, that family systems also go through a series of developmental stages. These include when a couple first meets and is married, when they have their first baby, when they have their second baby (and any subsequent children), when the children first go to school, when the child moves into adolescence, and when the children leave home, leaving behind an empty nest. Other major transitions happen when one or both partners retire, when one of the partners becomes sick or dies, and at any time throughout the chronological sequence if the marital couple separates and one of them leaves the nest. Changes in living or parent job situations may also require families to make adaptations. For the family system to continue to function in a healthy way, at each developmental stage, family members have to adapt to the changing demands and circumstances. It is when families encounter difficulty in adapting to these developmental transitions that families are most likely to come to therapy.

Interactions From a Developmental Perspective

As families grow and develop, changes occur, not only in family composition but also in the behavioral interactions that present themselves in families with different compositions or those undergoing major developmental milestones. When a couple first meets and marries, all their attention is on each other. When the couple is expecting their first child or when the child is born, some attention tends to be redirected from the marital couple to the child. However, if trouble is to be avoided, this shift should be handled in such a way that does not neglect either the marital needs of the couple or family or the needs of the baby. When a second child is born, attention is once more redirected to incorporate the second child. Again, this requires a balancing act in that the couple must now attend to themselves, each other, the first child, and the new baby.

In addition to normal developmental transitions within the family, other milestones outside the nuclear family might affect the family, such as events that occur in the extended family, the community, or the society at large. An example might be police brutality against a member of a racial or ethnic minority. These events may create waves of anger in persons of the same group that can affect a family member, thereby stressing the whole family.

Major developmental transitions are found in the break-up of parents' marriages (or common-law marriages of parent figures); the loss of a job and income; the temporary custody of children by one or another parent, grandparent, or foster parent; the reunification of portions of a family; and the many other permutations that families undergo as members are added and subtracted, with the dramatic changes in family roles that such transitions require.

Scientists who have studied families have noted that major flare-ups and family crises occur when developmental milestones are encountered. Of all these natural milestones, those when children reach adolescence and middle school appear to be the riskiest and critical developmental stages for externalizing and internalizing symptoms (Bava & Tapert, 2010; Steinberg & Morris, 2001). This is when a large number of families develop symptoms because they are unable to make the necessary shifts from overinvolved monitoring and regulating to a more democratic style that includes listening and negotiation and from direct guidance to leadership. This is also the time when adolescents often experience difficulty in making the transition from smaller, more personal elementary schools to large, more impersonal middle schools. This is also when parents have difficulty adjusting as their children transition from being family oriented to peer focused, which requires a new set of skills for monitoring children and a higher tolerance for the teens' increasing demands for autonomy. When the family is unable to adjust to this transition, the adolescent is the member most likely to behave in problematic ways, although the family as a whole experiences difficulties in adjusting to the conditions required by this developmental transition.

> Developmental transitions may be stressful. When a developmental transition occurs, if the family attempts to address the new situations in an old way, family conflict and symptoms are likely to develop. Most often, families come to the attention of therapists precisely at these times.

Is the Family System Organized in a Way That Is Appropriate to the Family and the Children's Developmental Stage?

Each time a developmental transition is reached, the family is confronted by a new set of challenges. As the family attempts to adapt to the new circumstances, it experiences stress. Failure to adapt, to make the transition, to give up behaviors that were used successfully at a prior developmental stage, and to establish new behaviors that are adaptive to the new stage will cause some family members to develop unwanted symptoms. Thus, behaviors that were adaptive at one time become maladaptive when circumstances change. For example, although it is appropriate for parents to bathe their infants, it is not appropriate for parents to be in the bathroom when their teenage children are bathing. Similarly, although it is necessary for appropriate monitoring of toddlers to leave their bedroom door open at all times, by the time they reach preadolescence, it is developmentally appropriate to allow them some privacy. Perhaps one of the most stressful developmental changes occurs when children reach adolescence and begin to individuate. We use the term *individuate* here to mean that the child's self is consolidated as a separate person. Parents must be able to continue to be involved and monitor their adolescent's life but now from a distinctly different perspective that allows for increasing autonomy in the youth.

Many other developmental "mismatches" can occur, such as when a parent behaves like a child and is treated as such by the other parent, children are held back in development by being infantilized, or children are given responsibilities that are well beyond their developmental stage. The family's ability to adapt to changing circumstances and developmental stages will have a profound impact on the quality of family interactions. Ability to adapt will permit the family to take on necessary new roles, tasks, and interactions to meet changing demands. Families that rigidly maintain previous behaviors often encounter difficulty. Such problems in being able to cope with the challenges of life's changing demands usually lead to symptoms in one or more of the family members. For example, when a child reaches adolescence, if the parents have not yet learned the art of negotiation, the adolescent is likely to rebel.

At each developmental stage, certain roles and tasks are expected of different family members. One way to determine whether the family has successfully overcome the various developmental challenges that it has confronted is to assess the appropriateness of the roles and tasks that have been assigned to each family member, considering their age and position within the family. When a family's developmental stage is evaluated, there are four major sets of tasks and roles to be assessed: parenting tasks and roles, how the parenting couple relates to each other, sibling tasks and roles, and the extended family's tasks and roles.

To assess parenting tasks and roles, a therapist observes whether parents are parenting at a level that is consistent with the age of their children and whether one or both parents are acting immaturely. To assess how the parenting couple relates to each other from a developmental systems perspective, we assess whether one parent is acting like a child and/or being treated by the other parent as a child. This is particularly relevant when a parent and a grandparent are coparenting, and the grandparent treats the other parent as a child.

In terms of sibling tasks and roles, are the children acting in a way that is appropriate for their ages? Are children being given too much or too little responsibility for their age? Are their family roles appropriate to their age? If the family includes extended family members such as grandparents, aunts, and godparents in parenting roles, the functioning of the extended family must also be assessed: Are extended family members usurping the parent's authority? When there is shared parenting, do parents and extended family members have clear agreements on shared parenting?

The Intersection Between Development and Culture

One of the issues that makes it challenging to determine what is developmentally adaptive is that culture greatly influences what a family may consider developmentally appropriate. For example, it is useful to know that some traditional African American and Latinx families tend to be more involved for a longer period with their children than mainstream families. Thus, it would not be unusual among traditional Latinx groups to have a longer period of dependence for their children compared with mainstream children. Similarly, it would not be unusual for an African American caregiver of a 9-year-old to continue to behave in an authoritarian fashion without the child rebelling or considering it odd. In fact, researchers have suggested that African American inner-city youths experience an authoritarian command as caring, whereas a child from another cultural group might experience it as rejecting (Gaylord-Harden, Barbarin, Tolan, & Murry, 2018). However, as suggested earlier, regardless of the culture of origin of the family, as the child grows within modern culture, the parent has to moderate their manner of control and the kind of involvement or the child may rebel.

Among African American and Latinx families, extended family members such as aunts and grandparents are often active and involved in child-rearing. Thus, these family members might be much more involved in providing guidance and leadership than would be the case in mainstream families. This is culturally normative and quite appropriate as long as extended family members do not usurp or compete for parental authority with the child's parents. However, in those cases in which the child's parents are unavailable or severely drug addicted or when they have poor judgment as a function of severe mental illness, it may be both appropriate and constructive for an extended family member to take on parenting responsibilities and function as parents.

It is challenging to determine the degree and type of supervision and monitoring versus autonomy that children should have at each age level. This is a highly complex and conflictive area even for the best of parents because, as children grow older, they experience considerable pressure from their peers to demonstrate increasing autonomy. It is also complex because many parents are not aware of what might be normative in today's society and may allow too little or too much autonomy, based either on their comfort or discomfort level, their experience, social conditions in the neighborhood, and/or their culture. Moreover, children's peer groups may vary considerably in the level of autonomy they expect from parents.

In summary, developmental stage functioning is one of the most complex areas for a parent and a therapist to determine what is adaptive. The decision of what is adaptive has to take into consideration the impact of family composition, the cultural streams involved (parents' and children's), social context (e.g., safety of neighborhood), physical and mental faculties of the parents and children involved, and even urban versus rural setting (i.e., in a rural setting it is typical to give the children more duties from an early age).

IDENTIFIED PATIENTHOOD

The *identified patient* (IP) is the youth who the family presents as having the problems that need fixing. The IP is typically someone who displays a symptom that is easily visible to all family members. It is easier for adults to come to therapy using a child as the excuse rather than to bring themselves to therapy. Children are often the symptom carriers, as in the case of depressed, suicidal, drug-using, or delinquent children who might have been referred by schools or the law. In this way, children become the reason or excuse that brings families into treatment when there is family conflict, lack of guidance and nurturance, or even abuse or neglect.

Even though the family comes into therapy identifying one family member as the one who needs fixing, it is not always clear who the family members are who are in most pain or experiencing the most severe symptoms. It is also important to note that the IP is not always what might be expected—that is, a person who is less powerful and can easily be blamed for the family's problems. In fact, acting-out youth, who express the symptom for the family in a way that is most visible to outsiders, often pay the price for carrying the symptom in exchange for the advantage of being the most powerful member in their families.

In BSFT, we view identified symptoms as reflective of systemic problems in the family—that is, maladaptive patterns of interactions. The more the family insists that their entire problem is embodied in a single person, the more difficult it will be to bring about change. A family that insists that a single person is the cause of all their problems will be more challenging to the therapist in bringing about family-wide changes. In contrast, families who more readily adapt to new interactions will have an excellent prognosis for a faster and more successful treatment.

> The *identified patient* is the family member who shows the most visible symptoms. The identified patient is the repository for the blame for all that goes wrong in the family.

The other aspect of understanding a family's identified patienthood is that families with problematic behaviors usually identify only one aspect of the IP as the source of all the pain and worry. For example, families of drug-abusing youths tend to focus only on the drug use and possibly on accompanying school and legal troubles that are directly and overtly related to the drug abuse. They usually overlook the fact that the youngster may have other problems such as depression, attention deficit disorder, and learning deficits.

The BSFT therapist diagnoses four types of interactional patterns that indicate the severity of identified patienthood. We start with the recognition that all families who come to therapy have already identified a specific person and problem that is the presenting complaint. In BSFT, the job is to evaluate the severity of this identification because the more fixed a family is in its definition of who and what constitute the identified patienthood, the harder it will be to help that family change. Therefore, an early step in restructuring family interactions focuses on diminishing and/or shifting the family's focus onto "the problem," which facilitates the rest of the therapeutic process. In other words, rigid identified patienthood interferes with other aspects of the therapeutic process. To diagnose the severity of the identified patienthood, we assess several behaviors, described next.

Negativity Toward the Identified Patient

Families of acting-out adolescents exhibit high degrees of negativity toward the youth. This negativity often takes the form of blaming the IP for all the pain of the family. When the therapist starts the first therapy session by asking, "What brought you here?" a parent might start the session by giving the therapist a long laundry list of complaints about the IP. When the therapist asks which issue the parent wants to work on first, the parent is likely to respond, "Everything he does that is a problem." This suggests that there is not any one problem that the family wants to work on but rather that the family sees the IP as the problem. If that were the case, it would imply that for the family, the only solution is to fix the IP.

Centrality of the Identified Patient

The centrality of the IP is another way to determine the severity of the identified patienthood. By *centrality*, we mean that the IP and identified patienthood are the most frequent topic of conversation in the family. In systems, as we have noted, all interactions are complementary. That is, the interactions are sustained because multiple family members collaborate in their perpetuation. This suggests that when the family places an adolescent in an IP role, the IP may act in ways that contribute to his centralization. An example of this occurs if the family were to discuss a topic other than the IP, and the IP calls attention to himself unwittingly, which results in redirecting the conversation back to himself. It should be noted that from a systemic perspective, we would not ask, "Why does the IP call attention to himself?" In systemic thinking, we observe that the family is trapped in a repetitive set of interactions in which the whole family contributes to the formation of and are subject to the family structure (i.e., patterns of interactions) that bring the focus of attention to the IP. As a result of the family structure that has evolved, if any family member tries to move out of their designated role, the family system will return that family member to his designated role. Family systems, like any other system, are designed to preserve themselves, and they do so by protecting its homeostasis or status quo. The reason families need therapy is to help them overcome their homeostasis to move them outside of their current family structure.

Overprotection and Nurturance of Identified Patienthood

In some fields, such as in substance abuse, the notion of overprotection of an IP is called *enabling* (Fagan, 2006). Enabling behaviors are those that support the symptom or the IP when he exhibits the symptom. In the case of the Ray family, the child is truant from school, and because the mother does not want him expelled from school, she sends notes to school excusing his absences. Although the mother is trying to prevent a worse outcome, she is actually protecting the youth's current behavior. The pattern will continue after the youth is expelled, with the mother protecting her child, theoretically to prevent a worse outcome. The fact is that the mother's protection of the symptom results in the worse outcomes she fears. This illustrates the complementary nature of symptom and system and the circularity of the behaviors involved. The child continues to act out and has a stake in his mother protecting him so that he can get away with his misbehavior. The child may have even asked the mother to help him so that he will not get expelled from school. The school, in fact, may also be "playing along," knowing that the long string of excused absences may be a parent covering for a truant child.

Denial of Other Problems and Lack of Interactive Perspective

Many families report that they have no other issues or concerns other than their concerns over the IP and his or her behavior. The extent to which the family identifies other problems represents a more flexible system that will be easier to change. The extent to which the family does not identify any other problems represents a family system that will be more difficult to change. The latter often insists on treatment specifically for the youth. When only focusing on the IP, family members do not perceive or are not willing to address other individual and interactional problems. Among the individual symptoms we might find are family members who are anxious or depressed or drinking too much or problems in another child. Interactional problems that are not initially acknowledged by the family may include conflicts between parent figures, domestic violence, constant fighting, and lack of awareness of the role of the families' behaviors in the IP's symptoms.

CONFLICT RESOLUTION

Although solving differences of opinion is always challenging, it is so much more challenging when it is done in the context of high negativity. Any two people are likely to have two different opinions. Two different opinions represent a disagreement. Disagreements are inherent in human relations. It is natural to disagree. However, when people disagree, they also have to find a way to resolve their disagreements in ways that do not give rise to chronic dissatisfaction and/or chronic negativity. In addition to dissatisfaction and negativity, it is constructive to resolve conflicts as they occur to avoid the accumulation of unresolved conflicts that tear at the family's cohesiveness. In the following sections, we describe five different ways in which these conflicts can be handled by a family.

Denial

Denial refers to a situation in which underlying conflict is not allowed to emerge. In this instance, the family members experience the differences of opinion, but they are not willing to express them. The classic denial case is the one in which the family says, "We have no problems." The truth may be that Juanito, the son, is in trouble with the law, Mother is depressed and Father drinks heavily, Juanito has little daily supervision, and discipline is, at best, erratic. Yet, the family claims that "all is rosy" or "we never argue."

Another classic family situation in which denial is the modus operandi occurs when an alcoholic parent claims, "I am not an alcoholic. I can stop drinking whenever I want. In fact, I have stopped drinking many times!" and the other parent agrees with this, declaring that she has "seen him stop many times."

Another important example of denial occurs in cases when a child is frequently and repeatedly abused, either sexually or physically. Either the other parent is completely marginal and unaware of what is happening in the family, or more likely, the other parent acts as if nothing of concern is happening. Outside observers often ask how it can be that a fully involved and caring mother would not know that her second husband is molesting her daughter from a prior union who lives with them. How is it that the teenage daughter who is being abused does not speak out to get herself out of the situation? Therapists adopting a system perspective instead ask whether all family members may be locked inside a pattern of interactions from which they cannot escape without outside help. There may be reasons that could be given for why the denial is occurring. However, none of them matter. Denial serves to perpetuate painful situations in which one or more family members are paying the price.

Avoidance

Avoidance refers to instances in which a conflict begins to emerge but is stopped, covered up, or inhibited in some way. For example,

- "Let's not fight now" (postponing),
- "You're so cute when you're mad" (humor),
- "That's not really important" (minimizing),
- "There would be no problems if Dad got a raise" (blaming),
- "Let's not argue; you know what can happen" (inhibiting), and
- "I don't want to talk about it now" (shelving).

Diffusion

Diffusion refers to situations in which conflict begins to emerge, but discussion about the conflict is diverted. The argument starts with one issue, and other issues are brought into the discussion, which results in moving away from discussing, much less resolving, the first issue. For example, Mother says to Father, "I don't like it when you get home late," and Father changes the topic by responding, "What kind of mother are you anyway, letting your son stay home from school today when he is not even sick!" The personal attack is a strategy used frequently for diffusion. One person begins to talk about the problem, and the other person responds with a personal attack to divert attention from the topic of conversation. Another classic strategy for diffusion is triangulation. The role of the triangulated individual is to diffuse conflict by attracting attention (usually) away from the conflict among adults and toward the self.

A BSFT therapist was working with a family that constantly diffused—that is, changed the topic of the discussion. When the therapist asked, "What do you want to discuss today?" Mother would say, "I want to speak about no one ever helping me at home." Two minutes into that discussion, the oldest son would say, "Mother is never home," to which Mother's romantic partner would insist (to the oldest son), "Your mother and I wish you had a job." In this case, each family member is expressing their concerns. The challenge with this is that it does not allow for the family to come to a resolution on how the family can address any one of the issues that were brought up.

Conflict Emergence Without Resolution

Conflict emergence without resolution occurs when different opinions about the same topic are clearly expressed, but no final resolution is achieved. Everyone knows exactly where everyone else stands, but little is done to reach an agreement. Sometimes this occurs because the family, although willing to discuss the problem, does not have the skills to negotiate a solution. Conflict emergence without resolution can be visualized as a ping-pong match that never ends. There is a topic (the ball) on which the family expresses different points of view. The ball goes back and forth with each player's opinion, but it never stops. There are no winners and no losers. Family members are more interested in expressing their opinion than in coming to a resolution.

Conflict Emergence With Resolution

Conflict emergence with resolution is the best solution for differences of opinion on topics that are important to the family. First, separate accounts and opinions regarding a particular conflict are clearly expressed. Then, the family can reach a solution by selecting an option that is accepted by all family members involved. The solution could be reached through negotiation or persuasion. It is the BSFT therapist's job to help families who have the four types of unsatisfactory conflict resolution styles described earlier to develop the skills to resolve conflicts in ways that are satisfactory to all family members involved.

Culture and Conflict

Sometimes a family member might say that in their culture, conflicts are handled in a particular way—for example, "We don't disagree with parents in my culture." This is truly a major challenge for a therapist because we respect our families' cultures. However, unless a youth can discuss with her parents significant issues on which they disagree, the parents' wish for their child to stop acting out might not be fulfilled. How can we work with parents who have strong cultural views that adults and parents cannot be confronted by their kids? One way is to elicit the parent's love, concern, and protective feelings toward the child, and in this context, have him ask for his child's opinion. In this way, the parent is fully in charge of asking the child rather than the child challenging the parent. The job of the therapist is to bridge the culture of the parent and the modern-day culture in which the youth is growing up.

LIFE CONTEXT

Although the dimensions of family functioning discussed up to now are all within the family, *life context* refers to what happens in the family's relationship to its social context. The life context of the family includes the extended family, the community, the work situation, schools, courts, and other groups that may affect the family, both in terms of stressors as well as support systems. A few examples are discussed next.

Youth Peers

Adolescence is a time when, developmentally, youths turn their attention from the family to the external world. As such, adolescence is a time at which youth, in their drive for autonomy and individuation, turn their attention to their peers (Ryan, 1993). In BSFT, although we focus mostly on intrafamilial interactions, an issue that requires attention is the parents' monitoring of the youth's worlds. The worlds of the youth include the family but also school and peers. When the family is not cohesive, when there is conflict at home, when youths do not feel nurtured, and when parents are not effectively involved in monitoring youths' peer relationships, there is a greater risk of the youths seeking support and validation from their peers. Many of the teens who come to treatment may be involved in antisocial activities or other activities the parents do not support. Yet, another way in which children may move away from their parents is along a religious dimension: becoming secular when parents are religious or becoming religious when parents are secular. In the United States during the 1960s and 1970s, we also saw youth moving politically away from their parents; modern analogs might be generational shifts in attitudes toward public service, sexual and gender expression, and use of technology, to name just a few.

The field of prevention science (Institute of Medicine and National Research Council, 2015) teaches us that there are many tools parents can use to prevent their children from rebelling. These include, for example, positive parenting (praising your child whenever he is good; Carlo, McGinley, Hayes, Batenhorst, & Wilkinson, 2007; Vostanis et al., 2006), parental involvement (including monitoring) in the child's worlds of school and peers (Barnes, Hoffman, Welte, Farrell, & Dintcheff, 2006; Wagner et al., 2010), excellent conflict resolution skills that facilitate coming to resolution when youth and parents differ (Branje, van Doorn, van der Valk, & Meeus, 2009; Van Doorn, Branje, & Meeus, 2008), effective and developmentally appropriate behavior control (Adalbjarnardottir & Hafsteinsson, 2001; Peterson, Hawkins, Abbott, & Catalano, 1994), and a positive family climate that encourages the child to bond with the family (T. E. Duncan, Tildesley, Duncan, & Hops, 1995; Johnson & Pandina, 1991). Families should be encouraged to seek family therapy to support parents in these functions years before the child develops symptoms.

Parent Support Systems

Parenting is a difficult job. To do such a difficult job, parents need adequate knowledge and skills about parenting, as well as support for their jobs as parents. They need support from friends, extended family members or kin, and other parents. The therapist must assess a family's needs for and the availability of such support. When sufficient support for parenting does not exist, the therapist has to encourage or facilitate the parents to develop a support system. Second, parents may have a support system that stresses the family. Because parenting of a teen is challenging enough, it may be necessary to restructure the relationship with stressful extrafamilial influences to reduce or eliminate the stress on the parent(s).

Juvenile Justice System

Increasingly, probation officers and the courts are found to be critical players in the lives of families in which a child has problems with the law. It is the therapist's job to assess how these various players are interacting with the family (supportive or failing to do what is needed or impeding collaboration). Some juvenile justice systems are individually focused and do not provide any support for family treatment, whereas others have, at times, supported the role of families in correcting the youth's misbehaviors (Casey Family Programs, 2017). In BSFT, we encourage collaboration among all systems, including the family system, that are relevant to each case. Thus, the therapist encourages families and juvenile justice players to collaborate with the family's treatment in pursuit of common goals.

EXHIBIT 3.1

Family Systems Diagnostic Checklist

ORGANIZATION

Leadership—Family Hierarchy

- Who is in charge of directing the family?
- Who are the family members in positions of authority?
- Is this leadership in the appropriate hands?
- Is it shared between (or among) the appropriate people?
- Is the hierarchy assigned appropriately with respect to age, role, and function within the family?

Leadership—Behavioral Control

- Who keeps order in the family, if anyone?
- Who carries out and enforces discipline?
- Are attempts to discipline and keep order successful, or are they ignored?

Leadership—Nurturance and Guidance

- Are parents nurturant?
- Do parents provide guidance in the family?
- Are parents appropriate role models?

Subsystems

- Which are the subsystems in the family?
- Are the subsystems appropriate given the family composition?
- Who is a member of which subsystem (parental, older sibling, extended family, younger children, etc.)?
- Are subsystems formed by the appropriate members in terms of age and function?
- Are the boundaries between subsystems clearly defined while remaining permeable?
- What subsystem alliances are in place?
- Is triangulation occurring? If so, what conflict is not being resolved as a result?

Communication Flow

- Is communication specific?
- Is communication direct and occurring between the appropriate dyads?

RESONANCE

Enmeshment Behaviors

- Mind reading
- Mediated responses
- Simultaneous speeches
- Interruptions
- Continuations
- Personal control
- Physical loss of distance
- Joint affective reactions
- Undifferentiated responses

EXHIBIT 3.1

Family Systems Diagnostic Checklist (*Continued*)

Disengagement Behaviors

- Family members indicate that they do not do anything together
- Family members express their lack of concern or care for one another
- Family members express the desire to be apart or away from other members or from the family as whole
- Lack of any support or alliances between one or more family members
- Family members are not spoken about or spoken to
- Family members are not speaking or not getting involved

FAMILY DEVELOPMENTAL STAGE

- Is the parenting level consistent with the age of children?
- Are parent figures parenting together in a cooperative manner (i.e., do they share equally in the demands of the family as a whole)?
- Do parents treat each other as equals?
- Is one parent acting like a child and/or being treated like a child by the other parent?
- Are children acting in a way that is appropriate for their ages?
- Are children's family roles appropriate to their age (i.e., are they being given too much or too few responsibilities for their age)?
- Do parents and extended family members have clear agreements on shared parenting?
- Are there cultural considerations?

IDENTIFIED PATIENTHOOD

- Negativity toward the identified patient
- Centrality of the identified patient
- Overprotection or nurturance of the identified patient
- Denial of other problems and lack of interactive perspective

CONFLICT RESOLUTION

- Denial
- Avoidance: postponing, humor, minimizing, blaming, inhibiting
- Diffusion
- Conflict emergence without resolution
- Conflict emergence with resolution

LIFE CONTEXT

- Is the identified patient/peers relationship supporting or stressing the family? Or is it nonexistent?
- Is the relationship between parents and their support system stressing or supporting the family? Or is it nonexistent?
- Is the relationship between parents and the juvenile justice system stressing or supporting the family? Or is it nonexistent?
- Is the parent support system stressing or supporting the parents?
- Other significant contextual factors (e.g., school, disability, community conditions, health needs, employment)

KEY TAKEAWAYS

- Understanding the dimensions that characterize family system functioning is foundational in guiding therapists to diagnose the problem in terms of specific dimensions of family interactions.

- BSFT is a diagnostically driven therapy. Therefore, the treatment plan is directly derived from the diagnosis by directing intervention that will correct the maladaptive interactions diagnosed.

- Key to BSFT diagnosis is to observe enactments (family interactions) in the here and now, by focusing on the processes that emerge rather than attending to content or stories. That is, the focus is on the patterns of interactions that are maladaptive and linked to the presenting symptom because to eliminate the presenting symptom, it will be necessary to change these patterns and support adaptive interactions.

4

Applied Issues in Diagnosis

The previous chapter presented what needs to be diagnosed as adaptive or maladaptive interactions and the elements that go into the diagnoses of each of the interactional dimensions. In this chapter, we explain how to apply these concepts clinically. We describe how the diagnoses are achieved and how they can be used to formulate a treatment plan (Robbins, Szapocznik, Alexander, & Miller, 1998).

ENCOURAGING ENACTMENT

In the process of *joining* (see Chapter 2), the therapist uses tracking to encourage enactments in the family. That is, the therapist follows the family's verbal and nonverbal cues to stimulate them to interact with each other rather than with the therapist. Mother says, "Bernie is always in trouble," and the therapist asks Mother to talk to Bernie about that (or ask Bernie what he wants to say to his mother about what she said). The therapist tracks Mother's statement (cue) by tasking Mother to discuss it with Bernie, thus eliciting a dialogue and interaction between them. When Mother says, "You are always late for your curfew," the therapist might task the teen, "Please respond to what your mother is saying." When the therapist observes with the purpose of diagnosing, the therapist ignores the content and is only concerned with the process—the interactional patterns that emerge and the behaviors that constitute them. At this point, the therapist must also become completely decentralized to allow

http://dx.doi.org/10.1037/0000169-005
Brief Strategic Family Therapy, by J. Szapocznik and O. E. Hervis

the family members to interact among themselves, as illustrated in Figure 4.1. A centralized therapist is part of a conversation; a decentralized therapist is not. To allow for the family to interact, the therapist must move out and become decentralized. Becoming *decentralized* means that the therapist assigns the task but is not involved in the discussion regarding the task. This allows the therapist to observe the family enacting their usual patterns.

We emphasize that there are ways to ask a question or assign a task in a manner that the answer could come back to the therapist (e.g., "How did you feel when your mother said that?"), and there are ways to assign tasks interactionally that encourages discussion among family members and not with the therapist (e.g., "Tell your mother how you felt when your mother said that"). Even after tasking a family member to tell his mother, the chances are that early in the therapy (before the family has learned that, in this therapy, they are to speak with each other), the family member is likely to answer, "I have already done it" or "I have told her a thousand times" or "There is no use; she doesn't listen to me." The therapist using Brief Strategic Family Therapy® (BSFT®) has to be insistent, consistent, and persistent in redirecting the communication to the family by using statements such as, "Well, do it again so that I can make sure that you hear each other clearly." Diagnosis is possible when the therapist observes the family interacting as if the therapist were not there. Because we believe that families interact in overlearned ways, what the therapist observes accurately represents the family's typical way of interacting.

Before encouraging enactment, it is critical that the therapist knows who is who in the family. This is easy with a conventional family consisting of a biological mother and father and 2.3 children. However, families in America today have varying compositions. Blended families, for example, may have children from either parent or both parents. In families of siblings who are close in age, it is useful to know their order of birth. If a child is acting in a parenting role, it is important to know the difference in age between the parental child and the sibling she is supposed to parent.

FIGURE 4.1. Therapist Centralized Versus Decentralized

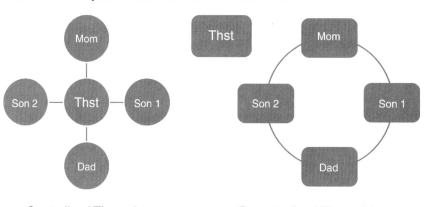

Centralized Therapist   Decentralized Therapist

Thst = therapist.

Enactments can last 10 seconds or 10 minutes. In an enactment, we want to observe fully how the family interacts. However, if the same interaction is repeating over and over again, particularly if it is a negative interaction, we must intervene therapeutically to transform negative interactions into more positive ones. For example, we might find a parent who is criticizing a child. If that happens continuously for 2 minutes, we intervene with a reframe to reduce negativity. In the first session, it is critical to not allow negativity to go unchecked for a long time because unchecked negativity in the first session often results in the family not returning for a second session. Having said that, we do want to allow the enactment to go on long enough to permit the therapist to diagnose who gets involved and, more important, how they get involved: Do they support a parent or the identified patient (IP), the family member with "the problem" who has to be "fixed"? Do they try to mediate? How does the rest of the family respond to that person supporting one or the other? How do they respond to the attempt at mediation?

DEFINING ADAPTIVE OR MALADAPTIVE PATTERNS

Family interactional patterns constitute a youth's most influential context. However, the family is nested within other contexts such as culture, societally defined adolescent transitions, and biological development. These contexts determine what the family may consider adaptive or maladaptive, which may not always coincide with what the youth considers acceptable in the youth's sociocultural context. In this section, we discuss two of the contexts we frequently encounter in conducting BSFT with troubled youths: culture and human and family development.

Promoting Biculturalism

Culture is a sensitive area because, on the one hand, it represents the heritage of a family, and on the other, it might not function well in a new environment. Most traditional cultural patterns have historically served families well. Examples of traditional cultural patterns include the value of the nuclear and extended families for all manners of support. Similarly, respect for older generations has always served families well. However, some traditional cultural patterns create cultural clashes within the family when they come in contact with modern cultures. An example of this occurs when a parent's culture dictates that children never talk back—which includes youths never expressing their opinions. This clashes with youths living as modern Americans who can generally expect to have their opinions heard. Another example occurs in cultures in which children may have been traditionally disciplined with harsh physical punishment. Such traditional customs come into conflict with modern American society, where harsh punishment of children is against the law.

There are also cultural patterns that emerge from catastrophes. Catastrophes such as slavery for people of African descent and the racism that persists, the exploitation and genocide of the native people of the Americas, and the persecution of the Jews in the 19th and 20th centuries in Europe left deep scars and consequent troublesome traditions. From these resulted patterns that have been detrimental to families such teen pregnancy (Crosby et al., 2002), children growing up with no stable father figures in the home (Ruggles, 1994), familial alcoholism (Evans-Campbell, 2008; Wall, Garcia-Andrade, Wong, Lau, & Ehlers, 2000), and overprotective or overinvolved mothers (Baranowsky, Young, Johnson-Douglas, Williams-Keeler, & McCarrey, 1998; Halik, Rosenthal, & Pattison, 1990).

In BSFT, we focus on the here and now of interactions. In this regard, we evaluate how cultural and historical customs and modern standards either support or stress families and how they may be contributing to the presenting problem. We thus assess customs and standards by how they contribute either to adaptive or maladaptive interactional patterns in family life. In BSFT, we must be respectful of the family members who cherish their traditional customs while helping to alter those current behaviors that prevent the family from resolving the presenting symptoms.

We support the practice of biculturalism, wherein individuals can maintain those cultural traditions that support positive family outcomes while simultaneously becoming skilled in using those behaviors that will help them succeed in their present cultural environment. At the very minimum, those individuals who can successfully function in modern society will be most successful in the new context. We support the practice of biculturalism because research demonstrates that those youths who maintain bonds to their family of origin and are also able to function in the host culture are most likely to be well adjusted (S. J. Schwartz et al., 2015; Szapocznik, Kurtines, & Fernandez, 1980).

In our experience, differences in levels of acculturation between parental figures or between parental figures and their children are often accompanied by maladaptive interactions, such as an imbalance in parenting and conflict, that prevent collaboration in parenting functions. In any family, regardless of their cultural origin, when parents are not "on the same page," problems with the children will occur. Any differences of opinion between family members who function in a parenting role are problematic and must be resolved. Resolution does not require persons to change their views but rather to compromise on their actions. Similarly, differences in acculturation between parents and their children exacerbate the usual intergenerational autonomy-related conflicts that occur in adolescence, thereby compounding intergenerational with intercultural conflicts between parents and youth. These conflicts often bring about a breakdown in communication, cohesiveness, and executive leadership.

Considering the Developmental Stage of the Family System

An important context of the family is its developmental stage. This includes the biological evolution of the child, the sociocultural definitions for the developmental stage of the family in the culture of the parents and their present context, and the age of the parenting subsystem. In biological families, the age of the parenting subsystem and that of the children are typically synchronous, whereas in blended families, the time parents have been together becomes relevant. By the latter, we mean that, for example, there is a difference in what constitutes adaptive patterns of interactions between a family in which both parents have been together since the child was born and parents who have come together only recently. Thus, when diagnosing the family process under "Developmental Stage," we assess how appropriate the child's behavior is to their biological age as well as how appropriate the parents' behavior is toward the child, given the child's development. Similarly, when diagnosing "Organization," the BSFT therapist must first determine the "age" (stage of development) of the parental subsystem—how long the parents have been together. In a family in which the child is the mother's biological offspring, and the father figure has only been in the family for 2 years, we would expect the mother to have more leadership in parenting a 10-year-old (whereas for a 3-year-old it might not make a difference). If a stepparent has been with a child since she was 2, we expect the biological parent and stepparent to have equally shared parenting responsibility and rights when the girl is 15.

Assessing Appropriateness of Rewards and Consequences for Children

Another difficult area that requires careful evaluation concerning developmental appropriateness is the nature of the consequences applied to youngsters of different ages. Frequently, parents may be unsuccessful at attempting to apply the same consequences to a 16-year-old that might have worked with a 10-year-old. The determination of what may be a developmentally appropriate consequence is no easy task, even for the experienced therapist. In fact, what works as a reward or consequence varies considerably from one youth to another. One strategy for determining what is appropriate for each youth is to elicit from the youngster what may be important rewards and consequences. Siblings in the approximate age range or older provide another useful source of information. Typically, however, the focus should be on positive consequences when the children do well (Dishion & Kavanagh, 2003; Stanger & Budney, 2010). Instituting a regimen of negative consequences should only be used as a last resort when positive consequences have failed.

In determining what may be developmentally appropriate consequences, other aspects of the nature of the relationship between parent and youth also have to be evaluated. For example, if a parent tells an adolescent that he is grounded, how is the parent to enforce the consequence if the adolescent chooses to get up and go out anyway? A consequence that requires physical containment becomes increasingly difficult, if not impossible, with an adolescent who is unwilling to cooperate. A more appropriate consequence may be taking away a phone or videogames and not letting the youth into the house when on drugs.

Ultimately, consequences in an adversarial relationship have limited success. The true power that parents have over an adolescent is their loving bond with the youth. This is a bond that makes the youth wants to listen to the parents' advice and guidance. It is a bond that elicits in the youth a sense of emotional responsibility for the well-being of the parent. That is, the child does not want to make their parent unhappy because she cares for the parent.

PLANNING TREATMENT ON THE BASIS OF DIAGNOSIS

Now that we have a better understanding of the cultural, developmental, and contextual nuances that must be considered when reaching an accurate diagnosis, we can discuss how to use BSFT diagnosis to create a treatment plan. Understanding the dimensions that characterize family system functioning is foundational in guiding therapists to diagnose the problem in terms of specific dimensions of family interactions. Then we are ready to develop a treatment plan to correct problems along these dimensions. BSFT is a diagnostically driven therapy. Treatment planning directs the interventions needed to correct the maladaptive interactions diagnosed. In each family, we are likely to find some dimensions that are more problematic than others and thus have to be the greater focus of the intervention. For example, in the Guerrero family, we illustrate how the BSFT diagnostic schema is crucial in treatment planning because it directs the therapist immediately to those interactional patterns that are maladaptive and linked to symptomatic behaviors. We illustrate how it is possible to conduct BSFT in cases involving troubled youths within our usual treatment duration of 12 to 16 sessions. One powerful reason for the brevity of the counseling is the preciseness of the treatment planning. Such preciseness is made possible by the clarity of the diagnosis.

> BSFT is a diagnostically driven therapy.

The Guerrero family consists of a mother, stepfather, two sons ages 11 and 12 who are biological children of both, and a 15-year-old son who is the mother's biological child. They were referred for family therapy after a truancy meeting with school administrators as the last step before the 15-year-old's case went to juvenile court. Observations of their initial enactment revealed the following interactional patterns organized according to the BSFT diagnostic schema (see Chapter 3).

Organization

There is a strong alliance between the mother and the 15-year-old youth; the father (the teen's stepfather, hereafter referred to as *father* for simplicity) is uninvolved. All three children communicate with the father mostly through the mother. The mother and father do not share much time as a couple. The mother is responsible for child-rearing nearly all the time. The mother and father ally occasionally but only regarding unimportant issues such as what to eat for dinner. Although the mother does not permit her 15-year-old (the IP) to go out, the IP nevertheless leaves home at night, reflecting the mother's lack of behavior control over the IP. The spousal and parenting subsystem is characterized by low levels of mutual support, and there is an imbalance between the level of parenting responsibilities, with the mother having all the responsibility. The IP is more powerful than either parent due to his alliance with his mother and her ineffective behavior control.

Resonance

When the 15-year-old is asked about his favorite foods, the mother indicates what he prefers to eat. The mother and the 15-year-old son giggle together when not appropriate, a sign of enmeshment. Another sign of enmeshment is the mother's interrupting her son, such that when the son tries to speak, she breaks in and says, "Let me talk; you are not going to tell it like it is." The father's only comment (a sign of disengagement) is to say, "I'm too busy, and I don't have time to get involved in all this." Complaints of family members about other family members during the interview are highly specific, a sign of adaptive functioning on this aspect of resonance. It is thus clear that the father is outside the mother–child alliance. He and the family are emotionally distant from each other. In contrast to this, the mother and the 15-year-old son are overinvolved emotionally and psychologically. Whether or not we define mother and son as enmeshed and/or mother–son and father as disengaged, it is obvious that there is a difference in the psychological and emotional distance that exists between father and mother and father and son on the one hand and mother and son on the other.

Developmental Stage

The three children do not have household chores as would be appropriate for their age. However, the mother uses the 15-year-old son as her confidante in her many complaints about the father. The IP is burdened with emotional responsibilities that are more appropriately assigned to a spouse.

Identified Patienthood

The mother constantly berates her 15-year-old son for being rebellious, refusing to do chores at home, having problems at home and in school, coming home late and often in an excited and irritable state, and staying up much of the night playing video games and then sleeping late, which makes him late for school. The mother tells her younger children how wonderful they are. Identified patienthood is sometimes lodged on the troubled son and sometimes to the father. Although the negativity toward the father functions to keep the father and the rest of the family distant from each other, both the mother and father blame their current problems on the IP.

Conflict Resolution

The mother and father avoid arguing with each other by staying out of each other's way. However, the mother and the 15-year-old recriminate each other for a multitude of sins, which effectively diffuses attention on any one topic so that nothing is resolved.

Life Context

The father has a demanding job, whereas the mother finishes her work early and is home by 3 p.m. The family lives in a high-crime neighborhood with drug-dealing gangs that recruit in the neighborhood. The mother and father are not involved in arranging or supervising activities for the adolescent with his peers. The 15-year-old son is associating with antisocial youth in the neighborhood.

Systemic Diagnosis

In the Guerrero family, the parents have assigned themselves separate role responsibilities, with the mother having full responsibility for all child-rearing and the father having responsibility only as breadwinner. This is maladaptive for child-rearing issues because the father and mother do not cooperate on parenting functions. Despite their constant conflict, the mother and troubled son appear to be allied, with the father marginalized. As is typically the case, we expect to find that the same patterns of interactions occur with content areas other than child-rearing. In fact, these kinds of interactive patterns or structures are almost always found to reoccur in most aspects of family life. The lack of a strong parental alliance with regard to child-rearing issues undermines the parents' ability to chart an effective and successful course of action. This is particularly troublesome when there are forces external to the family that contribute to the development of the youth's behavior problems. These forces include the adolescent peer group and the behavioral expectations to which the youth is exposed outside the home. These ecological forces provide training and opportunity for a full rebellion.

In this family, we have diagnosed the following maladaptive interactions:

- the lack of a parental subsystem—the parents do not work together;

- a cross-generational alliance between the mother and IP;

- maladaptive resonance in which the mother and IP are too close (enmeshed), whereas the father is distant from the rest of the family (disengaged);

- the developmental dimension is maladaptive in that the IP is burdened by being in a spousal role (confidante to his mother), whereas the other children do not have the level of responsibilities that would be expected for their age;

- the family identifies both the father and the youth as being problematic;

- there is high negativity toward the youth IP;

- each time conflicts emerge, the family avoids or diffuses them; and

- the IP is involved with a deviant peer group.

Treatment Plan for the Guerrero Family

The *treatment plan* is the overall Strategy (with a capital S) to achieve treatment goals in a manner that is specific (referred in Chapter 1 as strategy with a lowercase s) to each family and that family's context. The treatment goal is always to correct the maladaptive interactional patterns that have been diagnosed that maintain the presenting problem. In the case of the Guerrero family, all the maladaptive interactional patterns linked to the presenting problems are listed in the previous section. The solutions implemented in therapy are targeted specifically for each of the identified presenting problems and are summarized in Table 4.1. For example, if the family diffuses when conflicts arise, we must help the family stay on topic until that conflict is resolved. We repeatedly keep the family on topic regarding different contents until they solve each conflict and repeatedly do so until the family has developed conflict-resolution skills. If the parents are not in alliance and there is also poor behavior control, as in this case, we give directives that result in the parents forming an alliance regarding the behavior-control problem. If there is negativity (i.e., criticizing, rejecting), we transform negative affect with the underlying positive emotional connections (e.g., we criticize because we care).

The implementation of the treatment plan is broken down into interventions that take us "from here to there." This requires restructuring that involves changing cognitions, affect, and behaviors and interactions from maladaptive to adaptive. At the same time, the therapist capitalizes on the family's strengths, which in the case of this family, includes parents who are ultimately concerned that the IP does better at home and school and does not get in trouble with the law. Strengths often also include good sibling relationships and direct communications within each dyad. We discuss how treatment plans are put into effect in Chapter 5 on restructuring.

INTERRELATIONSHIP BETWEEN DIMENSIONS

BSFT has many technical aspects, but the ultimate goal of our technical diagnoses is to provide a road map for change by using intervention techniques that capitalize on adaptive interactions or strengths to transform interactions from conflictive to collaborative, from anger to love, from negative to positive, and from habitual to proactive. Families ultimately change because the love that is trapped behind the anger is allowed to flourish.

As can be seen in Table 4.1, the BSFT diagnostic dimensions occur in an interdependent fashion. Thus, for example, identified patienthood reflects the family system's need to take the focus away (i.e., distance themselves) from

TABLE 4.1. Treatment Plan for the Guerrero Family

Maladaptive interaction	Treatment plan
Negativity toward IP	Transform mother's negativity into concern for her child. Redefine her connection with IP from negativity to positive interactions (e.g., concern, caring, praising).
Lack of parental subsystem	Build an alliance between mother and father regarding parenting, which may require improving the spousal relationship.
Ineffective behavior control	To improve behavior control, the triangle between mother–IP–father has to be broken. This is done by stimulating a relationship between father and son that equalizes the father–IP and mother–IP alliances. The therapist identifies the specific behaviors in which parents are rendered ineffective (e.g., sabotaging each other, inconsistent messaging and consequences) to reverse them. Parents are helped to collaborate in formulating rules and consequences that are appropriate to the IP's stage of development and the family's environmental context. After parents are allied, they and the IP negotiate rules and rewards for compliance with the rules. The therapist supports firm and consistent implementation of rules and consequences.
Enmeshment/disengagement	Rearranging alliances already impact resonance.
	Eliminate enmeshed behaviors such as speaking for each other, interruptions, and so forth. After evaluating that speaking for each other is culturally accepted in the Guerrero family, which caused family members to not listen to each other, it was restructured sufficiently to ensure that each family member has an individual voice, is heard, and has their wishes and wants considered by other family members.
Children assigned age inappropriate roles: IP is mother's confidant, whereas younger children have no age-appropriate responsibilities	Removal of IP from this role must be part of the reorganization of alliances. Structure responsibilities for younger children.
Conflict avoidance and conflict diffusion	When conflicts (i.e., disagreements) emerge, we prevent families from avoiding or diffusing by refocusing the family on the topic of disagreement, facilitating negotiation until they agree on a solution. Through repeated interventions, the family learns conflict resolution skills.
IP has antisocial peers	As parents rebuild their relationship with the IP, rebuild the youth's bonding to the family, improve the quality of interactions, and increase the effectiveness of behavior control, parents regain their ability to monitor the youth—all critical steps in moving the youth away from antisocial peers.

Note. IP = identified patient.

the parents' marital problems. Similarly, inappropriate developmental stage (i.e., son as mother's confidante) is interlinked with the emotional gap left by the spousal distance.

Frequently, cross-generational alliances represent a problem both in the organization of the family (maladaptive alliance) and in resonance. In this case, the child–mother dyad was too close (enmeshed), and the father–family relations were not close enough (disengaged). Our six dimensions, or catego-ries, of family functioning are like the proverbial elephant described in the legend of the four blind men. Each man, as he touched a different part of the elephant, provided a true but different perspective of what the elephant was. Similarly, each of our six family functioning dimensions provides a slightly different perspective of the same overall family process.

> The same interactions can be viewed from different diagnostic perspectives. Hence, one set of interactions may give rise to several diagnoses.

Although the dimensions of family functioning are interrelated, there is a great advantage in diagnosing the same interaction from different dimen-sional perspectives. This is the case because it offers the clinician options. That is, it provides the clinician with the opportunity to strategize the best ways to intervene to change an interaction, such as, for example, from which dimen-sional perspective to initiate the change intervention or who is more available or flexible to initiate change in an interaction.

The next chapter describes the techniques and strategies that BSFT uses for bringing about change in interactional patterns.

KEY TAKEAWAYS

- BSFT diagnoses adaptive and maladaptive interactions using the former to support change in the latter and using the latter to create the treatment plan.

- Do not allow a negative interaction that repeats itself to go on for a long time. In the first sessions, after 2 minutes, intervene to transform negative interactions into positive interactions. In subsequent sessions, the therapist must intervene as soon as the negative interaction emerges because negative interactions are not constructive.

- Assess culture, customs, and standards by how they contribute either to adaptive or maladaptive interactional patterns in family life.

- BSFT has many technical aspects, but the ultimate goal of our technical diag-noses and intervention techniques is to transform interactions from conflic-tive to collaborative, from anger to love, from negative to positive, and from habitual to proactive. Families ultimately change because the love that is trapped behind the anger is allowed to flourish.

- Diagnostic dimensions present different aspects of a whole and are conse-quently interrelated.

5

Orchestrating Change

Restructuring

As we have mentioned before, the family structure is the script for the family play. In this chapter, we discuss how to change the family script from maladaptive to more adaptive by transforming the network of patterns of family interactions that we refer to as *family structure*. The method we use for changing the family script is called *restructuring*. Restructuring is nothing more than replacing maladaptive interactional patterns with more adaptive interactions; however, the devil is in the details: how to make change happen.

In this chapter, we talk about how to bring about change in families and the strategies and techniques that make it possible. However, the most important message we want to give the reader is that Brief Strategic Family Therapy® (BSFT®) is a love therapy. A focus on love and other positive connections among family members, such as trust, are well beyond what strategies and techniques can yield. Another important aspect of changing family interactions is that, as we have said earlier, homeostasis hinders the family from changing. To overcome the powerful forces of homeostasis, we must recognize that the momentum of change has to be greater than the inertia of homeostasis. Therefore, the pace of change interventions must be swift. A hesitant therapist will not be able to build and maintain the momentum needed to bring about change.

In BSFT, we find ourselves working with powerful adolescents, and we have learned that powerful adolescents cannot be overpowered. Because teenagers are too powerful in the context of their peers, because they are often bigger and stronger than their parents, and because their brain is at the developmental

http://dx.doi.org/10.1037/0000169-006
Brief Strategic Family Therapy, by J. Szapocznik and O. E. Hervis

stage that propels them to be increasingly more autonomous and independent, it is neither possible nor desirable for a parent to overpower the adolescent. As a side note, teens brains are also at a stage when the teen's ability to say "no" to oneself has not been fully developed, which results in impulsivity and variable judgment (Casey, Jones, & Hare, 2008; Casey, Jones, & Somerville, 2011). We propose that the most effective influence a parent can have on a teenager is in the context of the love in their relationship, which provides the philosophical context for this chapter. The rest of the chapter describes the principles and steps of orchestrating family change.

BUILDING ON JOINING AND DIAGNOSIS

The first step in BSFT is to establish the therapeutic system. The therapist, by taking the lead in establishing the new system that includes the family and the therapist, becomes the leader of the therapeutic system. At the beginning of therapy, this is done through joining, as described in Chapter 2. Joining is the proverbial foot in the door. The therapist is then ready to encourage family members to interact with each other. When they do so, they enact the family script. As we have noted, the family script is likely to have been played out thousands of times. Thus, when the family enacts the family script, the therapist's job is to observe the interactions that emerge and, guided by the BSFT diagnostic schema presented in Chapter 3, identify the maladaptive family interactional patterns that are linked to the problem behavior and the adaptive interactions that can be used to support the change process.

Having joined and diagnosed maladaptive interactions, the therapist is ready to formulate a treatment plan for those maladaptive interactions that have been diagnosed and are linked to the presenting symptom(s). One of the features that make BSFT brief is that we can intervene in maladaptive interactions as they emerge, even though we may not have certainty about the full interactional diagnosis. For example, when it becomes evident early on that family members interrupt each other constantly, the therapist might respectfully say, "You all have important things to say, and I want to make sure that you hear each other. You are so excited to talk that you interrupt each other. Please speak one at a time. Allow one person to finish before the other one speaks." In this early intervention, the therapist is careful in her language because there is much she does not know about the family, and thus, she wants to intervene in a way that does not erode her rapport with the family.

We call the interventions used to create a more adaptive script *restructuring*. In restructuring, the therapist orchestrates and directs change in the family's patterns of interactions. To bring about these changes, the therapist assists family members to think, feel, and behave differently. In the next section, we discuss two important principles that are fundamental to effective restructuring.

- We work in the present, in the context of enactments, and as maladaptive interactions emerge, we stimulate, elicit, and direct new and more adaptive interactions.

- BSFT is a skills-building therapy. For this reason, the therapist never does for the family what the family must learn to do for itself.

WORKING IN THE PRESENT

What do we mean by "working in the present"? We mean that in BSFT restructuring interventions are made in the here and now—that is, at the time that the maladaptive interactions occur in the session when the family is enacting. The most important point we would like to make with regard to working in the present is that we do not want families to talk with the therapist about their problems. Rather, we want family members to discuss the problem with each other. Why is this? Because when family members interact, the interactions occur in the present.

> The "how" of the interactions is in the present. The "what" families talk about is in the past or the future. Hence, present-oriented BSFT focuses on "how" the family discusses their "what." The fact is that all we can change is the present. We have yet to meet someone who can change the past or future.

Two important aspects of working in the present warrant discussion. The first is that we assist the family to interact in the present during the session. The second is that we intervene to change maladaptive interactions in the moment in which they occur. We intervene in the family's present because we believe that change in interactions can only occur when interactions are occurring in the session, and we change them as they occur. This means that, in our view, changes in interactions do not occur when families go home. Rather, changes in interactions occur when we choreograph in the here and now the move from maladaptive to adaptive interactions.

Recognizing Consequences of the Past in the Present

When a family member is telling a story to another family member, the present is not in the content of the story but rather what the family does and how the family does it when telling the story. Sometimes, it is important to address something that has happened in the past, such as the sexual abuse of a child. We do so by recognizing that the consequences and scars of the past are still alive in the family's current interactions. Hence, by having family members discuss the past sexual abuse with each other, we can work on how the family is or is not interacting in ways that lead to healing from such a terrible experience, the consequences of which continue to live in the present.

Thus, our job as BSFT therapists is to help the family discuss the sexual abuse in a manner that leads to healing. This might include helping parents to listen and stop avoiding or whitewashing or treating the victim in ways that reinforce her feelings of being victimized. For example, if a well-meaning mother says to her 11-year-old daughter, "I know that you are now broken, but I am here to make sure you are made whole again," it could heighten the girl's sense of victimization. The therapist intervenes to correct the mother's language: "Mom, when you use the word *broken*, your daughter cannot hear anything else after that because she is feeling how the abuse has diminished her [see 'Highlighting' section]. Tell her [see 'Tasking' section] how she really is: a smart, strong, and wonderful girl [see the sections 'Reframing' and 'Tasking']." In response, Mom says, "Yes, you are right, she is a wonderful, loving human being, and I love her with all my heart." To her daughter, she says, "I am sorry. I did not mean it the way it came out. You're as wonderful in every way as you always were."

It is important to note that even small incidents that occurred in the past can still live in the present, such as "when you told me last week that you hate me." The past is present when it is unresolved. The unresolved past is alive in the here and now, when the emotions and cognitions that resulted from it continue to influence present cognitions, affect, and behaviors. Whether an incident in the past is small or momentous, we handle it similarly. We bring it into present interactions in which family members discuss and work on solving the problem in the present. And thus, we help the family work on the way they interact regarding the problem to enable them to reach a constructive conclusion.

We recognize that the past plays an important role in how we think, feel, and act now, but as therapists, we only have access to the present. More important, we can only change the present to create a better future for our families. By improving a family's ability to effectively communicate, listen to each other, care for each other, and stay on topic, the family is better able to work on the issues that are most important to them.

It is relevant to clarify that process (interactions) can happen only in the present. In present interactions, the past is always content. The action of breathing is process. The air I breathe is content. The air I exhaled is gone; it is definitely content. As in BSFT, if I have a breathing problem, my doctor will treat how I am breathing and not try to change the air itself. This is to say that process is the action that is happening now and can be changed. Everything else is gone. It is past. It is content. That includes everything that happened before this moment. This is important because a therapist can only change the present, the present of the family's behaviors, and the present of the therapist's behavior in relationship to the family's behavior. I can change my behavior now in ways that will change the way the family is interacting with each other now. Likewise, when interactions occur among family members in the therapy session, the interactions are always occurring in the present. For interactions to occur in the present, the therapist has to become decentralized to allow family members to interact with each other. When a family member is telling a story to the therapist, the therapist must move the family to interact with each other—in which case they will be enacting in the here and now, whatever their concern might be. Again, to be *decentralized* means that inter-actions in the session are happening among family members and not between family members and the therapist.

Our emphasis and goal is to develop new interactional skills, and the development of these skills occurs by (a) finding the opportunity to modify an "old interaction while it is happening" by introducing the new interactional skill in vivo (alive, while it is happening) and (b) having the new family inter-actional skill rehearsed and practiced in session.

Reconnecting

There are times when creating a new interaction is difficult because one of the family members is not psychologically at a place where she can think, feel, or act differently. Reigniting the parent–child bond that once existed is an important goal of BSFT. This is the bond that will once again allow the parent to have a significant impact in guiding and protecting the youth. A technique referred to as *reconnecting* is useful in achieving this rebonding (Diamond, Diamond, & Liddle, 2000). Yet this is only one of the tools we have as therapists when we use the past to create a new present. We do this work sparingly and only to facilitate changes in interaction, never only for the sake of individual change.

An important instance of reconnecting can occur early in therapy when the parent and child are in adversarial roles. The parent is angry, may be deeply hurt by the behavior of the youth, and is withdrawn. One strategy to overcome the impasse in which neither family member is willing to bend is to ask the parent, "Can you remember when Roger was born? How did you feel?" The parent rolls her eyes back, a look of bliss comes over her face, and she says, "He was such a beautiful child. I was so afraid of labor, but once I saw him, I realized that it was all worth it. I loved him so much I thought my heart would burst."

When the parent is hardened by the difficult experiences she has had with a troublesome youth, to overcome the impasse in which neither the parent nor the child is willing to bend first, we sometimes use the strategy of recon-nection. *Reconnection* is an intervention to help the parent access the positive affect that once existed toward the child. After the parent expresses her early love for the child, the therapist turns to the youth and says, "Did you know your mother loves you so much? Look at the expression of joy on her face."

As can be seen, we recreate in the present an individual experience of the past for a short time to reconnect the parent and child as a springboard to new interactions. Hence, the therapist must move quickly to use reconnection as a bridge that moves the therapy to a more positive interactional terrain. The reconnection permitted us to transform the mother's experience character-ized by resentment to an experience of the child characterized by affection. As in most cases, these interventions to bring about positive affect may have to be used repeatedly to foster new habitual interactional patterns.

Are there other examples of using the past? Another example occurs when some emotional wound has emerged, such as infidelity. Sometimes the offended person (often called *victim*) must express her hurt (e.g., how betrayed she felt when this happened) to bring her current experience of old events to the present to explain why she does not trust her husband. Hence, in BSFT, we transform the storytelling of the emotional wound and betrayal to a "now" interactional experience. Although debriefing of a trauma by itself has value, we emphasize moving the couple to a new way of interacting in the "here and now." The therapist might ask an emotionally wounded spouse, "What would you like to hear from your husband?" and receive a response along the lines of, "He has never admitted it; he has never even told me he is sorry." This opens the possibility of a healing conversation. Alternatively, the wife might say, "I am so angry that I will never trust him again," to which the therapist may respond with a question to the spouse, "Did you know how your wife felt? Let your wife know how it makes you feel to hear that from her." This again opens up the possibility of a new here-and-now interaction about the wife's feelings that could lead to a better understanding by the spouse of the depths of the anger and resentment, thereby providing the context for the couple to develop effective communication.

DEVELOPING MASTERY: HELPING THE FAMILY BUILD COMPETENCE IN ADAPTIVE INTERACTIONS

The purpose of BSFT is to replace maladaptive patterns of interaction with more effective and adaptive interactions. As we mentioned, *interactions* are behaviors that are linked with each other as actions and reactions of various family members. Maladaptive interACTIONS (an interplay of interlinked actions) consist of behaviors that occur as reactions to each other that are linked to negative cognitions about each other, negative affect, undesirable behaviors, or a sense of inadequacy, among other disabling experiences. Maladaptive interactions are also characterized by their stifling influence on individual development.

Our aim as therapists is to help families achieve *interACTIONal mastery*—that is, the ability of family members to act with each other in adaptive ways that rid the family of its symptoms. Interactional mastery can only be developed by encouraging family members to interact in more adaptive ways. Families increase their interactional mastery when the therapist helps the family transform its interactions from negative to constructive. By definition, families can only increase mastery when they practice new behaviors with each other. The skill of a family member speaking to a therapist is, in our view, a skill that does not help the family to develop mastery in interacting in new and more adaptive ways. For that reason, we alert the therapist that whenever a family member is talking to the therapist, we do not consider it a change-producing intervention.

Neither is it a change-producing intervention when the therapist does for the family what the family has to learn to do for itself. For example, a therapist who behaves like a nurturing parent to a child fails to provide the parent with the opportunity to develop that skill. What about modeling? From an interactional perspective, modeling does not teach interactional skills. We have found that parents are always happy to have the therapist do what they do not know how to do themselves. Learning new ways of behaving only occurs when families interact in new ways. Never use modeling of say, nurturance, by nurturing the child. Nurturing the child is always the job of the parent because it is the parent who must learn the skill. Even in the case of the parent, the therapist never becomes the parent's nurturer, except as a springboard to help the parent nurture herself and her children.

In BSFT, rather than assuming that nurturant behavior is not available in the family, we find ways of eliciting the nurturant behavior within the family. In the case of a mother with four children who has just lost her husband, the mother started the session by saying, "I feel overwhelmed because I have to work two jobs and take care of all the children by myself and do many of the things my husband used to do." The oldest son (not the identified patient [IP], the family member with "the problem" who has to be "fixed") responded, "Well, you also are not paying attention to me. I brought you wonderful grades, and you are not looking at them." Both mother and son were feeling emotionally neglected. Rather than modeling, our BSFT therapist helped build up both mother and son by validating their need for nurturance. The therapist then provided specific direction to encourage family members to nurture each other. This was all done with a nurturant stance on the part of the therapist and always with a focus on building the skills within the family.

The therapist's job is to validate the emotional needs of both and encourage them to find a way for mother and son to attend to each other in a mutually nurturant way. For example, the therapist might say,

> I hear that both of you are in great need of support, and I see that both of you have a lot to give and are sensitive and emotional people. Mother, you do so much for this family. Son, you do so much to make your mother proud. You are both incredible persons, already giving so much to your family. Mother, can you let him know how proud you are of your son's good grades?

After the mother does so, the therapist turns to the son and says, "Son, I can see how much you love your mother, and you can see how much she does for all of you. Please tell her how much you appreciate all that she is doing for the family." To which the son responds, "Mom, thank you." The therapist says, "Son, tell your mother three things you want to thank her for." The son responds, "You work hard to get us food and pay the rent." Although the therapist asked the son to tell his mother three things for which he wanted to thank her, as often happens, the task is not completed exactly the way the therapist intended. However, in this case, by providing thanks for two things, the son made considerable progress toward expressing appreciation for his mom. The therapist says, "Mother, children, talk with each other about making a plan of how all of you can have some quality time together each week." This example, we hope illustrates that even when nurturance is needed, the therapist's job is to elicit nurturance from the family rather than providing it herself.

The alert therapist might ask their BSFT supervisor, "What if the family does not have it within them?" The BSFT supervisor would respond,

> We are always providing plentiful nurturance when we are joining and in the manner in which we intervene. In joining and in intervening, we are always validating, saying that we are here to help you, that we are concerned about your family, and that we are here because we know you have good qualities within yourself and in your family, and so forth. We are nurturant in our tone of voice.

When it is culturally sanctioned and developmentally appropriate, and the circumstances permit, a therapist might put her arm around a parent in a caring fashion. In our culture, we, as Latinx, find that it is often acceptable to put our arm around clients of certain backgrounds and ages. However, we know that touching a family member in a professional and caring fashion is fraught with complexities and has to be done cautiously and judiciously, particularly in America.

What to do with families in which there is not the experience of nurturance? We might take (usually) a mother and help her step by step. This might include guiding the mother in the steps she has to take to express nurturance. First, she should sit next to the child, talk to the child, eventually take the child's hand, and so forth. Slowly, cautiously, and judiciously, we help the parent move toward behaviors that look and feel like nurturance. Unless the therapist is going to adopt the family and take them home, the therapist must help the family develop the skills they need for a happy life. We cannot stress enough that, as therapists, we are here to teach family skills. When we do not and instead nurture the family, we are doing a terrible disservice to the family because, when we have completed our work, they will be as unskilled as they were when we first met them.

> Some skills are more complex than others, but even the simplest skills can only be mastered by doing.

Reinforcing New Adaptive Behaviors and Interactions

After these more adaptive behaviors and interactions emerge, the BSFT therapist praises them and encourages family members to validate the new behaviors in each other. Subsequently, the therapist gives the family the task of practicing these new behaviors and interactions in different naturally occurring scenarios to generalize mastery of skills to the family's home. In the earlier case example, the therapist asked the mother and her children to find a time every week for them to have quality time.

This mastery over more adaptive interactions releases the family members from the web of maladaptive behaviors, including the youth's symptomatic behavior. The newly acquired mastery in more adaptive interactive skills promotes positive affect, a sense of competence, and individual development. Because these more adaptive behaviors and interactions are reinforcing in and of themselves, they are more sustainable. The family masters the skills to behave in adaptive ways as a result of family members reinforcing each other in more adaptive skills and the therapist also reinforcing these more adaptive interactions. The process, then, is one of validating adaptive behaviors and interactions as they are put into practice across various contents and contexts. Mastery is not achieved by criticizing, interpreting, labeling, pathologizing individuals, or belittling. Rather, it is achieved by incrementally shaping and praising positive behaviors.

An example is the case of Kamisha, an HIV-positive young adult who had recently learned about her illness and was in drug abuse treatment. When she left drug abuse treatment, Kamisha moved back into her father's house—the only sober place that would take her, in a Southern U.S. community with few safety net resources. The father had lived alone since Kamisha's mother had died 5 years before. However, the father belittled Kamisha. One issue about which the father would belittle Kamisha was her mishandling of money. She would get her welfare check and spend it right away on clothes and cosmetics.

The therapist had to help Kamisha and her dad build skills in the context of a new and positive relationship. The therapist worked with Kamisha and her dad to encourage him to teach her how to manage her money. After some coaching and when the therapist was present, Kamisha asked her dad to help her to learn to manage her money. After some grumbling and grunting, Kamisha was able to get him to begin to lay out the steps. The first step was to make a budget. With the therapist's guidance to keep the focus on working cooperatively on the budget, one was developed in the session. Most of the therapist's efforts were dedicated to reframing Dad's belittling of Kamisha as "his deep concern for her, and his desire that she would do everything 'the right way.'" Dad had suggested a bank account as a solution for Kamisha's difficulty holding onto money. After the success of working collaboratively to develop a budget during therapy, the therapist reinforced this new relationship and further tasked the father and Kamisha to plan the next step in which Dad would accompany Kamisha to open a checking account where she could keep her money. After Kamisha and Dad had experienced success in collaborating to develop a budget and a plan for Kamisha to manage money, the therapist turned her attention to obtaining additional system support for Kamisha. Dad went to church twice per week. Kamisha was interested in visiting the church. Thus, the next session was devoted to talking about God and church, a subject dear to Dad's heart. With some nudging from the therapist, Dad offered to take Kamisha to church with him, which had the potential to provide her with a prosocial support group.

Our intent here is to highlight that had Kamisha gone from treatment to the only place that would receive her, her dad's home, and had Dad continued to belittle Kamisha instead of supporting her, it would not have provided a sober healing environment in which she could thrive. The therapist's work was to transform the relationship into a mutually supportive relationship that would sustain Kamisha in staying away from drugs. By practicing mutually supportive interactions, Kamisha and Dad developed mastery in establishing a supportive relationship in which Dad could guide Kamisha's recovery.

Promoting Change in Affect to Change Behavior

In BSFT, we build the skills a family must master to improve the well-being of its members in the context of the families' interactions as they are occurring. In BSFT, learning occurs at the moment in which a particular new skill is needed in a presently occurring interaction. While the family process is occurring and evolving in front of the therapist, the therapist first changes the family's views and perspective regarding the process in such a way that it drives a change in affect. The change in perspective and affect is then used as a springboard to provoke a change in behavior. The following example illustrates how this can work.

Doris is a single mother with three children, Joan who is 15 years old, Kevin who is 14, and Mike who is 10. Joan and Kevin do not mind their mother. For example, Joan recently told her mother that she was going to a sleepover at her best friend's but was back home at 2 a.m., saying she had been thrown out of the house. Doris did not want to have her children sleep over, but she changes her mind from time to time. The same occurs with curfews and other rules. She enforces rules according to how she feels at the moment. The case was referred to the clinic because Joan was missing school regularly.

In the first session at her home, Doris launched into a rant to the therapist about her children not minding her, providing the therapist with a long list of complaints about what her children had failed to do. When Doris introduced the children, the therapist learned that one of the four children in the room was a 6-year-old cousin who lives with his family in the same household. Doris complained that she did not want the children's cousin in the session, but the child remained. The therapist noticed that Doris complained but did not act to have the cousin leave the therapy session. The therapist highlighted to Doris,

> Mother, you are talking to me, and that is not going to change what Joan is doing. To get done what you want to get done here, which I agree with you about, you need to take one child and one problem at a time. Tell Joan what the most important thing is that you want her to do differently.

Doris looked at Joan and continued to rant about a litany of problems. Joan and Kevin looked at each other and giggled. The therapist politely stopped the mother and said,

> Let me help you here. I want you to achieve your goal. Notice that they are giggling. They are not taking you seriously. I want you to get things done. So, remember, one thing at a time and in a serious voice. Now let's try again. What is the most important thing that you want Joan to do differently?

As soon as Doris started speaking to Joan, Joan began to giggle, Kevin joined, and soon they were both laughing. Doris joined them in the laughter. Laughing is a way to diffuse the conflict that occurs when Doris makes an expectation clear. Diffusing through giggling derails the path to change. This kind of joint affective reaction is a sign of enmeshment; it reflects that the mother is like one of the children, and therefore, the children do not take her seriously.

The therapist said, "Mom, I see you as the parent in the family. But by laughing with the children, you are acting like one of them. Tell me about your wanting to be taken seriously and be respected and obeyed." Because Doris was having a difficult time behaving as a parent, the therapist, in an effort to elevate Doris, prodded her to see herself as a parent. Prodding Doris to recognize the attitudes and behaviors that are appropriate for a parent was done as a way to induce her to take the role of a parent. Doris responded, "I do want to be taken seriously, but I think they are funny." It is important for the therapist to continue to develop the theme that for the mother to be taken seriously as the parent, she has to become comfortable with effective parenting behaviors. Among these are to be clear on what she wants from her children and to take herself seriously. The therapist highlighted what did not work for Doris, "If you don't take yourself seriously, the children won't either," which she followed with a reframe: "It is fine to have fun with the children, but not at a time when you mean business, when you are trying to set rules."

Several tasks followed, but they had to be given one at a time. To begin to develop skills in behavior control, the first task the therapist gave the mother was to "get Joan's attention, make sure she is looking at you, and in a serious voice, let Joan know the one most important thing you want her to do." Doris looked at Joan and said, "Joan, look at me." Kevin also called out to Joan. The therapist said to Doris, "Tell Kevin to stay out, that you are only talking to Joan." Doris said to Kevin, "You are stupid; don't you hear the lady that I am talking with Joan?" Kevin started laughing, and so did Joan. The therapist placed her hand on Doris's shoulder, "Mom, the first thing you have to do is to get them to stop laughing." The therapist, while keeping her hand on Doris's shoulder and looking in her eyes, said, "Mom, you can do this." Skills building in behavior control in this family requires encouragement and building the parent's self-confidence. "You can tell them to stop laughing, that this is serious." Doris said seriously, "You better stop laughing right now, and I mean it." Even though this intervention did not yet have any teeth (i.e., consequences), the children responded to their mother's changed behavior and her alliance with the therapist. This is the beginning of step-by-step skills building in the area of behavior control. The therapist said to Doris,

> Mom, you did great. Good job. You see, you can do this. Okay, let's go back now. Get Joan's attention and tell her in a very serious voice one thing that you want her to do. Don't make it a long list because Joan won't remember any of it. Tell Joan only one important thing that needs to change right now.

Therapist Behaviors That Support Skill Building

A great deal of micromanagement was needed to guide, direct, and cajole this parent into completing the behavior control task successfully. The first task here was for Doris to talk seriously to Joan. To achieve this task, the therapist had to manage the process with a number of small subtasks, such as getting Doris to talk seriously and telling Kevin to stay out of her conversation with Joan. This constant management is not unlike keeping our rafts upright when going down rapids. While not taking over the roles that belong to the family, the therapist must maintain a role as director and active facilitator to keep the raft afloat and moving forward. Equally, in the case of a task, the therapist, while keeping the focus on the family's interactions, may have to be on the lookout for processes that might emerge that interfere with the successful completion of the tasks and opportunities to intervene to move the larger process forward. Teaching the skills of behavior control is no less challenging than teaching someone to keep a raft upright while going down rapids. When the therapist is persistent, consistent, and insistent, she achieves it.

Helping a family develop new skills is somewhat like teaching someone to ride a bicycle. Lectures are not helpful. Neither is it helpful to ride the bicycle for them. Rather, the way to be helpful is to assist the person to learn to ride the bicycle on her own, with the therapist's role as the trainer remaining decentralized (i.e., not riding the bicycle). The trainer may move in to help the person sit on the bicycle seat, grab the handlebars, and so forth, and coach to "now pedal slowly and steadily," but soon she has to move back and let the new rider be the one who rides the bicycle, albeit with the therapist's support and encouragement.

> The BSFT therapist is never central but, rather, acts as a choreographer. The therapist's job is to assist the family in developing skills by choreographing the opportunity for skills to be practiced.

Although the therapist facilitates, supports, and encourages, she remains decentralized by allowing interactions to remain among family members. Her role is to assist the family in developing skills—the skills of new behaviors that lead to more adaptive family interactions. And her job during the family session is to orchestrate the opportunity for these skills to be practiced. In other words, in a therapy session in which the family members are talking, yelling, fighting, and nurturing each other, the therapist accomplishes an important part of the job by getting them to interact with each other and not with her.

As we mentioned before, most families come to treatment expecting the therapist to "fix" the child. We gently and politely violate the families' expectations because we empower the family to develop the skills it needs to rid the child of the symptom(s). We give families the skills that we expect they will need for effective parenting, for all time.

THE PROCESS OF RESTRUCTURING

This section discusses the three restructuring steps—highlighting, reframing, and tasking—that are always used in an integrated fashion. We define these steps next, but we explain their integrated use here to create a better understanding of how the three steps are a single process of restructuring (see Figure 5.1). The first step, *highlighting*, is intended to increase the negative affective charge of a maladaptive interaction. This, in turn, decreases the family's comfort in an interaction to which the family has become accustomed. Families develop a tolerance for maladaptive interactions. Highlighting is intended to decrease the family's acceptance and tolerance of the interaction and, thus, increase their discomfort with the interaction. The second step in the restructuring process is *reframing*. Once the therapist highlights an interaction to create discomfort with the interaction, the therapist uses reframing. Reframing, if successful, changes the opinions, views, and perspectives that family members attribute to a family member, interaction, or circumstance. Although highlighting changes the affect regarding an interaction, reframing moves cognitions and affect from negative to positive in a manner that readies the family to engage in new interactions. Once this preparation for change has been made, the BSFT therapist gives the family a *task* that transforms the interaction (that was also the target of highlight and reframing) from maladaptive to adaptive.

Effective and lasting change requires changes in cognition, affect, and behavior. For that reason, the three restructuring steps—highlighting, reframing, and tasking—are always used in sequence to bring about affective, cognitive, and behavioral change, respectively. To successfully bring about change, the three steps are used congruently to construct a single intervention that seamlessly includes changes in affect, cognition, and behavior.

Often families are in intense interactions with each other that may take the form of arguments or long tirades or preaching. Before the therapist can

FIGURE 5.1. Restructuring: Highlighting (H), Reframing (R), and Tasking (T)

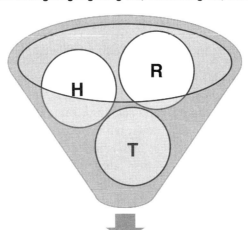

engage in the restructuring process, he has to get the family's attention. To make room for the therapist's intervention to be heard, the therapist interrupts by asking the family to stop for a moment, like a clever therapist did with a preacher who was ineffectively preaching to her daughter, "Reverend, please forgive me, but I need to interrupt a minute to be truly helpful to you."

Highlighting

Families develop a tolerance to maladaptive interactions and become "anesthetized" to how maladaptive interactions hurt the family and its members. *Highlighting* is intended to increase the negative affective charge of an interaction in a manner that increases the family's discomfort with a maladaptive interaction to which it has become accustomed. Highlighting is intended to focus on a specific interaction in a way that decreases the family's acceptance and tolerance of that interaction and, thus, increases their discomfort with that interaction. Highlighting is one of the intervention techniques used for increasing motivation for change.

Highlighting Without Eroding Rapport

What about keeping your joined position while highlighting? Highlighting, if not done carefully and correctly, can indeed erode our joined position. It is, without doubt, the riskiest intervention we do because it challenges the family. However, we have developed ways to reduce the risk. An essential way to minimize the risk brought about by highlighting is to present it in the context of a positive reframe. Thus, highlighting is always accompanied by a positive reframe. It is also important to point out that intensified joining should always precede a highlight. There are some other options for maintaining a joined position when challenging with a highlight. The most important of these is to ask permission of the family or family member before introducing the highlight, for instance, by saying, "May I be honest with you because I truly want to help you." However, the "yes . . . and" technique can also be helpful, as we illustrate next.

A 15-year-old IP calls his mother a bitch, and the mother does not respond. The therapist recognizes that if left unchanged, this type of interaction will further diminish the mother's credibility and leadership of the family and her accompanying lack of behavior control. In the first option to reduce risk, the therapist says to the mom, "Because I know that you are so committed to helping your son to complete his probation without getting into more trouble [reframe], may I be totally honest with you [asking permission]?" When the mother says yes, the therapist highlights the interaction by saying to the mother, "Wow, Mom, when your son called you a bitch, that was very disrespectful, and you just took it." The highlight communicates to the mother that the child is being disrespectful and she is not doing anything about it. There is a purpose to the pointed wording on the part of the therapist, which is to be supportive of the mother while raising her discomfort about the child's disrespect and her tolerance for it. If the mother responds affectively—for example, with her frustration and anger about the youth's lack of respect—we are ready to go to the next step. However, if the mother's affect does not change—which she may demonstrate by excusing the youth or minimizing the disrespect—the therapist has to further intensify the highlight until the mother expresses her feelings of hurt. For example, the mother might say, "All kids behave this way today."

Exercising Option 2 for reducing risk, the therapist would say, "Yes, you are absolutely correct; so many kids are rude and disrespectful today, and I know that is not what you want the relationship between you and your son to be" (yes . . . and). The therapist may have to deepen their intensification of the discomfort about the interaction until the mother's affect about it changes from tolerance to a feeling that reflects that she is no longer comfortable with this behavior. Mother says, "He always treats me badly, like I am not his mother who gave birth to him, who changed his diapers."

Highlighting signals to the family that this is a place to stop, look, and listen. It changes the tempo, voice, and threshold of sensitivity that the family has developed that had allowed for more of the same to continue to occur. The therapist wants her highlighting words to stand out rather than just blending in. The intensification required by highlighting challenges the family's threshold and calls attention to the interaction in a way that also lowers the family's tolerance for the interaction. Through experience, we have developed several ways to bring to the family's attention the interaction itself and its maladaptiveness:

- by using a word or phrase that indicates surprise, alarm, concern, or disbelief (e.g., *wow*; *gee-whiz*; *goodness*; *oh, my God*);

- by changing the volume (if they are talking loudly, talk low, or vice versa);

- by deepening through repetition of the highlight using different words;

- by extending the normal duration of a transaction (e.g., to the son, "Say it again and this time slowly, and Mom, you listen because I am not sure you heard him right");

- by changing the tone (e.g., if they are laughing, get serious, and vice versa);

- by changing the speed (e.g., speeding up or slowing down your speech); and

- by finding words that will get an affective reaction by rephrasing what was said with more jolting words (e.g., changing what the mother says from, "Sometimes he doesn't treat me well" to "That is verbal abuse").

The alert reader may have noticed that highlighting is the opposite of mimesis. In mimesis, we want to blend in with the family. In highlighting, we want our observation to stand out. Family members become so used to repetitive interactions that, on occasion, they must be jolted to get their attention. By highlighting, the BSFT therapist sends a message to the family that says,

"This is important, this is significant, this is tolerated, but should it be?" When a mother dismisses the fact that her son has not been telling her about his failing grades by saying, "Sometimes he doesn't tell me everything," the BSFT therapist, changing the tone and speed to slower and more serious, says back to the mother, "You mean he LIES to you?" She repeats to the mother, "You mean he just plain tells you a lie and makes you believe he is passing when he is not?" To enhance more, the therapist might say, "And how much or how long has he been lying to you?"

Highlighting Positive Interactions

Highlights are not just intended for negative interactions. They are also intended to highlight positive opportunities for interactions. In these cases, the highlight runs little or no risk of eroding rapport. A positive interaction that is being overlooked and requires a highlight to be noted by a family member is found in the following example when a husband in a marriage that is in trouble says in a low voice, "I do love him, but I don't tell him." Meanwhile, the other husband has been talking over him and did not hear it but is instead involved in the usual recitations of everything that is wrong with their marriage. The BSFT therapist stops all conversation, turns to the husband who is giving a list of all that is wrong with the marriage and says in a soft, warm voice, "Did you hear what he just said? This is VERY important, and I think you need to hear it." Then, to the first husband, "What you said was very important and beautiful, but you said it very softly. I know that your husband will want to hear it. Please repeat it directly to him."

Reframing

Reframing refers to changing the meaning that a person attributes to a situation or person (Barlow et al., 2017; Beck, 2011; Minuchin & Fishman, 1981). A reframing intervention changes the way a person or family views or understands people and situations. Reframing, a cognitive restructuring intervention, also results in changes in affect (Robbins, Alexander, Newell, & Turner, 1996). The immediate effect of reframing on client attitude in family therapy is that it becomes the springboard for tasking the family to behave in a new way.

Reframing is the essence of BSFT's strength-based focus. In reframing, we unearth the positive experiences that underlie families' routines (Minuchin & Fishman, 1981). We peel back the ugliness of an interaction to reveal its beauty and its strength, the love that lives below the anger, the hurt that lives below the fury, the caring that lives below the rejection.

Reframing reveals the hidden bonds of affection that are present below the surface of routine negative interactions. A family's frame exists in the realm of cognition. It is a set of opinions, perceptions, and beliefs that family members and the family system hold. An example of frames is our beliefs about what makes us happy (e.g., for a mother, it may be that her son does well in school; for a youth, it may be to have more freedom to be with his friends). Another example of frames is our opinion of each other (e.g., "My mother is a bitch," "My mother is always blaming me for everything") and of ourselves ("I am a victim"). Reframing is an intervention that changes the cognitions about an interaction, a person, or a situation in ways that change that person's views, perception, and beliefs. To reframe, a therapist creates a different perspective or frame of reality than the one that the family or any specific family member had. The existing frames support the family members' affect and behaviors, which together maintain the current interactional patterns. The therapist presents a new frame to the family in a convincing manner—that is, she "sells" it to the family, and then she uses this new frame to facilitate change. The purpose of systems-oriented cognitive restructuring (reframing) is to change perceptions and/or meaning in ways that will enable a change in affect, behaviors, and therefore, interactions. At a deeper level, the purpose of reframing is to bring forth the love and bonds that exist in families but have been buried behind anger and bickering.

Reframes must always open the door to new possibilities by giving a more positive perspective. For example, if a son calls his mother "a liar," and the mother responds by yelling at her son, "There you're mouthing off again," and the son follows by saying, "Oh, Mom, you are also mouthing off with your yelling," the therapist highlights by pointing out to the mother that "yelling is not working for you" and reframes by saying, "I understand that you are yelling because you are hurt when he calls you a liar." As we will see in the next section, highlighting and reframing is followed by a task (e.g., "Tell your son about your hurt when he calls you a liar") that deepens the new frame of the mother being hurt.

Research on BSFT shows that the families that are most likely to drop out of therapy are those families in whom negativity is high and remains high during the first session (Robbins, Feaster, Horigian, Puccinelli, et al., 2011; see also Hogue, Dauber, Stambaugh, Cecero, & Liddle, 2006; Robbins et al., 1996; Robbins, Alexander, & Turner, 2000). For that reason, it is essential to reduce negativity, but this cannot be done by just blocking the family's negative affect. From the first session, it is essential to transform negative interactions into positive ones. Reframing is the optimal tool to achieve this. An important function of reframing is to transform negative interactions into positive ones. When families are high in negativity during the first few sessions, it is essential to change the negative tone of family emotions and the negative content of their interactions to retain the family in treatment.

Reframing is among the safest interventions there is, and consequently, we encourage the beginning therapist to use it abundantly. Research has shown (Robbins et al., 1996) that reframing is an intervention that usually does not cause the therapist any loss of rapport. For that reason, the therapist should feel free to use it even in the most explosive of situations—and maybe particularly in the most explosive situations.

There are some standard reframes we have learned are useful in certain situations. There are a limited number of negative situations that occur in families, and thus, we present in Table 5.1 useful reframes for the most frequent ones.

TABLE 5.1. Negative Frames and Positive Reframes

Negative frame	Positive reframes
Anger	Hurt, intense, passionate, energetic, caring, desperate, involved
Sadness	Sensitive, hurt, tired, caring, thinks deeply, is deeply touched, emotional
Aggressive	Energetic, assertive, up front, bold, confident
Isolated	Scared, protecting, shy, sensitive
Anxious	Caring, careful, concerned, perfectionistic, needs assurance, cautious, intense
Fearful/afraid	Cautious, asking for protection and support, needs reassurance, mindful, caring
Worried	Caring, careful, organized
Indifferent	Sensitive and hurt, afraid to hope, wants to be heard
Hopeless/pessimistic	Asking for help, asking for reassurance
Fed up	Tired, afraid to hope, asking for help and support
Helpless	Asking for support, wants something new, asking for attention, tired
Controlling	Caring and wanting to make sure it goes right, is a leader, creative
Resentful	Hurt (old not repaired)
Frustrated	Desiring something new, caring, perfectionistic, has perseverance
Nagging	Persistent, caring, helpful, concerned
Embarrassed	Conservative, sensitive, aware, has high expectations
Obsessed	Perfectionistic, passionate, has perseverance, focused, determined
Suspicious	Curious, protective, worried, wants truth, hurt
Weary/tired	Asking for help, needs a break or rest
Overwhelmed	Needs new solutions, needs to learn how to prioritize, takes on too much
Giving up	Needs support and help, needs to reenergize, needs new ideas
Numb	Protects emotions, hurt, copes, needs to feel safe
Needy	Wants attention, wants love, wants help, wants support, needs new solutions

Reframes are much more than single words. Hence, the reframes that we show in the right column of the table are intended as themes, not as words to be repeated verbatim. Effective reframes are the ones that we introduce initially but continue to develop throughout therapy. If a reframe fits early, it is likely that it might continue to be useful with a family (e.g., the hurt child). Often patterns of interactions emerge over time in regard to different contents. It is helpful for the family to experience a consistent reframe across contents because it increases the likelihood that the reframe will generalize to their lives. This, of course, does not mean that new reframes cannot be added as the family evolves and new interactions emerge. Various reframes can also be combined in a theme because negative emotions are complex. A father who is frustrated with his child may sound angry and nag the child. These are signs of a caring, worried parent. Such a situation can be reframed as a desperate dad who loves and worries about his son. These several reframes can be used through therapy in an integrated fashion until the family shows that they have adopted these new frames as shown by their new, more adaptive interactions, which exhibit an increase in the nurturance and bonding within the family.

A family with a drug-abusing adolescent comes to their first session. They describe her as disobedient, rebellious, and disrespectful, a girl who is ruining her life and going nowhere. In BSFT diagnostic terms, we would diagnose that family behavior as negativity toward the IP. Family members are angry and rejecting toward the teen, and they blame her for all the pain in the family. In BSFT diagnostic terms, we would diagnose the denial of other problems. There are no signs of warmth or caring for her as an individual. In BSFT diagnostic terms, we would diagnose lack of nurturance. They are fed up. The girl withdraws into a fetal position, tears rolling down her face.

In this instance, the BSFT therapist first highlights to change the affect that is missing in the family's complaints. To do this, the therapist states with emphatic concern, "Oh, look at those tears." The therapist uses the highlight as a springboard to introduce a new frame: "She seems so sad. It looks like behind all the acting out there is a lot of hurt."

The highlighting and reframing were intended to open the family to new behaviors toward the young woman, which are caring and nurturing communications. Invariably, reframes in BSFT are used to move communications from negative to positive affect, from parents who see their child as upsetting to parents who can view their child as sad. A critical question at this point is whether the parents have "bought" into the reframe. This is a question that therapists should always ask themselves when they reframe: Has the family bought into the reframe?

When the mother does not respond, the therapist might ask her, "Do you see what I see: a sad child?" Does anyone in the family see it this way? No one responds, and thus, the therapist adds, "If it is not exactly sad, what is it that you are seeing in those tears?" Often this will work, but sometimes it does not, such as when the mom says, "She is being manipulative." When the family does not buy into the reframe, the therapist has to determine whether she wants to continue to pursue this new frame or move to a different frame that would elicit nurturance and care from the mother.

The therapist must always be careful not to get into a power struggle with a family member or the whole family. In this case, the whole family is not buying into the therapist's reframe, even though the mother is the mouthpiece for the family. At moments like this, it is best that the therapist takes a step back and look for another opportunity to sell this frame or look for a new reframe that the family would accept. One option is to consider that it was much too big a leap for the mother and family to view this troublesome girl as sad. A possible way to proceed might involve breaking the reframe into smaller parts. As a first step, the therapist might begin with, "The daughter has isolated herself in the family," or "A lot of bad things have happened to this girl lately, right?" This might get the family talking about the bad things that have happened to the IP, such as getting kicked out of school. This might provide the opportunity for the therapist to say, "Bad things can have a very negative effect when a teen is so fragile and unsure of herself. It hasn't been an easy life for her." The mom says, "She brought it on herself." The therapist replies, "You are right. Sometimes these young people do not realize how painful it is for them once they get into trouble." The mom adds, "She had it coming. She made it happen." The therapist responds, "Yes, she may have brought it on herself, but it still hurts just the same. She looks so sad and feels so hurt. Am I right?"

> Successful highlighting and reframing results in cognitive and affective change. The successful completion of a task is behavioral change. Together, these constitute the kernel of "the beginning of change." Therapeutic change occurs when families repeat and sustain these changes over time.

Tasking

Tasks are the final ingredient for successful restructuring. What is a task? Everything we ask the family to do is a task ("Please take a seat," "Tell me what you want to work on today," "Let your son know how you feel about what he said").

In BSFT, there are two types of tasks. We already discussed what we refer to as *exploratory tasks*. Exploratory tasks are those we give family members when we are tracking for diagnosis. They are intended to encourage or direct family members to interact with one another, rather than with the therapist and thus elicit enactments. In these tasks, we do not direct how the family should interact; rather, we allow their structure to emerge as is, which is why we call these tasks *exploratory*. Their primary use is for observation and diagnosis, and thus, we want the interactions to emerge without interference from the therapist.

This section is about the second type of tasks, which we refer to as *restructuring tasks*. Restructuring tasks are directives the therapist gives the family to guide the family to interact in new and more adaptive ways. Building on the interactions that have been effectively highlighted and reframed, the therapist gives a task that is quite directive and specific to transform interactions from maladaptive to adaptive. Restructuring tasks must always be given first during the session with the therapist present. Once the therapist assigns the appropriate restructuring task, the therapist is persistent in helping the family to accomplish it. This is part of creating a sense of competence and achievement in the family. Consequently, tasks should be given early enough in the session to allow the therapist to work with them throughout the session, if necessary. Once accomplished, we must always give positive feedback to consolidate the family's sense of achievement.

Only when the family has been successful in interacting in the new way during the session can a similar task be assigned to be carried out at home. By having a task carried out in a natural environment such as the home, the likelihood of the change in interactions to generalize to different contents, circumstances, and settings increases, as does the likelihood that the change becomes permanent.

All tasks are intended to bring about a reversal of an existing maladaptive interaction. When considering what task to use, a simple rule might be helpful: Use a task that reverses the behaviors involved in maladaptive interactions. For example, when there are triangles in the family, in the long term, the triangle has to be broken. If the emergent process is a two-parent conflict in which one parent diffuses to the child while the other parent and the child allow it, the therapeutic intervention of breaking up the triangle could be done through a task that reverses any of those three aspects of the triangle. Option 1 might be to task the parent who diffuses and turns to the child to keep the child out of the parental conflict. Although this is the preferable intervention, it is the hardest to accomplish. The second option is to task the second parent to ask the child to stay out or ask the other parent to stop involving the child. The third option is for the therapist to task the child to stay out. These, then, are all reversals of the three types of behaviors that together result in a triangle.

In another example, a mother complains to her oldest son that the youngest son is misbehaving, causing the oldest son to confront the youngest son in an aggressive manner, triggering the mother to step in and protect the young one by telling the older child he is too rough. Here we have a sequence of events that constitute a triangle and results in the youngest son's behavior remaining unchecked and uncontrolled. Like all triangles, there is a failure to manage the misbehavior of a child. The therapist tasks the mother to manage the youngest child's behavior without involving her other son. Because the young son is spitting in people's faces, the therapist asks the mother,

> Mother, tell your older son not to get involved, that you want to talk with your little one by yourself. Then, tell your little one not to ever spit in people's faces again, that if he does it again, you will take his phone away for the rest of the day.

Task Management

In response to a request for interactional change—that is, in response to a new task—families will often not be able to carry out the task successfully. This is to be expected because the job of a family system and its interactional patterns is to maintain itself unchanged—that is, to maintain its homeostasis. In other words, families may not exhibit the new behaviors required by the task because old habits die hard. As the leader of the therapeutic system, the therapist must take responsibility to choreograph and facilitate the successful completion of the task. One of the first steps for the therapist is to determine what he has to do to enable the family to complete the task. When obstacles emerge, it is the therapist's job to correct those that are interfering with the successful completion of the task as they emerge. This may require attention to emerging intertwined processes that have to be corrected to enable the larger goal of therapy to be accomplished. For example, to get a mother and father to collaborate, it may be that several different maladaptive interactions have to be corrected in the process of completing the major task by, for example:

- stopping diffusion by returning to the topic at hand;
- not allowing one person to speak for another but instead encouraging each one to speak for themselves;
- undoing maladaptive alliances, including but not limited to removing triangulated parties from a dyadic relationship; and
- creating adaptive alliances allowing the conflicted dyad to come to a resolution.

When we chunk a task into subtasks, we are in effect task (micro)managing. Task management is the process of dismantling the components that together contribute to creating the maladaptive interactional patterns and that prevent the family from engaging in successful new and adaptive interactions. It is like unraveling a tangled roll of yarn by untangling each knotted loop to achieve a smooth flow.

When the usual highlighting, reframing, and tasking (with therapist facilitation) is insufficient, and the family is unable to carry out a new task, the therapist may have to exercise task management by (a) breaking up the task into smaller steps, (b) changing the direction of the task to achieve the same interactional change, (c) managing the behaviors that interfere with the completion of the task, or (d) attending to the interface between the individual and the interactions in the task that the therapist is seeking to elicit.

Breaking Tasks Into Smaller Steps

If the task is for parent and son is to negotiate a curfew, and the family is unable to carry out this task, the therapist breaks it up into smaller steps. The therapist might first ask the parent to get the son's attention. When this is accomplished, the therapist asks the son to propose curfew times to his parent. Third, the therapist asks the parent to let the son know what the parent thinks are the best curfew times and why. At this point, the therapist continues to encourage and facilitate effective negotiation until they come to an agreement.

Changing the Direction of a Task

When the therapist tasks a parent to ask her crying daughter what her tears are about, and the parent remains negative and not willing or able to be nurturant, the therapist might instead ask the daughter, "If your tears had words, what would they say?" or "Can you share with your family what your tears are about?"

Managing the Behaviors That Interfere With the Completion of the Task

Some common examples of managing diffusion and interruptions are by blocking them, or when family members are speaking over each other, by asking family members to speak one at a time, or by constantly reframing negativity or redirecting the manner of speech (e.g., "If you want to tell your son how you feel about his leaving the younger children unattended, say it in a way that he can hear you"). This may require the therapist to guide parents to change their tone, affect, words, and/or volume. When the therapist is working to empower the parent, and the parent carries out the task in an immature, silly, or tentative manner, the therapist will have to manage the parent's behavior by directing the parent to sound serious and firm.

Attending to the Interface Between the Individual and Interactions

Dealing with the interface between the individual and interactions may require working with individual family members to help them process their reluctance or inability to behave in new ways. We do not expect behavior to change easily. It is as hard on the part of the therapist to create change as it is hard and persistent work on the part of the family to protect their old ways of behaving. The therapist must be insistent, consistent, and persistent to identify the ingredients that are making family members reluctant or unable to accomplish the task. If a mother who describes her daughter's tears and fetal position as "manipulative" is unwilling to complete the assigned task of asking her daughter what the tears are about, the therapist can work with the mother to uncover what makes it difficult for her to perform this nurturance function.

The therapist is aware that the family fights against change because that is the nature of systems; their homeostatic force is trying to perpetuate themselves just as they are. Mother might say, "She cries all the time when she does not want to listen to me. I don't trust her anymore. Those are crocodile tears." If the therapist is well joined with the mother, the therapist might use her relationship to ask the mother to go beyond her threshold. The therapist might say, "Mom, I can see that it is difficult for you to trust her." However, if the therapist knows that the mother has reported that her daughter betrayed her trust several times, the therapist might say, "And, Mom, I also understand what makes it difficult to trust her. Mom, I understand, and I am asking you to give it one more try with my help here. I want you to ask her why she is crying [as the therapist places her hand on the mother's shoulder], and please do so [the therapist shifts her tone to be soft and gentle] in a soft and gentle voice so that she can hear your concern." Note that tasking has to be specific and clear to maximize the likelihood that it will be done correctly. Our task assignment should be brief, clear, and specific and given at the moment it is needed. We do not lecture. Lectures kill the present and the momentum of interactions. We merely reshape the direction of the present interaction with a brief intervention to transform the affect and propel the parent's new behavior that, in turn, transforms the nature of the interactions.

It is important to note that in one statement ("I also understand what makes it difficult to trust her"), the therapist joins and validates ("I understand"), highlights ("what makes is difficult"), and reframes manipulation into "it's hard for you to trust her." The therapist also joins by placing her hand on the mother's shoulder (which says to the mother, "I am with you"). The therapist then moves to tasking the mother to behave in a new way, clearly encouraging the mother to move beyond the kind of impasse in which this family finds itself.

Brief Individual Work in the Whole-Family Context

There is also a kind of individual work that may be needed to overcome the intrapersonal obstacles to creating new interactions. This kind of individual work, compared with individual psychotherapy, is typically brief, and it is nearly always done in the context of the whole family. This is not a therapy directed solely at changing any one family member; rather, it is working with the individual to change what happens between and among family members. To change the interaction between family members, it may be necessary to overcome the here-and-now impediments (that may have built because of the history between the family members) that prevent each of the individuals involved in that interaction to behave in a different manner. Why is this done in the context of the whole family? There are two important reasons: (a) other members of the family will be impacted in some manner by one member's experience, and (b) the therapist has to know how the rest of the family reacts to the work with the one family member. This will allow the therapist to observe how the family system as a whole responds to one individual's change and possibly how the family either undermines or supports that change.

In our earlier example of the crying teen whose mother said she was being manipulative, the therapist focused her attention on the mother and inquired, "What makes it difficult for you to ask your daughter about her tears?" thus, exploring what is blocking the mother from asking. Mom, with a tear running down her cheek, said, "I can't. She has hurt me too many times." The therapist said, "I can feel your pain, and I am so glad you are sharing your pain with your daughter." To remain decentralized, the therapist redirected the statement as if it had happened between mother and daughter (and not the therapist). And, as a way of further bonding mother and daughter, the therapist provided a reframe: "I can see that you are both in pain." To the daughter, she said, "Did you know that your mother feels the same as you? Your mother is going to ask you now, and this time, be real and be open with your mom." To the mom, she said, "Please ask her again about her crying" (the therapist kept her hand on the mother's shoulder all this time). We note that mother and daughter were at an impasse, where the daughter had withdrawn and was crying, and the mother was too hurt to reach out. The intervention was intended to create a connection between the two women to overcome the impasse.

The mom said, "This is very difficult for me to do because the truth is that all I get from you is bullshit. What are you crying about? And, like the lady says, be real." The therapist praised the mom to reinforce her new behavior: "Well done. I am proud of you. I know you took a chance here and that it was very difficult for you to do." The daughter told her mother what was making her sad. The therapist also praised the daughter for sharing with her mother (a new behavior). It is not rare with acting-out adolescents to arrive at this kind of impasse, particularly when the adolescent withdraws. Withdrawing is a way of maintaining a position of power in the family, as well as a way of expressing anger. When the daughter spoke, she ceded her position of power. The therapist encouraged a tradeoff: The daughter traded power for nurturance.

As this example illustrates, families are often unable to complete a task without the therapist's help. It is important for the therapist to understand this because too many therapists will say, "But I told the mother to do it, and she won't do it." From a systems perspective, the therapist is the leader of the therapeutic system and, as such, when the family is unable to complete a task, it is always (there are no exceptions) the therapist's responsibility to help the family to "make it happen." In fact, if the family were able to accomplish the assigned tasks, they would not have to be in therapy. When tasks are assigned, therapists should always hope for the best but be prepared for therapeutic challenges. In fact, when the family fails to carry out a task, the therapist's real job begins. After all, a restructuring task represents a new behavior for the family. It represents a behavior that is different from what the family has been doing for years. It also requires changes in how the family felt and thought, and initially, it is not supported by the other family members. Hence, once the family member, with the therapist's help, engages in new behaviors, the therapist must help the rest of the family to change their thoughts, feelings, and behaviors to allow, support, and reinforce new interactions.

In summary, as the family attempts a task, the therapist should assist the family in overcoming challenges to accomplishing the task. However, even then, in spite of the therapist's best efforts, the task is not always accomplished at first. We often think of these situations as requiring considerable therapeutic skill and therapist's active participation and involvement. While not taking over the roles that belong to the family, the therapist has to maintain a role as director and active facilitator to help the family accomplish new and more adaptive interactions. Thus, therapists are always on the lookout for emerging processes that might interfere with the successful completion of the tasks and opportunities to intervene to move the process forward. The therapist's job is to identify the obstacle(s) to task accomplishment and help the family surmount them. It is essential to keep in mind that a family seeks therapy because it is unable to overcome obstacles without help. Failed tasks are usually a great source of new and important information regarding the challenges a family faces that impedes them from doing what is best for them—that is, doing what will help the family achieve their goals.

> The therapist should never be surprised that family members fail to accomplish a task. In fact, more often than not, when a member is asked to behave in a new way, there will be obstacles to overcome before the family can comply with that request.

Artfully Integrating the Elements

To further illustrate the restructuring process as integrating highlighting, reframing, and tasking, we present the White family. Their 8-year-old boy, Barron, was referred by the school because his grades had dropped in the last 6 months, he had stopped interacting with the other children, and had stopped participating in class. In the first session, the parents reported that he has a lot of nightmares and ends up sleeping in the parents' bed because he is afraid to be alone. In the morning, he fights Mom when she tries to get him ready for school, and he typically does not want to go to school. The mother has to literally drag him out of the house to take him to school. This was always a problem but became much worse in the last 6 months. In the first session, the therapist asked, "What brought you here?" The father took the lead and said, "My son is turning into a sissy, and it is all her fault because she babies him." In response, the mother said,

> I may baby him, but you are treating him like he is 20 years old. All you do is to say to him, "Straighten up, you should not be sleeping in our bed. Start acting your age. What is there to be afraid of anyway? Sleep in your own bed."

It is clear to the therapist from this interaction that the mom and dad are not on the same page. They are not allied on parenting issues. In fact, they fight about parenting issues, failing to collaborate in developing effective parenting solutions. This lack of collaboration between parents, reflecting a lack of alliance between the parents, is, without doubt, the most frequent interactional pattern that is encountered by family therapists treating families that present with children that have internalizing or externalizing problems. Although the therapist knew in the first 2 minutes about an important aspect of the family's interactions that has to be corrected, the therapist has to wait to intervene until she has joined the family. As always, this is challenging when there are family members who do not agree with each other. The therapist has to join each parent without alienating the other. The therapist can start joining in regard to the issue presented by the parents: "Even though you have different views of what needs to be done with Barron [highlight], I can see that you are both very concerned about Barron [a reframe that accentuates areas of agreement]." They agreed. The therapist further joins by using an alliance-building reframe that changes both the affect and cognition about the parents being on two sides, suggesting that they are both on the same side by saying,

> It is wonderful to see that you both care deeply and want your son to succeed. You don't want him to be fearsome of being alone, and you want him to be doing well in school. I know you disagree on how best to help your son, and disagreeing is not helping your son reach these goals [highlight]. What if we try something different? Let's work on getting you guys to achieve your common goals for Barron [setting up the task]!

Giving tasks that have to be accomplished jointly is another way to build an alliance between two persons. The therapist frames the task broadly in her initial statement, but tasks that are vague typically do not get the desired results. For this reason, the therapist makes the task more specific: "I would like you to talk with each other about how to handle his nightmares in a way that you can both agree, keeping in mind what will work with an 8-year-old." Note that the therapist is straddling alliances with a couple that does not agree. By saying "an 8-year-old," the therapist allies with the mom, but by working on how to handle the nightmares, the therapist allies with the dad. Mom said, "What about all the other problems, like his not wanting to go to school?" to which the therapist responded, "Okay, let's start by working on one problem at a time." It is not unusual for families to want to diffuse. By trying to tackle all the child's problems at once, the family attempts to maintain the homeostatic pattern of interactions that has not worked for them. The therapist's job is to prevent the diffusion, to focus the family on working on one content problem at a time, thus, breaking up one the family's maladaptive patterns.

Notwithstanding the therapist's block of the mother's attempt at diffusion, the father made his attempt at diffusion. He said, "I want him to be a big boy, not a baby." The mom responded, "I think that is the problem. You want him to be 20, and he is only 8." Both parents diffused by changing the topic away from the task. To manage this diffusion, the therapist said, "Those are all important issues, but I want you to talk first about how to handle his nightmares. We'll get to the rest in time [managing diffusion]." The therapist thus brings the parents back to talking about how to handle the nightmares: "Mom, Dad, talk about what you want to do when he has a nightmare." The mom replied, "I want to help my little one." The dad countered, "I don't want him sleeping in my bed." Now the parents are focusing on the problem, and the dad is quite specific about what he wants. To this, the therapist responded,

> Dad, let Mom know your reasons why you don't want him in bed, and be very specific. Just saying that you want him to be a big boy could mean many different things. Give Mom some solid reasons why you want him in his own bed, for his own good and for the good of your marriage.

The therapist's work is always a balancing act by appealing simultaneously to both parents. The therapist is supporting the dad by clearly taking the position that an 8-year-old need not be sleeping in his parents' bed and supporting the mom in that he is only 8 and cannot be treated like he is 20. The therapist also gives the dad some things he might say, such as, "You don't want him in your bed for his own good and for the good of your marriage." The dad replied, "I want my bed with my wife." The therapist responded, "Dad, tell your wife why you want the bed for just the two of you." The direction of this conversation shifts the focus from the child to the parents and, moreover, to the parents' marital relationship, which is where we determined earlier that change was needed. In these few interventions, we moved the dad and mom from being on opposite sides of parenting the child to speaking about the dad's wish for privacy and intimacy. Moreover, we took the first step toward detriangulating Barron.

Homework Tasks

Once a successful change sequence has been completed, the same interactional change can be tasked to be repeated outside the therapy session. By repeating the new changed behaviors over different settings, the new behavior is practiced and generalized to different contexts. This is important because mastery is acquired through repetition. The student learns to play the piano (or shoot baskets) by practicing every day. Homework tasks are also used to extend the gains made in the session. For example, when parents first collaborate in setting a rule or two during the session, a homework task may be to determine what the rest of the rules would be before the next session. Another homework task consists of carrying out a plan that was made during the session. For example, an estranged mother and daughter are able during the session to reconnect emotionally and decide to have some quality each day. The homework would involve having at least 10 minutes of quality time for each of the following 3 days.

As we close this chapter, we feel it is important, once again, to remind the reader that although these components of BSFT have been presented here separately, the reality is that these components constitute the BSFT change sequence and include joining, maintaining a viable therapeutic system, developing enactments, assessing the family functioning, highlighting, reframing, tasking, managing the tasks, and praising. The therapist's use of these components is like a dance that seamlessly flows from one to another to create one therapeutic wholeness over and over again as we take the family from one session to another, from intake to termination, from turmoil to strength.

KEY TAKEAWAYS

- We work in the present, in the context of enactments. As maladaptive interactions emerge, we stimulate, elicit, and direct new and more adaptive interactions. All of us can only change in the present.

- BSFT is a skills-building therapy. For this reason, the therapist never does for the family what the family must learn to do for itself.

- Mastery is not achieved by criticizing, interpreting, labeling, pathologizing individuals, or belittling. Rather, it is achieved by incrementally shaping and praising positive behaviors.

- The BSFT therapist is never central. Rather, the therapist's job is to choreograph the family.

- When families are high in negativity during the first session, to retain the family in treatment, it is essential to change the negative tone of family emotions and the negative content of their interactions through reframing.

- Reframing is the essence of BSFT's strength-based focus. In reframing, we unearth the positive experiences that underlie families' routines. Reframing reveals the hidden bonds of affection that are present below the surface of routine negative interactions.

- A task should be brief, clear, and specific and assigned at the moment it is needed.

- The therapist, as the leader of the therapeutic system, is always responsible for helping the family overcome their obstacles to change.

- The momentum of change has to be greater than the inertia of homeostasis.

- The BSFT change sequence includes joining, maintaining a viable therapeutic system, developing enactments, assessing the family functioning, highlighting, reframing, tasking, managing the tasks, and praising.

6

Pitfalls to Avoid

In therapy, as in life, it is just as important to know what to do as what not to do. The youth in the families we discuss in this book were often unable to keep themselves from trouble. In this chapter, we wish to help to keep the therapist out of trouble. We recognize that a therapist "thinking on her feet" might make statements that will result in some of these pitfalls. For this reason, we make several suggestions here for how a therapist can avoid these missteps and, if she gets in trouble, how she can extricate herself.

In this chapter, we illustrate the following common pitfalls when practicing Brief Strategic Family Therapy® (BSFT®):

- content-driven therapy,
- about-ism,
- centralization of the therapist,
- lecturing and philosophizing,
- losing the leadership in the therapeutic system,
- doing for the family or playing a family role,
- failing to close the deal, and
- getting "sucked" into the family's frame.

http://dx.doi.org/10.1037/0000169-007
Brief Strategic Family Therapy, by J. Szapocznik and O. E. Hervis

CONTENT-DRIVEN THERAPY

BSFT is a process-driven therapy. *Content* is what people talk about, and *process* is how they interact about any content. Process is the repetitive interactional patterns of the family. The repetitive interactional patterns in the family constitute how a family is structured to handle any topic. BSFT diagnoses family processes and intervenes in changing those processes that are linked to the symptoms. In BSFT, content varies according to the family's concern of the moment, but processes (i.e., interactional patterns) remain the same regardless of the content or topic. In fact, for families who come to treatment, process has often become too rigid and thus does not vary sufficiently across different situations. We want to strengthen processes that are adaptive (e.g., nurturance) and correct processes that are maladaptive (e.g., triangulation).

Knowing all of this, however, does not change the fact that therapists sometimes forget that BSFT is only about observing, diagnosing, and changing process. It is all too easy for therapists to become concerned, seduced, and involved in content—which is *not* the focus of BSFT. By becoming involved with content, therapists become lost and overwhelmed by detail. Following the content is the proverbial "losing the forest for the trees." Though content can be important, it is the purview of the family, and therefore, the family has to resolve it. The purview, job, and responsibility of the therapist are to reshape how the family works with (or interacts about) their content in a manner that allows them to solve it effectively.

How do we get seduced and trapped by content? Most often, we fall into the trap by asking "why" or other lineal questions, inquiring about history, and focusing on facts and details (e.g., Mom says her son got arrested; the therapist asks, "What for?" or "Is this the first time?" or "Was he alone or with friends?").

Becoming content focused is the pathway to falling into many other pitfalls. If you are stuck on content, you are also liable to

- talk about "stuff" rather than being action and present oriented;
- be centralized;
- do some version of lecturing and philosophizing;
- lose your leadership of the therapeutic system by allowing the family's content to derail you from what should be your role: process change;
- perform a family role, such as giving advice; and
- be "sucked" into (and thus work on) the family's frame, which supports homeostasis rather than creating a new frame that allows for change.

We discuss these pitfalls in more detail later in this chapter.

How do you extricate yourself if you make the mistake of getting lost in content? The first step is to continuously ask yourself whether you are focused on process or lost in content. When you become aware that you are trapped in content, stop yourself for a moment, step back, identify the process in the here and now, and explain with a reframe why it is better for the family member with whom you are talking to discuss it with the appropriate family member and task them to do so. It is even permissible and, alas, even better, to say to the family, "Please give me a moment here to think about where we should best be going now." For example, Mom is discussing with the therapist whether her son should spend the summer studying or get a job. The therapist begins to give her opinion when she realizes that she is caught in content. The therapist redirects the conversation away from herself by saying to Mom, "It would be best to discuss this with Dad and your son [reframe]. Go ahead and talk with them about it [task]." Hence, by eliciting an enactment, the therapist extricates herself from being trapped in content.

ABOUT-ISM

BSFT is not a therapy of "talking about"; it is a therapy of action. The aim of any discussion is to move toward actual change in behaviors and interactions in the session. About-ism is about content, and while the family is talking about this or that content, no therapy is happening. Mother's about-ism may sound like, "I want to work on the poor communication I have with my daughter and how she doesn't respect me." The therapist moves from about-ism to a change-producing intervention: "Mom, tell your daughter what you just told me, and let's see how she wants to respond." The therapist sets up the interaction. The therapist would have fallen for about-ism if she had allowed the mother to continue to talk to her about the problem (e.g., instances [when does it happen?], examples [what does it happen regarding?]). Instead, to extricate herself from about-ism and move the therapy to action, the therapist redirects the mother to interact with her daughter about her concern.

CENTRALIZATION OF THE THERAPIST

We make the distinction between a centralized and a directive therapist. A *centralized* therapist is a therapist who elicits interactions toward herself: "Mother, how do you feel about what your daughter just said?" This is contrasted with a *directive* therapist, who is focused on choreographing interactions among family members. This therapist would keep the interactions in the family by directing the mother, "Tell your daughter how you feel about what she just said." BSFT requires a therapist who is active and involved in choreographing. For example, if a child is crying, a directive therapist would give the parent the task to comfort the child and ask about the tears. A centralized therapist, in contrast, would do the comforting or inquiring himself.

To be directive is to guide, show the way, and point out the right direction without doing the actual work that family members have to do. Many therapists believe they have to model behavior—for example, model for a parent how to nurture the child. A parent who is having trouble being nurturing with her child can be treated in the same way you want the parent to treat the child, but in our experience, that is not enough. Beyond giving the parent the experience of receiving nurturance, the therapist has to "sculpt" the parent's behavior to help the parent behave in a nurturant manner, even if the therapist has to direct the parent through each step. This is what we referred to earlier as *managing the task*. It requires a directive therapist who actively coaches the parent through the set of behaviors involved in nurturance. However, when Mom has to exercise behavior control, the therapist cannot engage in controlling the parent, much less the child. Rather, the therapist helps the parent to build the set of skills she needs to manage her child's misbehavior. In this case, the therapist can model some behaviors—for example, by giving the mother the appropriate tasks in the same firm and serious voice that the parent has to use in managing her child's misbehaviors.

How does a therapist get out of trouble when she becomes centralized? Correction can be done simply by stopping yourself and saying to the family, "There is no point in my doing this. I need you to take over. She is, after all, your daughter."

A common way of becoming centralized is to continue to have one-to-one conversations with a member of the family. If you view a videotape and, on review, you see that family members are talking with you, the therapist, you are not doing BSFT. Therapists have to be careful because talking with you, the therapist, is what families expect to do in therapy, and they will try to trap you into such a centralized role. To extricate yourself from this centralization, you have to redirect the conversation to the appropriate family member. Conversation and interactions should take place among family members and not with you, the therapist.

LECTURING AND PHILOSOPHIZING

Lecturing family members about what they have to do is useless. This is another form of about-ism, and thus, it is not BSFT. In our experience, it has not been effective with the families with whom we have worked. Therefore, it is a waste of precious therapy time. Moreover, it causes families to become distracted and bored.

If you find yourself lecturing, you most likely got there because you did not know what else to do. The way to get yourself out of this pitfall is to simply say, "But I am sure you know and agree, so give me a minute. I need to make sure where we need to go next." When the therapist says that, someone in the family will often come up with something that needs attention, which can restart a process-oriented therapy. If this does not occur spontaneously with a family member, the therapist can go back to the last content the family brought up and use it to create an enactment by tasking a family member to talk with another person in the family about the issue at hand.

One way therapists get in trouble with these kinds of pitfalls is by asking the family what they want to talk about. Instead, we recommend starting the session with, "What do you want to work on today?" or "What do you want to fix today?" Both of these immediately signal to the family that it is their work and that it is not just "talking about" but "doing."

LOSING THE LEADERSHIP IN THE THERAPEUTIC SYSTEM

Several common mistakes cause a therapist to lose her leadership of the therapeutic system. These are described next.

Failure to Maintain a Joined Position

One of the most common reasons therapists lose leadership of the therapeutic system is the failure to maintain a joined position with one or more family members. BSFT therapists should know that at the beginning and end of each session, they must be equally joined with each family member, although there are times during a restructuring intervention when the therapist has to ally more with one family member over another (e.g., "I am sorry, but I have to agree with your wife"). This temporary alliance has to be followed with a rebalancing of the therapeutic system by rejoining those who were left out of the temporary alliance (e.g., "I really admire how you were open to hearing what your wife had to say"). It is essential that the therapist continues to have a balanced alliance with all family members on an ongoing basis from one session to another and across sessions.

Getting Caught in a Power Struggle With a Family Member

Another leadership issue can occur when the therapist gets caught in a power struggle with a family member. Never get into a power struggle with a family member. You will typically lose the power struggle, which means that you will lose your leadership of the therapeutic system. We lose the therapeutic leadership because we lose the power struggle. A power struggle places you at the same level as a family member. Hence, when you enter a power struggle, you give up your leadership role. Therapists are likely to lose the power struggle because it occurs in an area in which the family member has considerable history, experience, and investment, whereas the therapist has none of these with this particular family. When someone does not agree or comply with the therapist, the therapist can either (a) explore and resolve what is triggering the family member's reluctance to complete the frame or task or (b) when that is not productive, simply drop the highlight, reframe, or task until next time the same maladaptive pattern repeats and then present it again using different phrasing. Because family patterns repeat, the family provides the therapist with another opportunity to address the same interactional pattern. If you find yourself in a power struggle, always give in as early as possible by saying, "You are probably right," and move on.

Relating to the Family in a Personal Rather Than a Strategic Way

A challenge to effective joining and leadership arises when the therapist forms an alliance with a family in a personal rather than a strategic way. What do we mean by this? The therapist may choose whom to ally with, support, or confront on the basis of personal reasons or feelings rather than on the basis of what is strategic to effect the changes in interactional patterns that the family needs. In BSFT, the therapist must make temporary alliance decisions based on strategy and not on personal feelings. Quite often, therapists have to ally with the persons that are least likable—for example, angry, negative, critical family members or people who may be acting in an apparently hurtful way. When working with a family in which a mother is angry about her child's acting out but at the same time is unable to effectively exercise behavior control, the therapist may feel sorry for the child who is being berated and respond by supporting the child, but in this case, the person who has to initiate the change and has the power to change the family's negative interactions is the mother. If the therapist's heart is telling her to join more strongly with the youth than the mother, the therapist will not be sufficiently joined with the mother to create changes in the mother's cognitions, affect, and behaviors that will allow for new and more positive interactions between the mother and child.

Enabling Maladaptive Interactions and Structure

The most frequent example of enabling maladaptive interactions encountered in family therapy is the case of the therapist who agrees to work with whoever is willing to attend therapy when an incomplete family wants to come into therapy. Often, those who attend therapy are the primary caretaker and the identified patient (IP), the family member with "the problem" who has to be "fixed." As we explain in the next chapter on BSFT Engagement, what typically occurs is that the family members who are allied with each other are the ones who are likely to attend therapy. If the therapist agrees to work only with this subsystem of the family, he is unable to diagnose the problem in the way it occurs daily at home with this family, and consequently, he is unable to change the critical interactional patterns that are linked to the presenting complaint. The therapist wants to help the family members who attend therapy to reach their treatment goals. But the therapist is depriving them of getting the help they need to achieve their treatment goals. This occurs because the therapist is unable to observe what happens in the daily life of the family. For example, in this scenario, the family member who came to therapy may fight with a marginalized family member who did not come to therapy. In this case, there could be a triangulated child or IP who gets the brunt of the anger of the marginalized family member who most likely lost the argument with the adult who came to therapy. This IP will continue to receive the brunt of the anger generated by these arguments and thus will continue to display symptoms (e.g., acting out, being suicidal) and cannot be helped unless all the relevant persons come into therapy.

Another type of enabling of maladaptive interactions and structure occurs when the therapist agrees with the families' frame of who or what is the problem. In this case, the therapist allies with the parent figure about the IP being the only one who has to change. This supports the family's frame that the IP is the only individual who has a problem and has to change and that the mother is the only person responsible for helping him change. A therapist who accepts this frame is preserving rather than changing the maladaptive interactional patterns that give rise to the IP's symptoms. Such a frame results in the therapist's neglect of BSFT's systemic interactional perspective. Unfortunately, by accepting the family's frame, the therapist supports what the family does that prevents it from correcting the maladaptive interactions that result in the IP's symptoms.

Premature Challenges to the Presenting Family Power Structure

Unpleasant as it might sometimes be, in addition to joining all family members, therapists must ally with powerful members of the family at the onset of therapy, even when the powerful person is an adolescent (a hierarchical malalignment) or an angry, critical parent. Unless the therapist joins with the powerful family member, the powerful person will take himself out of therapy or might take the whole family out of therapy. Once the powerful person has been challenged, getting that person back into therapy is much more difficult than if the therapist had initially respected that person's power. An extreme example of challenging the powerful IP too early in therapy occurred in a family in which the IP was a powerful 17-year-old girl of whom all family members were afraid. In the first session, once the therapist diagnosed this hierarchical malalignment, she directed interventions to empower the father (the stepmother wisely said, "It is not my place. She is your child"). The IP refused to attend the second session, which was conducted at home. At that point, the therapist encouraged the father to impose consequences if the IP continued to refuse to come to session. When the IP, who was in the next room, heard that her father had reluctantly agreed to take away her car keys, she ran to the door, took the car keys, and ran out to the car. The father ran after his daughter to take away the keys, the daughter fought back, a physical confrontation resulted, and the police had to be called. A wiser strategy for the therapist would have been to join the powerful IP early in therapy and engage her and her dad in discovering their positive bond and in a negotiation process. A negotiation process requires the daughter to give up some of her power and her dad to regain some of his. This would provide the opportunity to restructure the hierarchy in this family without challenging the IP's power too early in therapy. For the daughter to relinquish some power, Dad has to be willing to provide her, in turn, with other rewards. The IP attained her power by being the primary homemaker at home. A benefit she obtained through negotiation was to move out of that burdensome role to have more time for her adolescent interests.

Not Attending to Power Relationships

It may seem natural for the therapist to ally with a parent who seems overwhelmed by a child who is totally out of control. Although this parent needs support and encouragement, the power in this relationship rests with the youth, and thus, to bring about change in this interaction, the youth will have to be asked to give up some of her power. This can only be achieved by the therapist strongly allying with the youth. To counteract the temptation to rely on personal feelings, it is a good idea to focus analytically on who has the most power to change a maladaptive interactional pattern (e.g., the IP is more powerful than the parent).

Allowing the Family to Derail You

Families diffuse by changing topics of conversation as much at home as in the therapy session. As we noted earlier, diffusion is one of the ways in which families avoid staying on topic to discuss what family members perceive to be difficult issues. Typically, the therapy requires the family to keep on topic until a resolution is found for the issue at hand. There are times when families raise contents that cannot be postponed, such as abuse. However, these are extremely rare compared with the number of times a family diffuses for reasons the family may say are important but are merely habitual behaviors intended to prevent conflict from emerging or being resolved or hot topics the family avoids. Sometimes the family may even create a sense of urgency about a different focus than the therapist had intended to pursue, and at times, the therapist gets seduced by this sense of urgency or by the nature of the content in a diffusion attempt. This is one time the therapist has to attend to both the process and the content to determine whether it is merely an effort to diffuse or indeed a topic that merits urgent attention and cannot be postponed for a later discussion. Even when a topic may appear extremely critical, it may be possible for the therapist to say to the family, "That is extremely important, and we will discuss it today, but let's finish what we are working on now, and then we will talk about that."

DOING FOR THE FAMILY OR PLAYING A FAMILY ROLE

The families you are helping are not your family. Therefore, do not do for your families in therapy what you would do for your family. Performing a family role is like giving a hungry person a fish to eat—it is laudable, but it only feeds that person and his family for one day. In BSFT, our goal is to teach a hungry person how to fish so that we have fed him and his family for a lifetime. Therefore, the BSFT therapist never becomes a parent, sibling, or spouse. Instead, the therapist's job is to empower each family member to perform the job that is appropriate for their role in an effective and adaptive manner. How does a therapist extricate herself from playing a family role?

Just as before, it is by gaining awareness of what you are doing and redirecting the action from you to the appropriate family member who has to be the one who performs this role. If you find yourself performing a family task or role, simply say something such as, "As a matter of fact, Mom, why don't you do this? It's much better coming from you."

GETTING "SUCKED" INTO THE FAMILY'S FRAME

The family comes to therapy because they are stuck in their habitual ways of focusing on only a limited part of their cognitive, affective, or behavioral experience. The family comes with a frame that supports their homeostasis. Again, *homeostasis* refers to the inner forces in the family system that maintain the status quo. In this case, these inner forces present themselves in the form of a limited perception of their experience. The problem occurs when the therapist also falls victim to this limited perception. For example, the therapist sometimes allies with the parent figure about the IP being the one who has to be changed. When this happens, the therapist is supporting a maladaptive interactional pattern that designates one individual as IP and does not recognize that it is the family, not just the IP, that has to change. As such, the therapist is neglecting BSFT's interactional perspective. This is exactly what the family does to prevent it from solving its problems.

We can learn about the family's limited perception by the way they talk about their problems and their goals. Problems can be presented from affective ("We are here because my son, Johnny, is driving me crazy"), behavioral ("We are here because he throws things at me when I insist that he do his chores"), or cognitive ("Johnny has attention-deficit/hyperactivity disorder, and the school sent me here because he can't do any school work") perspectives. By focusing on the full human experience—including cognition, affect, and behavior through the intervention sequence of highlighting, reframing, and tasking—the therapist broadens each family member's experience of the problem.

When the therapist gets "sucked" in or "buys" the family's frame, he reinforces the family's "stuck-ness" by enabling the continuation of the maladaptive patterns that frame allows. Enabling the family's frame prevents the therapist from unlocking opportunities for therapeutic interventions. The therapist is as stuck as the family. Therefore, the therapist is unable to help the family to open doors to new views, feelings, and behaviors that can lead to more adaptive interactions.

For example, Mr. and Ms. Papos do not want to bring their well-functioning children to therapy. They are afraid they are going to be "contaminated" by the IP. They may also think that is "just not fair to get them involved in therapy when they are doing well." A therapist who gets sucked into or buys into this frame sees only the Paposes and the IP in therapy. This therapist is unable to diagnose the family system as it functions as a whole in the home.

The therapist will not be able to observe diagnostically how the sibling sub-system is functioning and how they may be reinforcing the IP's status. Once we brought the whole Papos family into therapy, we learned that one of the older "good children" was involved in drugs and often gave the IP drugs. While the older child did not seem to get in trouble for using drugs, the IP appeared depressed and was also doing poorly in school. From a treatment perspective, the other siblings who were functioning well could be a resource to the IP and his older drug-using brother. The way out of this particular pit-fall is to ensure that all who are part of the family system attend the first and other required sessions, as we explain in Chapter 7.

FAILING TO CLOSE THE DEAL

In BSFT, "closing the deal" is to complete the process of empowering a family to behave in new ways that result in a well-functioning system that does not require symptoms. This occurs when the family reinforces new interactions by praising each other.

To make this happen, the therapist has to ensure that her highlights, reframes, and tasks are accepted and owned by the family as each component of each change sequence occurs. This means that in the first change sequence when the therapist moves parents from focusing on the child to focusing on their relation-ship, the highlights, reframes, and tasks were effective in bringing about changes in affect, cognition, and behavior. At the end of this sequence, family members must praise each other's new behaviors. This continues for every subsequent change sequence until the family has changed all the maladaptive interactional patterns that were linked to the problem behavior.

Closing the deal is a process that occurs with each change sequence, but it also occurs when family members look back and praise the changes in each other that led to the new adaptive sum of the family interactions that had to be changed, and the symptom has been eliminated or reduced so that it is no longer a problem.

After the deal is closed, a homework task can be assigned. That is, once a successful change sequence has been completed and reinforced by both the therapist and family members, the same interactional change can be tasked to be repeated at home. By repeating the new changed behaviors, over different settings, the new behavior is practiced and generalized to different contexts. This is important because mastery is acquired through repetition. The student learns to play the piano (or shoot baskets) by practicing every day. Homework tasks are also used to extend the gains made in the session. For example, when parents first collaborate in setting a rule or two during the session, a homework task may be to determine what the rest of the rules would be, before the next session. Another homework task consists of carrying out a plan that was made during the session. For example, estranged mother and daughter are able during the session to reconnect emotionally and decide to have some quality time each day. The homework would involve their having at least 10 minutes of quality time for each of the next 3 days.

KEY TAKEAWAYS

- Every minute of a BSFT session is precious, and every minute has to be used to transform the family's current maladaptive interactions into adaptive ones. Getting stuck in the pitfalls described in this chapter wastes precious minutes.

- It is essential for the therapist not to lose her position of leadership, which allows the therapist to direct change.

- Therapy is always action, and the pitfalls illustrated here interfere with process and action-focused, present-oriented change.

7

Engaging Families Into Brief Strategic Family Therapy

Every therapist who works with troubled youths and their families has been challenged to bring whole families to therapy. Unfortunately, most of the families that need family therapy never reach the first therapy session. This challenge arises, in great part, because most families expect and want only the identified patient (IP; the family member with "the problem" who has to be "fixed") to be treated. The goal of this chapter is to present our evidence-based approach, which is effective in bringing whole families into treatment. We call our approach Brief Strategic Family Therapy® (BSFT®) Engagement. It is a specialized model that was developed and tested separately from the therapy model.

As systems therapists, we view engagement and retention challenges from a systemic perspective that includes the therapist. We define *engagement* as the whole family coming into family therapy and *retention* as the whole family continuing to be involved in family therapy until family and therapist agree that treatment is completed. As we noted in Chapter 2 on joining, the therapist is the leader of a new system that includes both the therapist and the family and which we refer to as the *therapeutic system*. This system is created at the start of therapy and continues throughout the therapy process. It is dissolved at termination. Our approach to engaging families into treatment begins with our initial interventions to provide leadership in building the therapeutic system. As in all systems, the members of this system influence each other. Hence, therapists' behaviors affect the behavior of family members. It follows, then, that when therapists change their behavior, they can

http://dx.doi.org/10.1037/0000169-008
Brief Strategic Family Therapy, by J. Szapocznik and O. E. Hervis

also change the response by family members. Consequently, when obstacles prevent the whole family from coming into treatment, if the therapist changes her behaviors in adaptive ways, the result can be that the whole family enters into treatment.

We also discuss throughout this book that families have patterns of behavior that are overlearned because they have been repeated thousands of times. We mentioned earlier that for every one of us, including our readers, our families most likely have a set place at the dinner table for each member. Our placement at the table is a harmless example of the kinds of repetitive patterns of interactions that occur in all families, but it is an example of something that gives us a certain comfort: knowing our place at the family's dining room table. A more dynamic metaphor is that families are interconnected in the way that gears are. Gears make a machine function in the way that family members make a family function. Each family member contributes in unique ways to how the whole family functions. If we were to have in the session anything less than the whole system—that is, all family members—we would not know how the family functions. As we can see in Figure 7.1 of Lola, Jake, Grandma, and Mom, every gear or family member is important to understanding how the machine or family functions. Hence, to help the whole machine or family work properly, we need access to the whole machine or family.

Families of troubled youth have developed repetitive patterns of interactions that are linked to the presenting symptoms of the youth. We know that these repetitive patterns are overlearned and difficult to change and that they occur in many different contents and situations. Perhaps *one of the most important discoveries that led to the development of BSFT Engagement is that the same patterns of interactions that are linked to a youth's symptoms are also linked to the family's inability to enter into treatment as a whole family.*

In previous chapters, we described the basic concepts of BSFT and our approach to the assessment and diagnosis of maladaptive interactions and

FIGURE 7.1. The Family as a System

their relationship to symptoms, as well as the intervention strategies we use in BSFT. These same concepts are the building blocks for the techniques used in BSFT Engagement to bring reluctant family members into treatment. This chapter defines, in systems terms, the nature of the problem of "resistance" to treatment and the use of BSFT joining, tracking, diagnosing, and reframing interventions to overcome the family's "resistance" to entering treatment. We place the term "resistance" in quotations to denote that we do not use this term as usually understood. Usually "resistance" refers to the behavior of a person, whereas in BSFT the key to eliminating the family's "resistance" to therapy lies in our understanding of the nature of the therapeutic system in which the family and the therapist are both members, and the therapist is its leader. It is the therapist's responsibility to behave in ways that will cause the family to overcome its behaviors that interfere with treatment entry.

CHALLENGES FOR THERAPISTS

Regardless of their professional orientation and where or how they practice, every therapist has had the disappointing and frustrating experience of clients missing or canceling first appointments. For the BSFT therapist, this becomes an even more common and complex issue because the whole family has to be engaged into treatment. What to do? First, we offer some insight into how therapists may unknowingly contribute to families' "resistance," after which we offer some solutions.

Going Along With the Family's Definition of Who Needs Therapy

Because of how challenging it is to bring whole families into treatment, many therapists find it more convenient simply to accept the "resistance" on the part of the family. In doing this, however, the therapist in effect complies with the family's definition or frame of who should be in therapy. Consequently, the initially well-intentioned therapist agrees to see only one or two family members for treatment. With adolescents, this usually means that only the adolescent and an overburdened parent follow through with therapy. The result is that the therapist has been co-opted ("sucked") into the family's maladaptive patterns of interactions and, therefore, is unable to establish her leadership of the therapeutic system.

Not only has the therapist "bought" the family's definition of the problem but she has also accepted the family's frame of who should be in therapy. When the therapist agrees to see only part of the family, instead of challenging the maladaptive family interaction patterns that kept the other members away, she is reinforcing the family patterns that have contributed to the family's inability to resolve their presenting problems. An example is the case of a mother who was referred for family therapy because her son was chronically truant. The mother has a chronic illness and often needs the grandmother to stay with the children: the son, age 11, who was not going to school but spending most of his time with Grandmother, and an older brother. The mother was seeking therapy for herself, insisting that she had serious personal problems and needed an individual therapist. She refused access to the grandmother and children until an individual therapist agreed to take her case. The mother placed her own needs above those of the child, who was trapped in a power struggle between parent figures, further complicated by what the mother perceived as persecution from the school attendance review board. These critically maladaptive interactional patterns contributed to the presenting problem in this family. If the therapist agrees with the mother's definition of the problem and how it should be addressed ("You give me therapy first, and then we'll talk about family therapy") and who is going to be in therapy, the therapist has failed to achieve the first and defining reframe of the problem.

> When the therapist goes along with the family's definition of who has the problem and who has to change, the therapist has failed to achieve the first and defining reframe of the problem.

At a more complex level, there are serious clinical implications for the therapist who accepts the family's version of the problem. In doing this, the therapist surrenders her position as expert and leader. If the therapist agrees with the family's definition of "who's got the problem," her expertise and ability to understand the issues will be perceived by the family as no greater than their own. Her credibility and competence as a helper are at stake. Some family members may perceive the therapist as unable to challenge the status quo in the family because, in fact, she has failed to achieve the first and defining reframe of the problem.

When the therapist agrees to see only a part of the family, she may have surrendered too early her authority to direct change, to move freely from one family member to another. Thus, if after beginning therapy with only a part of the family, a therapist eventually attempts to include another important member of the family, she will be at a great disadvantage because she has begun by establishing a therapeutic relationship with only a part of the family. At this point, the therapist may be seen by previously excluded family members as being in alliance with only one part of the family, and the others may never trust the therapist. Moreover, when seeing only part of the family, the therapist will not be able to observe the system as a whole as it usually operates at home. It is like going to buy a car without a motor or a battery. It is impossible to know what else is missing or how it drives. It is like "the sound of one hand clapping."

Neglecting Those Families Who Need Therapy the Most

Although some therapists respond to the "resistance" of whole families to come to therapy by creating a therapeutic alliance with only those family members who most readily wish to come, other family therapists have resolved the dilemma by taking an even more alienating stance: "There are too many motivated families waiting for help. The 'resistant' families will call back when they finally feel the need. There is no need to get involved in a power struggle." The reality is that these "resistant" families will most likely never come to therapy as whole families without our help. Ironically, the families who most need therapy are families for whom patterns and habits interfere with their ability to get help for themselves. In BSFT, we take a public health stance: We have developed a therapy model that will bring treatment to families that most need it. Accordingly, a more constructive alternative for approaching "resistant" families is presented in this chapter. This alternative is built on the premise that "resistance" to coming to treatment can be understood and treated within the BSFT framework that we describe in this book. In BSFT Engagement, we extend the concept of repetitive patterns of maladaptive interactions that give rise to and maintain symptoms of the problem of "resistance" to entering treatment by adding a new building block as follows.

When the family wishes to get rid of the symptom, such as by looking for professional help, the same interactive patterns that prevented it from getting rid of the symptom also act to prevent the family from getting help. We come to label these maladaptive interactive patterns "resistance." Yet "resistance" is nothing more than the family's display of its inability to adapt effectively, to help itself to seek help.

How does a family respond when the therapist threatens its homeostasis? It responds in the same way that all systems respond when they confront an external force that wants to change them. They try to avoid it. The family runs. Sometimes all family members run, other times only some of them run (usually powerful IPs and the disengaged members). In either case, the family as a whole system is not available for therapy. It runs as far away from the therapist as it can. In the past, therapists have explained this "running away from therapy" response by saying, "The family resisted getting well" or "The family resisted help" or "The family did not want to get well." In fact, what the family is resisting is change. However, from a systems perspective, we understand that the purpose of the system is to perpetuate itself as it is—that is, to perpetuate both its interactional patterns and the role of the identified symptom in protecting the family from change and all that accompanies change, including the uncovering and confrontation of issues that are feared. The adage "old habits die hard" comes to mind. There is comfort in the familiar and fear of the unknown.

Blaming Families for Nonparticipation in Treatment

Imagine there was an interaction between the therapist and the family. The interaction went sour. The therapist placed all the blame on the family, which was, after all, the weaker member of the therapeutic relationship. The therapist blames the family for not participating in treatment. Does this not sound just like the case of a parent wanting to get a teenager to change, and when the teenager refuses, the parent responds by blaming it all on the youth?

The key to eliminating the "resistance" to therapy lies in our understanding of the nature of the therapeutic system in which the family and the therapist are both members, and the therapist is its leader. When the therapist accommodates by altering her behavior in ways that are specific to the family patterns of interaction that prevent them from coming to therapy, she can overcome the "resistance," and the family will come to therapy. Fortunately, the same principles that apply to the understanding of family functioning and treatment also apply to the understanding and treatment of the family's "resistance" to entering treatment. And the same principles that apply to the therapeutic system also apply to the ways a therapist must change her behaviors to bring the whole family into therapy. For these reasons, in the remainder of this chapter, we no longer apply the term *resistance* to the family. Resistance is what can occur in the interaction of the therapist and the family. We now refer to these families as *reluctant*. We refer to the therapist as *resistant* when the therapist is unwilling to behave in ways that will result in the family coming into treatment. We, therefore, have changed the locus of the resistance from the family to the therapist and their work context. We recognize that therapists' behaviors are often constrained by the rules of the agency in which they work. Consequently, to achieve better engagement rates and engagement of whole families that lead to better outcomes, it is necessary to change both the behavior of the therapist and the rules of the agency which constrain the therapist's behaviors.

> When things go wrong in the parent–adolescent relationship, the family blames the adolescent. When things go wrong in the therapist–family relationship, the therapist is often tempted to blame the family.

Our research has demonstrated that when the therapist changes her behavior, the family also changes their behavior. Our research shows that the best way to bring about engagement of whole families into treatment is for therapists to behave in ways that circumvent the family's interactional obstacles to engagement (Szapocznik et al., 1988). This is, without doubt, one of the most difficult concepts in BSFT for therapists to accept. However, as therapists learn to think systemically, they recognize that resistance is a systemic process. To build a viable therapeutic system, the therapist uses joining, tracking, and reframing to circumvent the family's initial perception of therapy as a threat to its homeostasis.

Prematurely Challenging the Family's Way of Operating

Premature challenges are the opposite of good initial joining. Good joining includes blending in, mimicking the family style, and maintaining the presenting family structure. Obviously, challenging is the opposite of maintaining the presenting family structure. Sometimes the therapist says, "You have to come to therapy because you too are a part of the problem," and that kind blaming is not conducive to joining. Another important aspect of premature challenging is that we do not challenge until the family has accepted us as the leader of the therapeutic system. Consequently, any challenge before that happens is considered a premature challenge. Challenging happens during restructuring. As we noted, we first establish ourselves as the leader of the therapeutic system, which means that we are well joined; we have observed and diagnosed interactional patterns; and we strategically plan interventions that include reframing to create a motivational context for change. We cannot challenge before a proper motivational context for change has been established that is accepted by the family.

In a scenario similar to the family described earlier, another family was referred to therapy by the court because of their oldest child's delinquency. The mother, Elsa, was willing to come to therapy with her son, Javier, but the mother's live-in boyfriend, Felipe, did not want to have anything to do with therapy. Elsa decided that she would like to help Javier and sought the therapist's aid in obtaining transportation to come to the therapy session. After the therapist obtained transportation for them, Elsa informed Felipe that she would be attending the therapy session. However, because this was a direct affront to the status quo in which Felipe held the power in the family, it triggered him to restore himself as the power center in the family. Homeostatic forces raised their head. His power position had been threatened by the potential alliance between "his woman" and the therapist. Felipe reasserted himself by forbidding "his woman" from going to therapy. The result was that neither Elsa nor Javier showed up for therapy.

This is clearly a case in which the therapist did not take the time to understand who the powerful member of the family was. When the therapist failed to determine who all the critical members of the family were—that is, all the individuals who function in family roles—she ran the risk of alienating rather than joining the family as whole. The therapist also did not understand the critical importance of having all family members involved in the early stages of forming the therapeutic system from the first phone call.

The therapist can only establish an effective therapeutic system by engaging all members of the family and, particularly, the powerful member. In this example, by inviting the mother and son into therapy, the therapist challenged the family's way of operating too early, before she had properly joined with each family member, which caused the family to reject treatment. The easy way out would be to blame it all on the belligerent boyfriend, the weak mother, and/or the rebellious, angry son who runs out of the house whenever the mother and her boyfriend are fighting. However, a more constructive approach would consist of asking the question, "What could the therapist have done differently?" The therapist could and should have been more aware and respectful of the existing structure.

Respect, in this case, does not mean that the therapist approves of, or agrees with, the boyfriend's behavior. Rather, it means that the therapist understands how this family is organized and works her way into the family through the existing structure. In initial joining for the purpose of engagement, the therapist is not yet focused on changing the family system. Instead, during initial joining for the purpose of engagement, the BSFT therapist earns her way into the family system to build a therapeutic system that includes the whole family. For example, on hearing from Elsa that Felipe did not wish to attend therapy, the therapist could call him directly and say,

> Señor Gomez [Felipe], I am calling you because Javier was referred for treatment by the courts. We always work with the entire family. Elsa said that she was willing to come. But we know how very important you are and that without you there is little we can do. We need your help in getting Javier into shape.

As an individual, the therapist may not like the way Felipe behaves and might even dislike the way he comes across on the phone. But because Felipe is part of this family, a family therapist has the responsibility of establishing a therapeutic relationship with him also. In this family, as is the case in all systems, the most powerful member of the system must agree to participate in therapy. For that reason, the therapist's strongest alliance, initially, will have to be with the powerful member who often is the most challenging person to bring in.

In the process of initially establishing a therapeutic system, the BSFT therapist must not disregard any family member, particularly those in power.

DIAGNOSTIC DIMENSIONS OF ENGAGEMENT

Diagnosis involves identifying the nature of the relationship between maladaptive patterns of interaction and undesirable symptoms. In all the previous chapters, we focused on the relationship between interactional patterns and the presenting complaint. However, during engagement, we focus on the maladaptive patterns that give rise to the symptom of "failure to engage" in treatment. The first enactment of reluctant families are the interactions that keep the whole family from entering treatment.

In engagement, the purpose of diagnosis is to identify those particular patterns of interactions that are keeping family members from coming into treatment. However, because it is not possible to observe the entire family, the BSFT therapist works with limited information.

To identify the maladaptive patterns responsible for the family not coming into treatment, we have extended the use of diagnosis forward to begin before the first face-to-face family therapy session, with the first phone contact with a family member. Because at this early time, it is not possible to directly observe enactments of the whole family, BSFT diagnosis has been modified for use during engagement to identify interactional patterns blocking engagement. Two ways that we have found useful in our work are described next.

Ask Relational Questions

First, we ask relational (i.e., interpersonal systems) questions of the contact person that allow us to infer what the interactional patterns may be. For example, when the therapist asks, "How do you ask your son to come to treatment?" the mother responds, "I tell him he has to come." The therapist then asks, "And, what did he say?" The mother replies, "He tells me, 'You try and make me.'" The therapist asks, "And, when he blows you off like that, what do you do next?" The mother says, "I can't do anything. He will throw a fit, and I am afraid of him." In this way, we seek to identify the back-and-forth interplay between this mother and son contributing to keeping the IP out of treatment. From the mother's description of their interactions, we learn that the son is more powerful than the mother.

As we indicated earlier, we do not trust the stories family members tell us, but when we only have access to one person, we work with the person(s) we have—strictly for the purpose of engagement into treatment.

Assign Exploratory Tasks

Second, we explore the interactions that prevent completion of the task of coming into therapy. This is done by assigning exploratory tasks. For example, we might ask the mother whether the dad would come, and she says "yes," but then he does not show up. When we ask the mother whether she asked her husband, she says she had, and he had agreed to come. The mother then says with frustration, "He is always making promises that he doesn't keep." The therapist is able to diagnose that the mother and father are not allied, and consequently, the therapist will have to reach out directly to the husband to engage him. The purpose of exploring the interactional patterns involved in bringing the family into treatment beginning with the first phone call is to identify as early as possible the interactional obstacles that may exist to coming into therapy, with the aim of intervening in a way that gets around these obstacles.

Three diagnostic dimensions create obstacles to engagement and, therefore, must be diagnosed to allow for effective engagement planning: organization (hierarchy, alliances, triangles), resonance (enmeshment and disengagement), and identified patienthood (level of rigidity).

Assess Organization: Hierarchy, Alliances, Triangles

Hierarchy is important because it tells us who has the power in the family, and it is that person who has the power to bring the family into treatment or keep the family out of treatment. Clearly, the whole family will only come into therapy if the person in charge is convinced that it is a good path for him. If the reluctant member also happens to be the most powerful, it would be a waste of time to direct other family members to bring the most powerful member to come to therapy because they will be unable to do that. Therefore, when the caller is not the most powerful member of the family, it should be clear to the therapist that she must access directly the most powerful member right away.

We have to know which family members are close to each other. We have to know whether parents collaborate in parenting. Are some family members in conflict? If so, the therapist would not task one of the two parties in conflict to influence the other. Rather, the therapist has to reach out directly to the other party. Family members may not be in conflict in general but may not agree about who comes to therapy. In this case, the therapist can give one of two persons a directive to bring the other into therapy in a way that specifically reframes the unwilling person's views about therapy or about that person's involvement in therapy. For example, one person may not believe in therapy. In that case, the person who reaches out for therapy might be tasked or directed to reframe the skeptical person's reason for being involved in therapy by saying, "Come to support me, even if you don't believe in therapy" or "The therapist wants you to know that she needs your point of view of the problem to better help me."

When there is a conflict or disagreement between two parties and one family member allies with one of them against the other, a triangle is formed. In the case of engagement, this can be two adults in conflict when a child and an adult ally with each other about coming (or not) to therapy. The conflict can appear in different ways. For example, Mom may want to bring her teen to therapy, and the teen does not want to come, and Grandma allies with the teen: "Daughter, you are always blaming him for everything. This is not his problem. It is yours." In another example, Mom does not want her live-in boyfriend to come to therapy, and the teen supports Mom by saying, "If he comes, I won't go. I don't want him in my business."

Assess Resonance

Although resonance includes the whole spectrum from overinvolvement to noninvolvement, in the case of engagement, the typical presentation occurs when one member and the rest of the family are disengaged. In our experience, the person who is isolated from the family is often a father. Typically, the therapist will hear excuses from the other parent for the father's non-participation, such as, "I am the one in charge of the children" or "He does not want to be involved in all this trouble that Hector brought on the family."

Identified Patienthood

A rigid identified patienthood becomes a problem when others in the family insist that only the IP has to go to therapy: "We are all fine and doing very well. It is only Milagros who needs therapy because she is the person with the problem." It is not uncommon that, at times, the IP may not want the rest of the family in therapy with him. He wants privacy, and he wants to get away from his parents' nagging and anger and their fighting with him.

HOW TO ENGAGE RELUCTANT FAMILIES

BSFT Engagement is an integral part of BSFT treatment (Coatsworth, Santisteban, McBride, & Szapocznik, 2001; Santisteban et al., 1996; Szapocznik et al., 1988). BSFT Engagement capitalizes on the concepts and techniques used in the therapy model. The BSFT theoretical concepts of systems, structure, and strategy are used in engagement as they are in treatment. The BSFT techniques that are used for engagement are joining, tracking, diagnosing, reframing, and tasking. In the case of reluctant families, the focus is on identifying and getting around the family's interactional patterns that prevent the family from entering therapy. Thus, during engagement, the therapist works his way "around" the maladaptive interactional patterns long enough to bring the family into treatment. It is only when the therapeutic system has been successfully established after the whole family has come into therapy that diagnosis and treatment can occur.

During engagement, we do not use highlighting, and we do not use reframing and tasking for the purpose of bringing about interactional change. Why not? For several reasons. First, we do not use any intervention that challenges the existing system. Second, and relatedly, we do not use any interventions that might erode rapport at a time when we are struggling to build rapport with all family members. Finally, because to execute effective interactional change (i.e., restructuring), we first have to know how the system operates as a whole, and this can only be achieved when we observe the whole family interacting, which obviously cannot occur until the whole family has been engaged.

In the following section, we discuss each of the BSFT techniques used during engagement and how they are used specifically to bring the whole family into therapy.

Joining

Joining has to be designed to match the goal of the phase of therapy, which during BSFT Engagement, is to bring the whole family into treatment. Joining the family while first engaging them is a process that begins with the first contact with the family member who calls for help and continues throughout the entire therapeutic relationship with the family. Thus, joining does not begin with the first family session but rather begins with the first contact of the therapist with a family member.

As noted, joining is the technique used to build a therapeutic alliance. During BSFT Engagement, joining is done sequentially as the therapist gains access to the various members of the family. It must be recognized that what each family member wants and/or needs to achieve in therapy will vary from one member to another. An effective way to join with each family member is for the therapist to agree with each family member that their individual agendas and needs will be addressed by therapy. For example, the mother may want to get her son to quit drugs, whereas the son may want his mother to stop nagging him.

A therapeutic alliance is built on the individual goals for each family member, for which therapy can be offered as a solution. Aligning with each person's goal is one of the important joining strategies for engaging the whole family into therapy. Ideally, the therapist and each family member agree on an outcome each person wants, and therapy is offered in the framework of achieving each of those goals. Particularly in families in which members are in conflict, it is necessary to elicit what each of them wants to gain from participating in therapy. For the therapist, this can be framed as a negotiation in which different parties have different goals, but a negotiated solution can be found in which these different goals can be pursued.

For example, I want to buy a shirt that makes me look good, and you want to sell me a shirt that will make you a profit. We can both win by the transaction even though we have different goals. In the case of a family, the therapist can say to the mother that her son should stop using drugs, to the son that his mother should get off his back and stop nagging, and to the grandfather that the mother should stop making him constantly play the role of "bad guy." In each case, the therapist can offer therapy as a means for each family member to achieve their personal goal within the family.

We emphasize that our focus in joining during BSFT Engagement is always on the individual family members' goals. This means that the therapist never has her own content goals for the family.[1] If the youth is not going to school, the goal of the therapist is not the content goal of getting the child to go to school per se but rather to help the family change its interactional patterns in such a way that the family can succeed in getting the child to go to school. As we noted, during engagement, the therapist's goal is to get the family into treatment. After engagement, the therapist's goal will change to transforming those interactional processes that prevent the family from attaining its content goals.

Sequential Alliances

In engaging reluctant families, the therapist initially works with and through only one or, at most, a few family members. Because the entire family is not initially available, the therapist will have to form a bond with the caller and any other family members that make themselves available initially. However,

---

[1]In the context of the work in agencies funded by governmental institutions, the therapist is required to have content goals, such as stopping drug use, eliminating truancy, or increasing family safety. However, in BSFT, these are achieved by transforming maladaptive interactions into adaptive ones. Consequently, the focus of the therapist is on those maladaptive interactions that are linked to these content problems.

the therapist's focus during this early engagement phase is strictly to overcome the obstacles that are keeping a family member out of therapy. Starting with the alliance formed with the initial caller, the therapist uses her alliance with this contact person as a vehicle for joining the other members of the family. The plan is for the therapist to sequentially establish therapeutic alliances with each family member and thereby elicit the cooperation of the entire family in the engagement effort.

Reframing

The sole purpose during engagement is to create a new frame for reluctant members that overcomes barriers to entering therapy. Reframing can either be done when the therapist tasks an engaged family member to reach out to the reluctant member(s), or it can be done directly by the therapist when the therapist reaches out directly to the reluctant family member. Examples of such reframing directives that may be used for joining include, "Let him know that his objective understanding of the issues regarding his grandchild are invaluable to me [the therapist] in successfully treating Johnny," "Let her know that it would take me a very long time to learn important things about Susie that are needed to treat her that she could tell me in just two visits," or "Please reassure her that I will only be interested in discussing issues regarding Susie's drug use." Of course, all of these reframes can be given by the therapist when reaching out directly to the reluctant family member.

In the process of engaging reluctant families, the therapist initially talks with one or a few of the family members. The therapist listens carefully to the frame or frames that express the reluctance of one or more family members to come into treatment. The therapist then reframes those "reluctant" frames into new ones that help the family see and feel positive about everyone coming to therapy. In the case of Milagros, mentioned earlier, the therapist might say to the older daughter who is the parental figure for Milagros,

> Yes, we need to help her to stop her sexual acting out, and we can do it better and faster with the help of her family. You are her family, and so are her other brothers and sisters and her great aunt who also takes care of her when you are working.

Additional examples are included in Table 7.1.

The single most important message we would like the reader to take away is that a diagnosis of the interactional patterns and the frames that accompany them is critically important before determining how best to help a family overcome the obstacles that are keeping it out of needed treatment. This helps the therapist to understand what kinds of reframes would be required to engage this family into treatment.

Tasking

In the work of overcoming patterns of family interaction that interfere with engagement, tasks play a particularly vital role because tasks are the only

TABLE 7.1. Ideas for Engaging Reluctant Families in Therapy

Issue causing reluctance to enter family therapy	Reframing suggestion
Hierarchical problem: The IP's powerful brother does not want to come.	Therapist calls the brother and says, "You are a very influential person, and we need your help to make sure that your brother does not go through some of the hassles you have had to experience."
Alliance problem: A parent figure does not want to come to treatment and claims that "fixing" the IP or the family is not his job.	"No one knows this family better than you do, and if you help me by sharing your perspective, therapy will be much faster than if only Mom is present."
Triangulation: Two parent figures are in conflict; one wants to keep the other from attending therapy.	To the parent who wants to keep the other out, "We need to work together if we are going to be successful with your daughter because she is doing whatever she wants. We need to get your two heads working together to stop your daughter from taking so many risks."
Identified patienthood rigidity: A parent does not want to bring to therapy the other children who are asymptomatic.	"You will be surprised how helpful it will be to bring your other kids, precisely because they are doing so well."

Note. IP = identified patient.

therapy strategy that a therapist can assign to occur outside the therapy session. There are two ways that tasks are used during engagement: for initial diagnosis and for gaining access to reluctant family members. For diagnosis, tasks are particularly well suited for use during the engagement period, when the response to the task of coming to therapy by the whole family or by any one member can reveal family interactional patterns that have to be overcome for the family to come into treatment. Tasks given to engaged family members are intended to help the therapist join a reluctant family member by providing a compelling frame that is likely to bring the reluctant member into therapy or give the therapist access to that reluctant family member.

Leveraging Complementarity

Complementarity allows us to understand how the family interactional patterns fit together to keep reluctant family members out of treatment. As noted in Chapter 2, the behaviors of the parts of a system are always complementary. For the family system, this means that the behaviors of each family member must "fit with" the behavior of every other family member. Thus, within the family, for each action, there is a complementary action or reaction.

In the case of Felipe, Elsa, and Javier, described earlier, Felipe did not want to come into treatment (the action), and Elsa excused him from not coming into treatment (the complementary action). In her phone call, Elsa told the therapist that whenever she says anything to Felipe about therapy (the action), he becomes angry (the complementary reaction). The therapist has to know exactly what the caller's contribution is to this circular transaction. That is, what is Elsa's part in maintaining this interactional pattern that keeps the whole family from coming to treatment? When Elsa says that Felipe becomes angry when she talks to him about coming to therapy, complementarity alerts the therapist that Elsa must be contributing to keeping Felipe out of therapy. The therapist has to explore what Elsa does before and after Felipe gets angry.

First, how does she ask him? She may ask him by blaming him for the problems at home: "The therapist says you have to come to therapy because you are a big part of the problem." This allows the therapist to discover that Felipe may get angry as a response to the way he is being asked. As a result of this discovery, the therapist knows that she has to train and task Elsa to ask Felipe to come to therapy without blaming him but instead by elevating him, as in, "We cannot do this without you because you are so important to the family." However, complementarity may reveal that the engaged family member does not do enough to bring the reluctant member into therapy: When the therapist asks, "When Felipe gets angry, what do you do?" Elsa says, "I get scared and back away." In this case, the therapist may determine that she will have to reach out directly to Felipe because helping Elsa overcome her fear is too long a process during engagement.

WORKING WITH CHALLENGING FAMILY INTERACTIONAL PATTERNS

In this section, we discuss the types of interactional patterns we have identified as preventing families from coming into treatment, the process of getting these families into treatment, and the central role that diagnosing, reframing, and tasks may play in achieving this goal.

Much of our research with reluctant families has been done with families in which the adolescent was known or believed by the parents to be using drugs and engaging in behaviors associated with the use of drugs such as truancy, delinquency, aggressiveness, frequent fights in and outside the home, and disregard for curfew. The types of family interactional patterns presented in this section are provided as examples of the types of family structures that are difficult to engage in therapy. However, the examples are not intended to represent all possible configurations of family patterns and interactions that become obstacles to coming into therapy. Therapists working with other types of problems and families are encouraged to review their caseload of "difficult to engage" families and carefully examine the clues for diagnosing the systemic challenges to bringing those families into therapy. You may find that they are similar to those we have found, or you may find them different. In any case, you will be better equipped to successfully engage those families if you can recognize the role of diagnosing the patterns of interactions that interfere with coming to therapy and the kinds of reframes and tasks that are helpful.

Powerful Identified Patient

Even though the powerful IP is the most frequently occurring interactional pattern, we include in this grouping families in which there is a member who is powerful and unwilling to come to treatment. With powerful adolescent IPs, this is particularly a problem in cases that are not court referred and in which the adolescent IP has no external compelling force that facilitates engagement into therapy. These families are characterized by an IP who is in a powerful position in the family and whose parents, conversely, are unable to influence the adolescent. Powerful parents are able to bring the adolescent into therapy without having to lie about where they are taking the adolescent. This is not the case for families with a powerful IP. The parent of a powerful IP will often admit that he is unable to bring his daughter to therapy because she flatly refuses to come. We can assume that the IP resists counseling because

- it threatens her position of power and moves her to a "problem-person" position, and
- it is the parent's agenda to come to therapy, and thus, if the youth agrees to the parent's agenda, it would strengthen the parent's power.

In the first step in joining, the therapist shows respect and allies with the adolescent. With the parent's consent, the therapist contacts the adolescent by phone or in person (perhaps even on her own turf, such as after school at the park). The therapist listens to the powerful adolescent's complaints about her parents' unrealistic expectations and then offers to help the youth change the situation at home so the parents stop harassing her. This does not threaten the power of the adolescent within the family and thus is likely to be accepted. The therapist brings respect and concern for the youth but also brings an agenda of change that, by virtue of the alliance, is shared by the youth. That is, the youth comes into therapy expecting and encouraging change to happen.

To bring these families into treatment, the youth's power in the family is not directly challenged. Rather, it is accepted by the therapist. The therapist allies herself to the powerful adolescent so that she will be in a position to influence the adolescent to come into treatment. Initially, the therapist, in forming an alliance with the powerful adolescent, reframes the need for therapy in a manner that strengthens the powerful adolescent in a positive way. The kind of reframing that is most useful with powerful adolescents is a reframing that transfers the symptom from the powerful adolescent or IP to the family. For example, the therapist might say, "I want you to come into therapy to help me change some of the things that are going on in your family." If the therapist can develop and maintain a solid relationship with the IP, eventually, in treatment, the therapist can begin to restructure the hierarchical misalignment by helping the parent(s) become more loving and supportive of the IP and her prosocial interests in exchange for the IP giving up her powerful position.

It should be noted that in cases of powerful adolescents with less powerful parents, forming the initial alliance with the parent figure(s) is likely to be ineffective because the parents are not strong enough to bring their adolescent into therapy. Their failed attempts to bring the adolescent into therapy would render the parents even weaker, and the family would fail to enter therapy. Furthermore, the youth is likely to perceive the therapist as being the parent's ally, which would immediately be translated into distrust and disqualification of the therapist.

Contact Person Protecting Structure

The second most common type of interactional patterns that prevent families from entering treatment is characterized by a parent who protects the family's maladaptive patterns of interactions. These families are identified when the person making the agency contact to request help (usually the mother) is also the person protecting family members from entering treatment. How the identified patienthood is maintained in the family is also how entering treatment is undermined. The mother, for example, might give conflicting messages to the therapist, such as, "I want to take my family to therapy, but my son couldn't come to the session because he forgot and fell asleep, and my husband has so much work that he doesn't have the time." The mother is expressing a desire for the therapist's help while at the same time protecting and allying with her son's and husband's unwillingness to be involved in solving the problem. The mother "protects" these family members from getting involved by agreeing that the excuses for noninvolvement are valid. In other words, by supporting the arguments (content), she supports the status quo (process).

It is worthwhile noting that, ordinarily, this is the same conflicting message that maintains the symptomatic structure in the family: Someone complains of the problem behavior yet supports the maintenance of the behaviors that nurture the problem. For example, a mother may be worried that her son skips school and yet provides false excuses to the school for her son's absence so he will not "get in trouble."

To bring these families into treatment, the therapist must first form an alliance with the mother by acknowledging her frustration in wanting to get help and not getting any cooperation from the family member(s). Through this alliance, the therapist validates the mother's position by acknowledging that the other family members are busy—"I recognize how difficult it is for them to become involved"—and then asks the mother's permission to contact the other family members by saying, "You know, I have had a lot of experience doing this, and perhaps I can get luckier than you. And anyway, we have nothing to lose. No harm in trying." In this way, we can go around the mother's protection of the symptoms, albeit with her permission. Thus, with the mother's permission, the therapist calls the other family members and "separates" them from the mother regarding the issue of coming to therapy (to prevent her from

enabling their unwillingness to come to treatment). This is done by the therapist developing her relationship with other family members about the importance of coming to therapy. By developing her own relationship with these
other family members, the therapist circumvents the mother's protective
behaviors. The intention is to get around the interactional patterns that are
blocking entry into treatment. Once in therapy, the mother's overprotection of
the adolescent's misbehavior and the father's underinvolvement (and the
adolescent and father's eagerness that mother continues to protect them) are
interactional patterns that must be changed because they are typically related
to the adolescent's presenting problem behaviors.

Disengaged Parent Figure and Triangulation

These family structures are characterized by strong conflict between the parents and, therefore, no alliance between the parents. This often results in a
triangle in which the first parent and the child are enmeshed, and the child–
first parent alliance and the other parent are disengaged, as illustrated in Figure 7.2. In this case, the 15-year-old son was arrested when his dealer was
arrested for selling OxyContin to a minor. Emma, whose fertilized egg was
implanted and carried by Glen, refuses to come into therapy. Emma has typically remained disengaged from the child. Emma's disengagement from the
Glen–son alliance protects her and Glen from having to contend with the
challenges in their marital relationship, which is most likely the more troublesome of the two relationships being avoided. Glen and the IP are allied in
maintaining Emma's distance from parenting functions and role.

For example, if Emma attempts to exercise executive leadership to manage
the youth's misbehavior, Glen complains that she is too tough, or she creates
mythical fears about Emma's potential for violence. Emma does not challenge
this portrayal of herself. She is then rendered powerless when she relin-
quishes her parental role, thereby reestablishing the disengagement between

**FIGURE 7.2. A Triangulated Family Structure With an Enmeshed Parent–Child
Dyad and a Disengaged Parent**

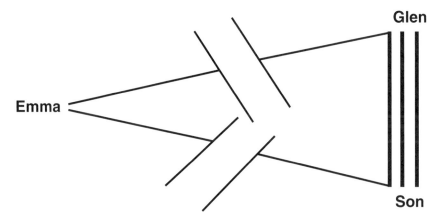

her and their son. In this family, alliances are of foremost importance in planning how to bring the whole family into therapy.

Because the mothers are not in agreement with each other, the child is getting different messages from each mother. The child is overprotected by Glen, and because she is not consistent in her behavior expectations, and her behavior control interventions are half-hearted and thus ineffective, the son does whatever he wants. To correct the conditions that encourage acting-out behaviors in the child, both mothers have to be brought into treatment. In a family like this, there is always the issue of whether the marital couple wants to stay together, but whether or not it does, while they are both in the child's life, they have to work together as parents.

The triangle happens because the two mothers are in conflict, and the conflict about parenting is avoided when Glen and her son, on the one hand, and Emma, on the other, remain disengaged. In this family structure, in which there is a disengaged parent, there is no pretense on the part of Glen when she calls the therapist and makes clear that she does not want her wife involved in therapy. In full complementarity, Emma does not want to be involved either. Thus, both mothers are contributing to the disengagement between Emma and the child. As usual, the therapist starts by forming an alliance with the caller. As the first step in getting both parents into treatment, the therapist begins by reframing the caller's view by stating,

> Glen, I want to respect the differences that you and Emma have as a couple, but unless she supports you as a parent, your son is going to continue to misbehave. I know you don't like how your wife disciplines your child, but I am going to help you with that so that we can help your son.

The therapist can choose to get permission from Glen to talk directly to Emma or might choose to give Glen the task of persuading Emma to come. The former is often easier. But if the therapist chooses to encourage Glen to persuade Emma, the therapist must coach Glen how to get Emma to therapy. The challenge, of course, is the conflict between them and the likelihood that Glen will speak angrily to Emma when asking her to come: "You've got to come because it is all your fault because you don't support me as a parent." To avoid this, the therapist coaches Glen on how to explain to Emma the need for her presence in a way that will cause Emma to want to come to therapy "because she loves Johnny." She might say something such as, "The therapist says that both of us who care for Johnny need to come if we are going to help him." We know how difficult this is for Glen, and we discuss with Glen that she will have to rise above her feelings for the sake of their son. Glen has to own the frame that both parents are needed to help Johnny before she can perform this task correctly.

Selling the frame is a challenging job, and it requires persistence on the part of the therapist. The therapist has to explore the obstacles that the parent is experiencing: "What's going on that you are having trouble seeing it the way I presented it to you?" Sometimes a parent may be reluctant because she knows that the other parent can become violent. If this is the case, it is essential for the therapist to understand what this parent experiences as dangerous. If it is indeed a case of domestic violence, the first step is to consider the safety of the other parent and the child. However, when this is not the case, the therapist can continue to explore the nature of what may keep one parent from feeling comfortable with the participation of the other. If we do not change the family interactions that maintain the symptom, the symptom will continue to worsen over time.

Once the therapist believes that Glen accepts the frame that Emma has to be involved, the therapist gives Glen the task of inviting Emma to come to therapy, focusing only on the issue of taking care of their son's problems. The therapist assigns tasks in such a way that is least likely to spark the broader marital conflict. These tasks are only intended to get around the interactional patterns in which Glen conspires with Emma to keep the latter from coming to therapy. If the task fails and Glen is unable or unwilling to bring Emma, the therapist, with Glen's permission, will reach out to Emma directly.

Conflictual Parent Relationship and Triangulation

Another form of triangle occurs when two parents are in high conflict with each other. This type of family differs from the one described previously in that there is no disengagement. These are parents who are continuously involved with each other in a negative way; hence, they are overly sensitive to each other's behavior. Yet they are unable to be distant from each other. In these situations, a child is highly likely to be caught in the middle of the warring parents, with both parents striving to get the child on their side by telling the child how awful the other parent is and using the child as part of their aggressive ploys against the other parent. This scenario is illustrated in Figure 7.3.

Many divorced couples have this kind of pattern. Although they no longer live together, they continue the fights that characterized their marriage, now using the child as the content and weapon of aggression. We think of these

FIGURE 7.3. A Triangulated Pattern With Parents in Conflict

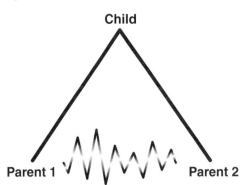

couples as divorced on paper but still "married" emotionally. The fighting is a way of continuing to be connected. Letting go represents a loss and causes the parent to feel lonely. Hence, continuing to be emotionally involved has many benefits, particularly avoiding experiencing the loss of the person they loved and built a long history with or the loss of recognizing that the couple failed. We do not agree with Neil Sedaka's song that "breaking up is hard to do" (Greenfield & Sedaka, 1963). What is truly hard to do is to move on beyond the connection of a past love, particularly when that past love involves a shared child. What makes it so difficult is that when children are involved, the parent couple cannot totally separate. Instead, they have to reinvent their relationship, which is extremely hard to do without professional help, particularly when there has been conflict.

The challenge to engagement is that these parents are reluctant to be in therapy together. A particularly difficult situation occurs when a parent obtains a protective order against the other parent that makes it illegal to be in the room with each other. Ideally, the whole family—in this case, the mom, dad, and child—should be seen together. However, when there is a protective order we have to slowly take steps to approximate that ideal. The protective order makes it necessary to start the therapy by seeing the child with each parent separately, alternating parents but having the sessions with each parent and the child in the same week. This is the one circumstance in which we begin therapy without the whole family present, although the whole family is involved in treatment. However, from the first call and the first session, we work with the parents to accept the need and responsibility to place differences aside to care for their child, first and foremost.

This is achieved, as in all engagement work, by intensive joining of both parents and copious reframes that emphasize the child's need for them to collaborate on the child's behalf, which is operationalized by collaborating on parenting:

> You have to understand that the child's symptoms are his way of letting you both know that he does not want to have to pick a side or do ugly things to either of you. You don't have to like each other, but you do have to collaborate on his behalf.

After a few sessions, as the therapist coaches the couple on how to best manage each other, and if the parent who requested the protective order is ready, she can approach the judge to request that the other parent participate in therapy over the phone, in which case separate therapy sessions are no longer needed. Once in therapy, it is critical to work with the family to ensure that the parents keep the child out of their adult issues—that is, to detriangulate the child from their relationship. The therapist continues to work toward bringing the parents together in the same session to facilitate their developing a mutually respectful relationship that is in the best interest of the child while not endangering the person who felt the need to obtain a protective order. The latter will be the person who, when she is ready, will have to make the request from the judge to allow the father to be in the therapy session under the supervision of the BSFT therapist.

Therapy as an Exposé

Sometimes family members fear what will happen if they attend therapy. Some of these fears may be real; others may be simply imagined. In some instances, families just need some reassurance to overcome their fears. Such fears might include, "They are going to gang up on me" or "Everyone will know what a failure I am." Having overcome their fear, they are now more likely to enter therapy. Another fear that family members may have is that dysfunctional behaviors on the part of the adults will be exposed, such as substance abuse. Therapy is sometimes threatening because it may expose deeper secrets kept by one or more individuals. Sometimes the person who resists coming is afraid that daunting secrets will be revealed (e.g., extramarital relationships, illegal activities). These individuals' beliefs or frames about therapy are usually an extension of the frame within which the family is functioning—that is, it is a family of secrets.

The therapist must reframe the idea or goal of therapy in a way that eliminates the perceived fear of exposure and replaces that frame with positive outcomes. One way to achieve this is to meet with the person who is most unwilling to come to treatment to assure him that therapy does not have to go where he does not want it to go and that the therapist will focus only on the problems of the youth and not on any issues that the family chooses to leave out. The individual is assured that in the session "we will deal only with those issues that you want to deal with. You are the client. I am only here to help you with what you want to achieve in therapy." In our experience, however, even if the therapist focuses on those aspects of the marital and parenting relationship that are directly related to the youth, on occasion, the family will reveal its deepest secrets during therapy. If so, the revelation makes it possible for the family to work toward a long-term resolution.

In reviewing these patterns, it is evident that considerably more engagement work is needed to mobilize some families than others. For example, families with disengaged parents require more complex work than families in which the contact person is protecting the structure. In turn, the latter type of families needs more work than those protecting a family secret, where a simple reframing from a position of a close therapeutic alliance will do the job. Therefore, the extent and type of engagement work needed by different types of family interactional patterns vary, not unlike the already accepted reality that some families in therapy need more thorough and deeper restructuring than others.

As we close this chapter, we want to remind therapists that, as we said at the beginning of the chapter, there may be other types of interactional patterns that create challenges to families entering therapy. The therapist should be alert to new forms of interactional patterns that may require new solutions. In whatever form a family presents, engagement is a tool to achieve the essential inclusion of whole families into treatment.

KEY TAKEAWAYS

- Family systems are like songs. Songs you have never heard before require that all the notes are played. If all the notes are not played, you do not know how the song sounds. We do not know what the family system is like unless we have all the family members present.

- What we have traditionally called *resistance* is nothing more than the family's display of its inability to adapt effectively, to help itself to seek help. We define resistance as what occurs when the therapist is unwilling or unable to change her behavior to get around the family's interactional patterns that result in the family not coming into treatment.

- The same patterns of interactions that are interconnected to a youth's symptoms are the patterns that prevent the family from entering into treatment as a whole family. There are four frequently occurring interactional patterns we have observed that prevent families from entering treatment: a powerful IP, a contact person who protects the family structure, triangulation due to a disengaged parent figure or conflictual parent dyad, and family members who view therapy as an exposé.

- The therapist's focus during the BSFT Engagement is to overcome the obstacles that are keeping a family member out of therapy. This is done by the therapist developing her relationship with each family member about the importance of coming to therapy.

- When making initial arrangements for therapy, ask questions and assign tasks to quickly assess power relationships, alliances, resonance, and how the family identifies who needs "fixing" the most. Diagnosing the interactional patterns and the frames that accompany them helps the therapist understand what is required to engage the family into treatment.

- Joining with the family occurs even before the first meeting, and alliances are built sequentially with each family member. As each one enters the therapeutic system, the therapist elicits what each of them wants to gain from participating in therapy and offers negotiated solutions that will benefit all family members.

8

Applying Brief Strategic Family Therapy to Different Circumstances

In this chapter, we review the application of Brief Strategic Family Therapy® (BSFT®) to different practice types, family compositions, and special circumstances or clinical conditions. The essential elements of BSFT do not change with different family compositions or circumstances. BSFT is sufficiently flexible and resilient that it can be adapted to many different situations, cultures, and clinical dilemmas. What makes BSFT flexible across cultures and family compositions is that it focuses on the process of how families interact in adaptive or maladaptive ways, with full recognition that specific interactional styles may vary across cultures and family compositions. Interactional styles vary across cultures, but family jobs typically do not. For example, how love is expressed varies across cultures, but when a child does not feel loved, it is important for the therapist to help the parents to express their love for the child in a culturally appropriate way. To illustrate the flexibility of BSFT and, hopefully, to help readers begin to envision how they might incorporate it into their practice, we provide some tips on how it can be applied across diverse contexts.

WHEN THE FAMILY'S HOME IS THE PRACTICE SETTING

BSFT can be implemented in a variety of settings, including community-based social service agencies, mental health clinics, health agencies, family clinics, schools, and churches, as well as in the home. These, in turn, can be located

http://dx.doi.org/10.1037/0000169-009
Brief Strategic Family Therapy, by J. Szapocznik and O. E. Hervis

either in rural, urban, or suburban areas. Because doing therapy in the family's natural environment presents special challenges, we discuss here in some detail specific recommendations for delivering BSFT in the home.

When working in the home, the issue of the therapist maintaining leadership of the therapeutic system requires special rules because families, as systems, always attempt to maintain the status quo (homeostasis)—and they may do this by using their territory to sabotage the therapy. For this reason, it is critical for the therapist to discuss these rules for home-based therapy in the first session. To introduce them, the therapist might say, "I know that we all want to get as much as possible from these sessions. To make the best use of our time together, I would like us to follow some rules."

First, everyone who is expected to participate in therapy must be present in therapy sessions (as in all BSFT). This includes all the persons who are involved in an ongoing basis in the interactions to be addressed in therapy sessions. This rule excludes neighbors, visiting cousins, girlfriends, and the like, who may often be in the home. However, some of these extrafamilial members are expected to be present for a specific session if they are involved in particular interactions that will be the focus of that session. The family system is distracted by the many people who come in and out of the home, and such distractions are not helpful in getting the family to focus on the internal family functioning. Consequently, we only include at the beginning of therapy the actual family members and bring in extrafamilial individuals if and when needed.

Second, no distractions are allowed—no phone use, no running to the kitchen to check on the stew, no radio or television, no answering the door, no running in and out of the session, and no use of electronic equipment, for example.

Therapists must consistently advocate for in-home therapy rules. The therapist must remember that rules have no value unless they are consistently followed. The implementation of these rules is part of the therapy plan. Family members sometimes challenge the rules as a way of sabotaging those other family members who support therapy. The therapist cannot get into a power struggle over these rules when they are broken during the session; thus, the therapist has to consider appropriate strategies for ensuring that families follow the rules. The rules are set at the outset, but how they are reestablished when they are challenged depends on the manner in which the family is organized, the treatment plan for that session, the extent to which the therapist is joined with the person challenging the rules, and whether there is a person at this stage of the therapy who can be tasked with enforcing the rule.

Early in therapy, the therapist might not be able to challenge a powerful family member, nor would the therapist ask a parent who is unable to manage a youth to challenge the youth. Rather, the therapist might intensify their joining of the challenger to persuade her to see the benefit of how abiding by the rules can be to her advantage. For example, the therapist might say to a 17-year-old adolescent who refuses to turn off her phone, "I am only going to be using your time for an hour at most, and I would like in this hour to give you an opportunity to bring to your mother's attention just exactly how angry you are."

FAMILY COMPOSITIONS

According to the U.S. Census Bureau (2016), the majority of America's 73.7 million children under 18 years of age live in two-parent families (69%), 23% of which are blended families. The second most common family arrangement is children living with a single mother, at 26%. What is not captured in these statistics is the full spectrum of family arrangements, such as kinship networks and grandparent-led families.

BSFT applies to this broad range of family compositions. The focus of BSFT on family process is the same across different types of families. The ways a family may carry out its essential functions—such as support, nurturance, guidance, and socializing children—to allow each individual to be the best that she can be differ as a function of culture and family composition. All family compositions and cultures have to be successful in performing these fundamental family responsibilities. However, different issues may come up in different family compositions and cultures. The role of the therapist is to help families develop their abilities, consistent with their family composition and culture, for family members to reach their potential. In the following sections, we address some of the particulars of different family compositions illustrating the common BSFT elements that hold true across this broad diversity.

Single Parents

The prejudice that single-parent families are handicapped can harm the therapist's opportunity to help. Single-parent families are whole systems capable of successfully undertaking the same responsibilities as two-parent families. In BSFT, we consider both the assets and liabilities of single- or two-parent families. Single-parent families, in general, have as an asset the increased opportunity for children to take on responsibility and gain autonomy at an earlier age. The frequently occurring issue of marital discord, which often is an obstacle to parenting agreement in two-parent families is, by definition, absent in single-parent families. Among the deficits of single-parent families, however, are the lack of support for the one parent, decreased opportunity for nurturance, and increased risk of poverty.

What are the clinical issues of single-parent families with troubled youth? An often-occurring issue is that the single parent is overwhelmed by work and family responsibilities and thus lacks energy and time to parent. The central therapy task is to enable single parents to be more fully engaged in all parenting functions, including nurturance, guidance, and behavior control. Another important issue is the possible lack of support for the parent. Two parents who get along can support each other. A single parent is like the CEO who feels lonely at the top, with no other parent with whom to consult and share parenting tasks and who provides emotional support. Therefore, in therapy, we look at the options available to the single parent. Extended family members can function as sounding boards and can share some parenting duties. Sometimes, a teenaged child who is well-functioning and responsible and about 5 years older than a younger sibling can be assigned certain parental responsibilities for the younger child. Such duties have to be assigned by the single parent in accordance with the age and stage of development of both children, the caretaking teen, and the care receiver.

The ultimate authority must always remain in the hands of the parent. Parental children are not coparents, nor should they be peers of the parent. As we said before, there is a certain risk of having a parental child—primarily that that child acquires too much power in the family and can no longer be managed by the parent. Therefore, we make a clear distinction between a parental child and a spousal child. The parental child can never be allowed to become a coparent or a parent's soulmate or confidant. This is an inappropriate burden to the child, preventing him from having a normal adolescence and giving him far too much power over the parent.

The BSFT therapist must also help single parents obtain the emotional support they need, either from parenting groups, church groups, or other groups interested in parenting, as well as from extended family members (never from a child). Often the therapist might have a session with the parent and an extended family member to enlist the extended family member into a support role while establishing the boundaries for this relationship in which the extended family member provides support but does not usurp the management function of the parent. There are other ways in which the parent may seek help in parenting, in the form of community activities that can supplement the single parent's parenting—for example, Big Brothers Big Sisters, 100 Black Men, sports with a caring coach that provide structured activities and emotional support and nurturance to the child, and a prosocial network within which the child can develop safely. In working with single parents, the therapist often finds herself having to encourage and guide parents to develop community supports for themselves and their children.

A frequently occurring parenting challenge faced by single parents is having their authority usurped either by a child, a group of the children, or an extended family member who is allied with at least one of the children against the parent. Authority is restored when the single parent achieves mastery of parenting skills and reassumes a leadership role. As in two-parent families, several interventions are required to restore a parent to a position of authority. These include

- building on the parent's self-confidence through validating statements by finding "what's been done right," highlighting it, emphasizing it, praising it, and repeating this process until she identifies herself with her accomplishments rather than her failures;

- orchestrating opportunities for the parent, incrementally, to successfully manage the behaviors of her children;

- in the case in which a child has usurped the parent's authority and has become powerful, realigning the hierarchy to place the parent back in the executive role (see Chapter 6); and

- in the case of an extended family member who usurps parental authority and is typically allied with a child against the single parent, the first maneuver is breaking the triangle and allying the extended family member as soon as possible to the parent. At the same time, the therapist rebuilds the relationship or alliance between the parent and the child. If that does not work, the extended family member, unfortunately, may have to be removed from the family. In this latter case, once this detriangulation has been accomplished, the parent's executive position can be restored.

An example of work with a single-parent family is found in the case of the Monte family. The mother had lost control over her children because she was overwhelmed by making a living, running the household, and caring for the children. The central therapy task was to restore the single parent to a position of authority. Alma is the 42-year-old single mother of Ricardo, a 14-year-old drug-abusing male. Alma has an older married daughter and two younger children, ages 9 and 7. Alma works as a salesperson in a department store, which requires her to work until 10 p.m. on weeknights. Ricardo has been truant from school and often arrives home well past midnight, in spite of his mother's requests that he stay home to watch over his younger siblings, making sure they do their homework and eat dinner. Ricardo refuses to cooperate, and the younger children are left unattended. As a result, the young ones have also become quite unruly and are getting bad grades. Alma came to her first session feeling disheartened and overwhelmed. She believes she has a choice between making enough money to house and feed her children or keeping a watchful eye over them to ensure their well-being. Meanwhile, Ricardo has been coming home with clothes that Alma knows are beyond their means, and he has been seen in the neighborhood in the company of older teens who are known troublemakers.

The first task of the therapist was to join with all members of the family. Because Ricardo is a powerful identified patient (IP; the family member with "the problem" who has to be "fixed"), the therapist took preliminary steps to ally with him by phone and made an appointment to see him alone on his turf. In that meeting, the therapist was able to convince him to attend a family session with the promise that she would help him eliminate the daily fights with his mother. The therapist appealed to Ricardo's Latinx cultural tradition of being the man in his family.

In the first family session, allying with the two younger siblings was accomplished quite easily by inquiring about their interests and praising them. Alma was quick to list the many sorrows and complaints she had been collecting, with a tone of pessimism and self-blaming for her many failures: "I have tried and tried, but it is just too much for me. I just can't go on trying to keep my job, pay the bills, and take care of these kids at the same time." The therapist was quick to move to Alma's side, empathizing with her situation: "I can imagine how hard this has been for you since your husband left; it is amazing that you have been able to keep your family together as well as you have."

Tracking and reframing, the therapist then elicited the support of Ricardo for his mother: "Did any of you know that your mother was feeling so desperate and so sad?" Ricardo took a while but eventually responded grudgingly, "She's having a bad time, but that doesn't mean she should take it out on me. I got a right to live my life too." The therapist said to Ricardo, "Please explain to your mother what you mean when you say, 'I have a right to live my life.' Tell your mother what that looks like. And don't just say, 'Leave me alone,' because you are smart enough to know that at 14, this is not something your mother can do." Ricardo explained, "I make my own spending money, and I got things to do with my time. And I am in charge of my own time."

The therapist remembered that conversations left at the level of behaviors do not overcome the mother–son impasse that brought them into therapy. This is what the family does at home, and the role of the therapist is to change that. To overcome the impasse, as is always the case, the therapist must move the conversation to a different level, to emotions:

> Mother, because you love Ricardo, you don't want him running around exposed to all the bad stuff that is going on at night. You want him home at 9 p.m., which is a reasonable time for a 14-year-old because you love him, and it is your job to protect him. Maybe you have been too busy fighting to remind him about your love for him. In your own words, let him know how you love him, why you love him, and what you particularly love about him.

After she did this, the therapist said, "Ricardo, let your mother know how it feels to hear these things from her, and make it more than just one word."

The love was always there but was buried by everyday stresses and hassles and by the bickering. The relationship has to be healed by bringing to the foreground the mother's love for Ricardo and Ricardo's love for his mother. Once this more positive bond is experienced by both Mom and Ricardo, the therapy can move to develop a more cooperative relationship between them.

Blended Families

The central and most unique issue for blended families is when the stepparent can become a full parent in parenting his spouse's children from prior relationships. The answer is simple. This process takes time, and it depends on the age of the child, but it has to be discussed on an ongoing basis. For a 2-year-old, it can happen relatively quickly; for a teenager, the process requires the development of a complex trusting relationship with a solid bond between stepparent and child. It also requires trust in the couple regarding parenting issues and negotiation about the rules that will guide their collaborative parenting.

At the beginning in a new blended family, the stepparent must allow the natural parent to do all the disciplining. It is only with the passage of time and the building of the stepparent and children's relationship that the stepparent acquires parenting rights and responsibilities. Most frequently, the problems encountered in therapy with blended families involve a stepparent (usually a man) who became involved prematurely or, at the other extreme, a stepparent who has been frozen out of parenting functions. In both cases, the work starts by facilitating a conversation between the stepfather and mother about their views on the stepfather's involvement in parenting functions to reach an agreement on parental role distribution.

SPECIAL CIRCUMSTANCES

Special circumstances require special consideration. Some of these include sexual abuse and domestic violence, when more than one family member has a clinical diagnosis, when a parent has a substance use disorder, and when family members attend sessions while intoxicated.

Sexual Abuse and Domestic Violence

In this section, we focus on two kinds of abuse: sexual abuse of the child within the family and domestic violence in the home. Among these situations, we distinguish between ongoing and past sexual or domestic violence. If either is present, the first order of business is to go into crisis-intervention mode to protect the victim. This is not BSFT. It is crisis intervention. After the victim and the rest of the family are in a protected environment, we begin BSFT, and in doing so, we have to make sure that the treatment plan includes a focus on the following three systemic maladaptations that characterize systems where sexual abuse and domestic violence have taken place:

- being part of an isolated family (the boundaries with the outside world are too rigid),
- having poor boundaries within the family (it is not clear where one person starts and the other ends), and
- keeping family secrets among family members that are also kept from outside family relations.

There are also cases in which the sexual abuse or violence occurred in the past, either within or outside the family. In families in which this has happened, there is often a dread of talking about it, and family members become somewhat withdrawn from each other—both of which are ways of avoiding talking about the problem. Because of the avoidance, the family is unable to process their traumatic experience, both as individuals and as a family. Individual therapies tend to focus on helping the individual process their experience, but this does not help change the avoidance that takes place in the family. Avoidance, by definition, does not allow the family to process the abuse. What is not fully recognized is that the violence is experienced not just by an individual but by the whole family. Therefore, the scars left by violence have to be healed at the family system level. For this to happen, we have to help the family overcome the hurt, fear, and embarrassment that feed the avoidance.

In the case of sexual abuse, when the abuser is a family member, there is likely complicity between the abuser and spouse or another authority figure in the family that permitted the abuse to occur. This "other" authority figure is often a spouse or wife who is so dependent on the abuser or husband financially and emotionally that she cannot confront the abuse. Most often, there is true denial in that the spouse or wife does not perceive the behavior as abuse or fails to accurately interpret the signs and symptoms happening in the family.

The live-in boyfriend of Ms. Ruru (Rosalina), Limont, has been insisting on having his 14-year-old stepdaughter, Sanaa, sit on his lap while watching TV, and he often "accidentally" comes into the bathroom while she is in it. He has been bringing her nice gifts, a behavior that Rosalina interprets as "trying to win Sanaa over as a daughter." Limont also comes to Sanaa's bed after her mother falls asleep. Since this started, Sanaa has been having trouble sleeping at night, her grades have suddenly dropped, and she tries to avoid coming home in the evenings by staying out late with her friends. She seems angry with her mother and snaps at her every chance she gets. Rosalina reports that when she tried to talk to Sanaa about her unacceptable behavior, Sanaa reacted strangely. First, she cried, then she verbally attacked her mother, and then she began to say things that Rosalina could not figure out, such as, "If you only had eyes for a change" and "You're so busy criticizing me that you don't know what's up." How is it that a mother does not see what is going on in her household? Rosalina had wanted to make this relationship with her boyfriend work. She had never been lucky in this regard: No relationship had lasted more than 2 years before this one. This relationship was now getting close to the 2-year mark, and she was hoping that everything would go well this time. This, in part, explains why Rosalina may not want to think negatively of the behaviors she may have observed.

Rosalina used to have women friends that she used to see after work and on the weekends. However, since she became serious with Limont, he has been jealous and does not want her to socialize when he is not with her. Consequently, she has lost contact with her women friends. Abuse grows and survives in an isolated family. It is often the abuser who encourages isolation. The first characteristic of families of abuse is isolation.

The second characteristic that occurs in families of abuse is a lack of interpersonal boundaries within the family. This is manifested in a bathroom that does not have a lock, allowing the boyfriend to walk into the bathroom when Sanaa is in the shower. In this family, there are no age-appropriate rules about protecting boundaries, and this allows Limont to ask his 14-year-old stepdaughter to sit on his lap.

The third condition for abuse is secretiveness. The abuser requires, demands, cajoles, and threatens the abused to ensure secrecy.

These families have all the mechanisms needed to allow sexual abuse and prevent it from being discovered. How to treat these families? Regardless of how families may differ, they all have in common the problems of isolation, poor interpersonal boundaries, and secrecy. The first step is to work with the mother and daughter, supporting the daughter to tell her mother about the sexual abuse. The therapist works with the mother to immediately file for protection that removes Limont from the home. The therapist will have to work with the mother's loss. Quickly, however, the whole family—the mother and two daughters—are brought together in therapy to help them talk openly and honestly about what happened to Sanaa and the family as a whole and how each of them feels about it. Issues that will be addressed include anger, resentment, forgiveness, apologies, reparation of the relationships, and reassurance that the mother will look after the safety of her daughters. The BSFT treatment plan must also address the other maladaptive interactional patterns that permitted the abuse. This includes reestablishing contact with extended family and friends, correcting the lack of adequate boundaries within the family, and committing to openness.

In her book *Sex, Love, and Violence: Strategies for Transformation* (Madanes, 1990), Cloé Madanes, a strategic family therapist, discussed the conflict between violence and love that gives rise to abuse, which in turn gives rise to relational trauma. She suggested that abuse affects the whole family, which makes the work on the family's relational trauma central to helping families of abuse. She also suggested that repentance and reparation have to precede forgiveness and psychological healing. When the abuse occurs between a teen and a younger child, Madanes works with the perpetrator to get him to ask for forgiveness, kneeling in front of his family. Every member of the family is then tasked to tell the perpetrator whether they think he is being truthful in his repentance and request for forgiveness. Then the family discusses how the perpetrator can make reparations to the victim. In a number of instances, the reparation has involved money, with the perpetrator getting a job to place money in the college fund of the victim. Then, each family member lets the perpetrator know whether they forgive the perpetrator.

Another important aspect of making the victim whole is that other members of the family have to take responsibility for their part. It is well known that when abuse occurs within the family, one or more family members had seen clues of what was happening, but often because of avoidance or denial, they either refused to believe what was happening or were too afraid to speak out. For this reason, relationships between the victim and other family members have also been damaged and have to be repaired.

From a BSFT perspective, the interactional changes that occur as a result of Madanes's suggestions include transforming the relationship between perpetrator and victim from hurt to healing. The power relationship between perpetrator and victim is reversed in that it is the victim who has the power to forgive. Denial and avoidance regarding the abuse are transformed when the family discusses the abuse and agrees to have the perpetrator ask for forgiveness, when each family member expresses whether they believe him, when each family member takes responsibility for their silence or blindness to the abuse, and when the family together determines a plan for reparation.

Dual Diagnoses

In our systemic perspective, we think of dual diagnoses as applied to an individual as well as to the family. In our experience with thousands of families, it is rare to find a family with a single problem. In families with an IP, typically more than one family member is symptomatic. When multiple family members have symptoms, it is difficult to address the problems of the IP alone without addressing the problems of other family members whose symptoms impact the IP. For example, families of acting-out children often present with a depressed parent. A depressed parent may be too hopeless and helpless to take charge of an acting-out child. Other times, when the parent has an agitated depression, the depression is displayed through high levels of negativity. Often the parent's depression has to improve for the relationship to improve and the acting out to disappear.

There is also a psychiatric definition of dual diagnoses that is applied to one person. In problem behavior or acting-out youth, different types of symptoms typically appear together in the same youth (Donovan & Jessor, 1985; Jessor & Jessor, 1977). Having worked with these youths for over 4 decades, we are puzzled by the thinking that dual diagnosis is something other than ordinary. It is rare to find a youth with one diagnosis who does not have a second diagnosis. Not surprisingly, all these symptoms recede when maladaptive interactions are transformed.

Drug- and Alcohol-Addicted Parents

In 2015, there were 7.7 million persons with an illicit drug use disorder in America, of which 855,000 were adolescents (Center for Behavioral Health Statistics and Quality, 2016). Our efforts are aimed not only at treating drug use and other problem behaviors in the youth but also at attempting to seek treatment for the youths' drug- and alcohol-addicted parents. As we indicated in Chapter 1, BSFT is not a treatment for severe adult drug or alcohol addiction. Nevertheless, depending on the severity of parental substance use, there are three potential approaches we have explored in our work. First, research has demonstrated BSFT's abilities to reduce alcohol consumption in parents with mild drinking problems (Horigian et al., 2015). This might occur in part because family interventions help reduce the stressful family events that trigger substance use in adults and reducing the enabling behaviors in family members that encourage helplessness or use in addicts.

Second, in the case in which the parent's substance use meets the criteria for moderate to severe diagnosis according to the *Diagnostic and Statistical Manual of Mental Disorders* (fifth ed.; American Psychiatric Association, 2013), we work with the family to get that adult into their own treatment. We have developed interventions that are specific to engaging adults with substance use disorders into treatment (Dakof et al., 2003). This does not preclude continuing BSFT because effective adult substance abuse treatment requires a family therapy component.

Third, when the substance-using adult does not want to enter their own treatment, it is not possible to successfully treat the child while the drug-using adult is living in the home. Effective treatment of a child's acting-out behavior, which may include drug use, cannot occur in the context of untreated parental substance use disorder. In this case, either the child or the drug-using adult has to be removed from the home. Although the therapist can encourage such a decision, the therapist typically does not have the authority to implement it. This requires either the family's firm action or the law to intervene. When a youth has to be removed from the home, the therapist can assist the legal system by identifying and engaging the extended family to explore with them the possibility of their taking responsibility for parenting the youth and thereby providing a drug-free environment.

Another important issue is that once the child is removed from the home of the substance-using parent, the parent may still disrupt the child's drug-free environment. An example is the case of an adolescent living with her grandmother. The adolescent's mother, the grandmother's daughter, is a methamphetamine user. The addicted mother "crashes" in her mother's home once every few weeks for several days, recovers, and then goes back on the street. When she comes into the household, she creates considerable havoc not only by demanding respect from her daughter but also because her drug-using friends are constantly dropping by, thereby sabotaging the grandmother's authority and the child's treatment.

The BSFT therapist must help the caretaking grandmother to establish firm boundaries with her drug-addicted daughter. This may take the form of a reframe in which the therapist suggests to the grandmother that because she loves her daughter, she should insist on her daughter going into treatment. The therapist might explain that the daughter is less likely to go into treatment when she has a warm and safe place in which to crash whenever needed. Thus, the grandmother's only possibility of ever helping her daughter is by making her home unavailable to the daughter as long as she is not actively in drug treatment. This action on the part of the grandmother has three functions. First, it keeps the home drug free, thereby protecting the recovery of her granddaughter. Second, it opens up the possibility that the daughter might be encouraged to go into treatment when she loses her safe place to crash. Third, it models the behavior that the granddaughter also has to follow to keep her drug-addicted mother out of her life as long as she is not in treatment.

Family Members Attending Sessions While Intoxicated

When a family member is intoxicated at the time of the family session, the therapist may make two errors. The first is to refuse to conduct the session. The second and more serious error is to conduct the session as if nothing unusual occurred. In BSFT, determining whether or not to have the session is a strategic decision for the therapist to make. The intoxicated family member may be an adolescent or an adult.

If an adolescent is intoxicated, it constitutes an enactment of what the family confronts at home that brought the family to therapy. It presents an opportunity to work with the family on how to respond to their adolescent at such times. The BSFT therapist can observe how each family member responds to this situation and look for the maladaptive interactions that allow this kind of behavior on the part of the adolescent to continue. The focus of the work is to diagnose the family's response to the intoxicated IP and restructure their maladaptive response. Often when the family responds as if nothing unusual is occurring, the first intervention is to highlight that the youth is intoxicated: "Wait a second, before we work on anything else, did you notice that this child is intoxicated? Talk about what you are going to do about it."

For example, the Hernandez family was referred to the clinic by the public defender at the time of Isabelita's third arrest, this time for drug possession. Isabelita was 15 years old. The therapist called the home and heard screaming and fighting in the background. The therapist spoke with the mother, who sounded overwhelmed. When the therapist explained that he was calling to set up a family session, Ms. Hernandez angrily told the therapist that she could never get Isabelita to come. The therapist asked Ms. Hernandez for permission to come to the home during a time in which she and Isabelita were both likely to be home. The therapist established that Mom, Isabelita, and a 12-year-old son lived at home and that Isabelita was not parented by anyone else. Because Ms. Hernandez worked as a domestic during the day, the appointment was set for 7 p.m. the next evening.

When the therapist arrived at the home, she found the mother alone with her son. Ms. Hernandez explained that Isabelita often stayed out with her friends, and she could not predict what time she would be home. The therapist began by joining with Ms. Hernandez and her son by listening to the story of their hardships as immigrants in this country. Mother discussed her concerns about Isabelita, who often gets home late and drunk. Ms. Hernandez expressed how overwhelmed she felt by Isabelita's behavior and that she did not know what she could do. In fact, she said, "It is all in God's hands now," as if there were nothing else she could possibly do. The therapist empathized with Ms. Hernandez and reframed the great concern that Ms. Hernandez was show-ing for her daughter, "You love your daughter a lot," to which Ms. Hernandez replied, "Of course, I do." The therapist said to the son, "Are you worried about your sister too?" He replied, "Yes, I am. And I hate to hear them fighting all the time." The therapist said, "Mom, when your daughter comes, I want you to not fight with her. Remember that you love her, and fighting has not helped Isabelita thus far."

A few minutes later, at about 7:30 p.m., Isabelita arrived intoxicated. It was obvious to the therapist that her gait was unsteady and her speech slurred. Her eyes were red. She barged into the home and went straight to the kitchen.

When Ms. Hernandez said to Isabelita, "Come here, there is someone here who has come to see you about your arrest," the therapist immediately said, "Hi Isabelita. I am happy to meet you." Isabelita answered, "F—k you both. I am hungry."

Ms. Hernandez went to the kitchen to serve Isabelita her dinner, screaming at her, "Your food is already cold. You are late again. We had dinner 2 hours ago." It is important at a time like this to help the mother make the choice that will set clear limits for Isabelita rather than enabling her being drunk. Enabling Isabelita takes the form of the mother giving Isabelita dinner at any time she comes home, drunk or not. Setting limits on Isabelita would require the mother to give her a clear message that when she comes home late and drunk, she does not get dinner here. The therapist guides the mother to help Isabelita get over her intoxication.

To address the enabling behavior, the therapist said,

> Mom, Isabelita came late and intoxicated, and I see you are serving her dinner. This sounds like you are giving Isabelita a confusing message. You are fighting over her being late for dinner and drunk, and yet, you are also serving her dinner. That doesn't make sense, Mom.

The mom replied, "I know, I know, but I don't know what I else to do. I tried everything. I have given up." The therapist continued, "Mom, you have not given up taking care of your daughter—you are still serving her dinner because you care for her and you love her. Right, Mom?" The mom responded, "Yes, of course, I care for her." The therapist said,

> You care for her, and you love her, but giving her dinner is the wrong thing to do when Isabelita comes home drunk. If you truly love her, you would not give her dinner, but you would help her to get out of her drunken state by putting her to bed. Let her know that you care for her and you love her. It would be best if tomorrow, when she is sober, the two of you talk about how you can best help her.

The therapist said to Isabelita, "Please know that I am looking forward to helping you in every way I can as soon your head is clear."

In a therapy process such as this one, where a dramatic reversal of the mother's usual response to Isabelita's drunkenness and lateness has occurred, the therapist works with the mother to discuss what may happen after the therapist leaves to empower and coach the mom to stand firm in her new stance. This will require exploring what challenges the mom expects after the therapist leaves, coming either from Isabelita or her protective feelings. We recognize that when giving tasks to the mother that have not been fully practiced before, the tasks may not be successful in the therapist's absence. Nevertheless, the therapist suggested to the mother,

> Mom, Isabelita may get up and demand dinner. What is important is that you not serve her dinner. If she wants to go to the refrigerator and eat, let her, but stay out and away from any confrontation. If she becomes violent, call the police. Mother, remember to be loving, and don't confront her or disagree with her. Tonight is not the time. Wait until she is sober.

If the mother says, "I don't know if I can do it. I've always taken care of my little girl," the therapist can respond,

> Mom, I know that you don't know what to do. That is why I am here, to show you something you have not tried before. What you have tried is taking care of your little girl by giving her dinner. Without you realizing it, the message she is getting is that it is okay to come home drunk.

Mom responded, "I know. She is getting worse all the time." The therapist said,

> Mom, I know how difficult it is for you to be firm with your daughter because you want to take care of her and give her dinner when she is hungry, even when she is drunk. We are going to try something you haven't tried before. I know you will do the right thing and not give her dinner when she is drunk because you love your daughter, and you want to do the right thing for her. Let's meet tomorrow again when she is sober.

The next day, the therapist came for the second session, and the same incident occurred with Isabelita coming home late, clearly drunk. Having already established a therapeutic relationship with Ms. Hernandez, while the therapist sat with her waiting for Isabelita to show up, the therapist used the time to coach the mom to be loving and firm with Isabelita when she arrived late: to remain calm, not let Isabelita engage her in a screaming match, and let Isabelita know that her mom loves her very much and that it is because she loves her and she is worried about her that she cannot act as if nothing is happening when, in fact, Isabelita is drunk. When Isabelita arrived, her portion of the family dinner had been placed in the freezer. As Isabelita came in the door, the therapist said, "I am glad you came. I have been looking forward to our work together." However, Isabelita, as usual, bolted to the kitchen and demanded food. Ms. Hernandez, encouraged by the therapist, continued to sit in the living room, which was just next to the kitchen in their small home. Isabelita came into the living room and began shouting at her mother about the food. The mother yelled back to Isabelita, "You are a drunk," and this began anew the cycle of blaming and recrimination. The therapist stood up, walked up to Ms. Hernandez, placed her hand on her shoulder, and said, "You have to stay calm and tell your daughter that you do not want to fight with her because you love her." After several such interventions, Ms. Hernandez finally looked at the therapist and said, "I am trying to do it, but it is very hard." This statement represented Ms. Hernandez's initial step in using the therapist to help her detach from the conflict with her daughter. The therapist said, "Yes, I know it is hard for you. Your love for Isabelita will help you. Tell her how much you love her and that you want the best for her." Mom did so.

Isabelita continued to scream at her mother without a response for another 15 minutes before storming to her bedroom in a fury. Having been unsuccessful in engaging her mother in a fight, she was frustrated and gave up. After the therapist gave the mother ample support and praise for controlling the situation and avoiding a fight and repeatedly telling her daughter that she loves her, the therapist moved the conversation to the next step of discussing with the mother other ways in which Isabelita is successful in getting her mother to act in ways her mother does not want to. The therapist gave Ms. Hernandez the task of using the newly learned skills on these other occasions.

This was a great gain for two sessions in 2 days, and the therapist followed up during the next session by praising Ms. Hernandez and Isabelita whenever they avoided a fight and offering empathy when they did not: "I understand how hard it is, but I know you tried." Mom and Isabelita had gone through 2 nights of nasty confrontation. They had done well since in minimizing their fights. Now it was time to rebuild their relationship.

When an adolescent comes into a therapy session intoxicated, we respond therapeutically differently than we would typically. Because Isabelita was intoxicated, we focused on having Mom change her behavior, do away with fighting, and tell Isabelita that she loves her instead, but she cannot serve her dinner when drunk. In the case in which any family member is intoxicated at the time of the session, the session is not conducted in the manner in which it was planned. This is also the case when an adult acts intoxicated. This is a time to refocus the session on the adult's intoxication. By the therapist making a statement such as, "Unfortunately, we won't be able to continue our regular work today," it serves to highlight to the family the severity of the problem that the adult is intoxicated. The therapist starts by pointing out why she is refocusing the session in a manner that opens up the discussion about the adult's intoxication: "I am so sorry that we cannot continue to do the work that we planned for this session because I need Mom's full brain during the session, and obviously she is not all here today." This typically opens up a conversation about Mom's substance use and the frustration the family feels about it. It also provides an opportunity to shift the identified patienthood from the adolescent IP to the mom. That in itself is a change in family focus from their frame about who is the IP to a relational focus in which family members discuss how Mom's problem is affecting the family, including the IP. As such, the therapist reprioritizes the treatment plan to focus on the parent who needs help. The first step is to determine whether the family recognizes Mom's intoxication as a problem. Provided the family does recognize the problem, Mom would be handled like anyone else the family recognizes as needing help. The difference here between a presenting IP and an adult is that with a presenting IP or adolescent, the family enters treatment having already identified and verbalized that the youth has a symptom. With the parent who uses, the first step is to help the family acknowledge that the parent has a symptom which is a jumping-off place to working on the family's problem that gives rise to the symptom.

KEY TAKEAWAYS

- When working with a family in their home, maintain leadership by setting clear expectations and boundaries and enforcing them consistently.

- Single-parent families are whole systems capable of successfully undertaking the same responsibilities as two-parent families.

- The central and most unique issue for blended families is when the step-parent can become a full parent in parenting his spouse's children from prior relationships. This process takes time, and it depends on the age of the child, but it needs to be discussed on an ongoing basis.

- When sexual or domestic abuse is ongoing, the first order of business is to go into crisis-intervention mode to protect the victim. After the victim and the rest of the family are in a protected environment, we begin BSFT.

- Families in which abuse has occurred typically present three problematic interactional patterns: isolation from the outside world, insufficient boundaries within the family, and secrecy. When sexual or domestic abuse occurred in the past, and they have avoided talking about it, the family has been unable to heal. A therapeutic goal is to help the family overcome the hurt, fear, and embarrassment that feeds the avoidance.

- In our experience, it is rare to find a family with a single problem or an acting-out youth with a single diagnosis.

- When a family member is intoxicated during the session, it is an important enactment of a crucial problem in the family. Such an enactment provides the opportunity to restructure the patterns of interactions that maintain the substance use by redirecting the session to the substance use problem.

Bringing It All Together

The Case of JJ

Many social systems interact with each other in ways that support or stress the family as a system. In Brief Strategic Family Therapy® (BSFT®), we choose to focus on the family because it is the most powerful and influential system in the development of its members. The family can reorganize itself to protect its members from social stressors. The family modulates the impact of the social context on its members. The more adaptive (e.g., nurturant, supportive) it is, the better the family can moderate the impact of social context influences on individual family members, particularly the young.

To be successful at moderating social influences, families have to support, love, and respect each other, communicate effectively, and parent children in a manner that results in healthy and adaptive development. The family's job is to create the conditions that allow each of its members to be the best person they can be. The family system should be at the service of the individuals. But as we have seen throughout this book so far, in clinical families, individuals' welfare is sacrificed for the sake of maintaining the family system's status quo, giving rise to symptoms in individual members.

The case vignette that follows elaborates on how an Afro Caribbean family was able to prevent their 15-year-old son, JJ, from becoming another incarcerated Black man in the U.S. prison system. We illustrate and provide commentary on the family systems at work and how the BSFT therapist worked with JJ's family to restructure their family script.

Our purpose in presenting JJ's extended case is twofold. First, we want you to challenge yourself to begin integrating what you have learned so far about

http://dx.doi.org/10.1037/0000169-010
Brief Strategic Family Therapy, by J. Szapocznik and O. E. Hervis

BSFT. As you read the vignette, stop reading periodically and put yourself in the position of JJ's therapist. Ask yourself, "What would I do?" or "What process is effectively being stopped in its tracks because of the rigidity of the family's interactional pattern? How might I join with this family member? What social issues directly affect JJ's family?" As you consider this latter question, reflect on the social contexts of the clinical families you see in your practice. How can you empower a parent to take charge? How can you empower adults to support one another and get on the same page? How can your families use social supports to cope with challenges such as long work hours, violent communities, minority stress, and more?

Our second purpose in including an extended case vignette here was to give you an idea of how the complete 12- to 16-week arc of BSFT works, from engagement to termination. We include transcript material for some sessions and summarize others. In this way, we hope to facilitate your ability to consolidate and synthesize what you have learned about BSFT in terms of its goals and prioritization of restructuring interactions, how to separate content from process, the importance of joining, the responsibility of the therapist as leader in the therapeutic system, and how the therapist elevates parents to leadership in the family system.

JJ'S CASE

Jamell Johnson (called JJ by his friends) was born in Jamaica of an African American mother and a Jamaican father. JJ came with his mother to the United States when he was 3 years old. He was 15 when he was referred by his juvenile probation officer. His family brought him to therapy with many complaints. He was not going to school, he had recently physically attacked his mother, and his mother said that he often came home drugged and was hanging around with older kids who got in trouble with the law. Mother had said that JJ lived with her and three younger siblings.

JJ was arrested for stealing a car to go for a joyride with his friends. He was taken to the juvenile assessment center, where a probation officer did an evaluation and determined that because the family was constantly fighting—JJ's mother told him to never come back—and there is such chaos at home, JJ should go to residential care. However, because Florida had at the time a program to divert youth to family-based interventions, JJ was reassigned to an agency that provided BSFT. In this case, none of the names are real.

ENGAGING THE FAMILY

The BSFT therapist assigned to JJ contacted the probation officer to learn more about the case. The therapist learned who JJ lived with and the reason for the referral and, of course, got contact information. The therapist then contacted the mother by phone to set up the first appointment. Remember that in BSFT, the therapist is interested in the first phone call to learn about the members of the family—that is, who is involved with JJ in caretaking or child-rearing roles and who else is involved in the daily life of the family, such as mom's live-in boyfriend, siblings, and other live-in extended family members.

In the following transcript, the left column shows what each person says, and in the right column, we explain what the therapist is doing and why.

Setting Up the First Appointment: The Phone Call With JJ's Mom

When the therapist called Ms. J (Mom), she introduced herself and explained that she had been assigned to the family.

THERAPIST:	I am your family therapist.	
MOM:	[*Angrily*] What? What do you mean the family's therapist? The only one that needs fixing here is JJ.	
THERAPIST:	Ms. J., you are angry, and I don't blame you a bit. You have every reason to be angry.	Joining by validating and empathizing with Mom.
MOM:	You damn right that I'm angry. I already told him I don't want him home. He is too much trouble. I have had it. He called me a bitch, and then pushed me, and I fell and hit my head and needed three stitches.	The therapist begins to diagnose high levels of negativity in the mom–son relationship.
THERAPIST:	Ms. J., you have had a very tough time. I am sorry that you have gone through so much, and I understand why you feel that you have had it with JJ. It sounds like you have tried everything. You have done all the things a mother could possibly do.	The therapist hears the pain behind the mother's statements.
MOM:	I sure have. I tried and have tried, and nothing works with that kid.	
THERAPIST:	I am sure you have! I have something I want to offer you, which has worked for many families that have gone through the same troubles you have. I am asking you to give me a chance to work with you and your family. I know that you and I working together are	The therapist engages Mom into family therapy by framing therapy as successful in families like hers, thus instilling hope.

	going to set your son straight. He has to respect you. I only need you to give me 12 weeks.	"Working together" strengthens the therapist–mom alliance.
MOM:	What? You gonna fix my kid? He is a mean kid.	
THERAPIST:	I know that you have had it with him. Most of the kids I work with are just like JJ. They don't respect their Moms. I have ways to turn that around. Just give me a chance. When would be a good time for me to come and meet with you, JJ, and your family? By the way, who lives at home?	
MOM:	Why do you need to know? The only one that needs fixing is JJ.	
THERAPIST:	It works better and faster when the whole family meets with me.	
MOM:	My other kids are doing fine; they are smaller, and I don't want them mixing with JJ's mess.	
THERAPIST:	Your kids live in your home. They see what's happening at home. They see when JJ pushes you. Because they see the JJ mess, they need to see how we fix it. They must also be upset, and we need to hear how they feel and what they would like to see happen.	The therapist reframes by providing a rationale why the other children have to be in therapy sessions, while reaffirming mom's view that the other children are fine.
MOM:	I have three young'uns. Lila is 11, Rod is 10, and Lanisha is 6.	Mom's response about her younger children shows that she accepted the reframe.
THERAPIST:	Oh, great. And who else lives in your home?	The therapist continues to explore who else might live in the home or be involved with JJ.
MOM:	No one.	
THERAPIST:	Anyone who takes care of the children besides you?	
MOM:	Yeah, their Grandma Louisa picks them up from school and takes care of them when I am at work.	

THERAPIST: Grandma is very important, and we need her help too. Can you get her to be home when I come to see you?

[*Mom and therapist agree to meet after her work, when she gets home and Grandma is still there. The therapist reviews with Mom that she and JJ, the three other children, and Grandma will be at home.*]

The therapist emphasizes the need for Grandma to participate by framing her as needed and important.

The therapist wants to ensure that Mom can bring everyone to the first therapy session.

MOM: Heck, I can't get JJ to be here. I can't get him to do nothing.

THERAPIST: I know all kids these days have cell phones. What is his phone number? It will be my job to get him to the meeting. You don't need to tell him anything.

The therapist diagnoses that JJ is more powerful than Mom. He will have to be engaged directly by the therapist.

MOM: Okay.

THERAPIST: Thank you, Mom, for your cooperation. I know that with you and I working together, we won't fail. It is great to see that you are willing to give me a chance.

The therapist is humble: "You are willing to give me a chance."

Setting Up the First Appointment: Phone Call With JJ

The therapist prefers in a case like this for Mom not to invite JJ to the meeting because Mom is likely to be angry and say something such as, "The lady is coming to help me fix you." That would likely increase JJ's desire to avoid the meeting. As in other cases with a powerful family member, the therapist reaches out directly to JJ, calling him on his cell phone. Accepting the identified patient's (IP's; the family member with "the problem" who has to be "fixed") power is an important aspect of joining. Even while accepting his power, however, note how the therapist positions herself as an expert and reframes "the work" as more helpful when the family is involved, just as she did with JJ's mom.

THERAPIST: [*Calling JJ on his cell phone*] Hello, JJ, my name is Ada. I work at Sanders Family Services. We are in your neighborhood, and we are the agency that your probation officer referred you to. Now, I am calling to set up a meeting with you and your family.

JJ:	You work for probation? What do you want?	
THERAPIST:	No, I don't work for probation. I work for Sanders Family Services. Whatever you and I talk about is confidential. That means that I cannot tell your probation officer about anything you say. The only thing I can tell your probation officer is how many meetings you came to.	The therapist reassures JJ that she is not part of the probation system, and that she will maintain JJ's confidentiality.
JJ:	So, what you want?	
THERAPIST:	I want to meet with you and your family. How does next Tuesday at 6 p.m. work to you?	The therapist defers to the IP's power by asking him whether the time is convenient for him.
JJ:	What you want to meet with my family for?	
THERAPIST:	Because I know they are giving you a hard time! I have worked with many kids who have these kinds of problems, and I always can help them when we work with the family.	The therapist reframes (sells) the therapy by attending to the IP's perspective and potential goals.
JJ:	Maybe I will be there, and maybe I won't.	
THERAPIST:	JJ, could you give me a more definite answer, please?	The therapist is respectful but insistent.
JJ:	OK, I will be there, but just one time.	
THERAPIST:	It will only be an hour. I am very much looking forward to meeting you. I'll see you then, next Tuesday at 6 p.m. at your home. Do you mind if I call you to remind you?	The therapist minimizes the inconvenience to the IP (i.e., "only an hour").
JJ:	Okay.	

THE FIRST THERAPY SESSION

The therapist's plan for meeting with JJ's family the first time is to create an effective therapeutic system with the therapist as its leader and develop enactments to observe the nature of interactions and thus diagnose the family system. During the first session, she will also begin to reduce negativity. She will begin to create a relationship with each member of the family.

One of the first steps we must take in therapy is to transform the negative interactions into positive ones, even before we fully understand the nature of the interactional patterns in the family. When strong bonds are present, even if they are negative, this work is easier because bonds are available to be transformed.

At 6 p.m. on Tuesday, JJ is not there. Mom is present with her three younger children, and so is Grandma. When JJ has not arrived at 6:05, the therapist calls JJ's cell phone.

THERAPIST:	Hello, JJ, I am here at your house. Are you on your way?	The therapist reaches out directly to JJ. Later in therapy, she will ask Mom to reach out, but in this first session, she continues to defer to JJ's position of power, while avoiding Mom calling and pushing JJ away from therapy.
JJ:	Yeah, yeah!	
THERAPIST:	[*To the family*] Is it okay with you all if we meet in half hour when JJ gets here? [*The therapist makes sure that JJ can hear her asking the question.*]	
MOM:	I told you JJ is no good.	
THERAPIST:	Mom, I know it is an imposition, but could we meet in half an hour?	The therapist minimizes the negativity by not responding to the "no good" comment and politely asks whether the session can be postponed to accommodate JJ. She does not want to set the precedent of initiating the session without everyone there.
MOM:	Okay, but he better be here.	
THERAPIST:	[*To Mom*] Thank you.	
THERAPIST:	[*To JJ*] Your family agreed to wait for you. We will all meet you here in half hour. Thank you, too.	
THERAPIST:	[*At 6:30 p.m.*] Thank you all for your willingness to reschedule the session.	
MOM:	You see, JJ can't be counted on. He comes and goes like he wants to. [*JJ comes in, and the therapist starts the session by thanking him for coming.*]	
THERAPIST:	Mom, I am going to get to know every-one a bit. I had a chance to talk with you earlier. Do you mind if I spend a bit of time with the rest of your family? Let me introduce myself. My name is Ada, and I like to work on first-name basis.	The therapist engages in maintenance (a joining technique) by making contact with every member of the family.

I am from Sanders Family Services, and I have come to work with your family. Who would like to introduce me to the Johnson family?

The open question is an exploratory task to allow the family's usual structure to emerge unaltered (enactment). This way, we can observe the patterns of interactions that will inform our diagnosis later on.

[*Lila, the 11-year-old, takes the lead in introducing the rest of the family. She introduces the children first, the grandmother, and the mother last.*]

A first glimpse of the hierarchy in the family is that Lila may be the second most powerful member of the family.

That Mom and Grandma did not take the lead suggests that they are not in powerful positions in the family.

[*In the conversation, Lanisha, one of the young children, mentions Milton. The therapist is interested in learning who Milton is and whether he is someone that lives in the household. As it turns out, Milton is Mom's live-in partner.*]

The therapist is alert to any other family members that might have to be included in treatment.

THERAPIST: [*To Mom*] How long have the two of you been together?

MOM: Five years about.

THERAPIST: [*To Lanisha*] You were really little when he came into your life. Do you ever do things together?

The therapist explores the extent to which Milton might be involved with the family, specifically, the children.

LANISHA: He takes me to school sometimes. And he takes me to the park sometimes.

THERAPIST: Gee, I am happy to learn about Milton. He seems to be important to many of you.

GRANDMA: He don't pay the bills, but he help out.

THERAPIST:	I would like for him to join us. Is he at home now?	Having determined Milton's role in the family, the therapist asks to include him in the session.
LILA:	I'll go get him.	Another show of Lila's leadership.
JJ:	I don't want him here. I thought this was about me, and I have nothin' to do with him.	The spontaneous enactment reveals hostility in the JJ–Milton relation-
THERAPIST:	I understand how you feel, JJ. How you feel is very important to me. And it is just because of how you feel about him that we need him here.	ship, which is another sign of how important Milton is to include in therapy.
		Joining is followed by reframing aimed at getting JJ to allow Milton to be part of the session.
MOM:	I am sick and tired of the fights between the two of you [*JJ and Milton*].	Confirmation of the JJ–Milton conflict and a possible indication of mother, Milton, and JJ being in a triangulated relationship.
	[*Milton walks in. The therapist thanks him for joining and lets him know they are just getting started with the meeting.*]	The therapist joins with Milton.
THERAPIST:	Now that all the family is together, let's start our work. What would the family like to fix?	Although the therapy started with the first phone call, the therapist emphasizes that the work happens only when the whole family is present and indicates to Milton that he has not missed anything.
		"What would the family like to fix?" is the "work" signal to the family that indicates that in this therapy we "don't just talk." Rather, we work to find solutions.

MOM:	We're here because JJ gives nothin' but trouble. He got arrested last time for stealing a car. He don't help at home. He don't listen. He pushed me, and I fell on the floor and had three stiches on my head.	Mom brings the focus back to JJ's identified patienthood.
JJ:	Because you threw a pan at me. Almost hit me on the head. Look, you still see the bump.	The therapist diagnoses that Mom and JJ are direct and specific with each other—a healthy communication flow. However, there is a lot of anger expressed in the form of blaming.
		The intensity of the interaction shows a strong connection between Mom and JJ, even though it is negative. The high levels of reactivity between Mom and JJ suggest an enmeshed relationship.
THERAPIST:	[*To Mom*] Wow, that is a lot of trouble. Sorry to hear the two of you are having such an ugly time with each other. But I hear something else. Even though it is not pretty, you two are very connected with each other. You immediately respond to each other. You both care what the other does. I have to believe that there was a time when you had a very nice relationship.	The therapist notes that JJ and Mom have strong affective bonds (that are negative now but may have been positive in the past) and that these bonds make working together possible, though not easy.
MOM:	You're right, it's not pretty. I am f---ing angry with JJ. I don't deserve how he treats me.	
JJ:	I don't deserve how you treat me either.	JJ diffuses by changing the direction of the conversation, moving the role of the greater victim from Mom to himself.

THERAPIST:	Yep, you sure have a lot of feelings about each other. And you know that families that feel so much anger are families that care about each other. I bet you're never so angry about the neighbor down the street. That's because you don't care as much. Grandma, when you hear them fighting like this, let them know how it makes you feel.	Dyads with so much negativity are usually enmeshed. The therapist has a choice of continuing to work on the dyadic conflict or moving the focus away from the conflict for a moment and toward how the conflict may affect other members of the family.
GRANDMA:	Makes me feel bad when they're fighting. They used to be so close when JJ was little. JJ's not so bad. She never listened when she was young, either.	
THERAPIST:	Grandma, please say that to your family instead of me.	The therapist decentralizes herself and tasks a family enactment. The therapist wants to reframe that mom and JJ's relationship was (is) close and was positive at one time.
GRANDMA:	They heard me.	
THERAPIST:	But I want you to tell them directly with me here because what you said is important, and I want to make sure they hear you.	The therapist insists on redirecting the conversation and emphasizes the importance of Grandma's statement.
GRANDMA:	[*Looking at Mom*] I can't stand your fighting no more. JJ's not so bad.	
THERAPIST:	Mom, what do you want to say to Grandma about that?	
MOM:	[*To Grandma*] What you talking? You were always busy with the little ones. Never minded me.	Mom diffuses by changing the topic to her relationship with Grandma when Mom was a child.
THERAPIST:	[*To Mom*] Do you agree with Grandma that you and JJ had a great relationship?	Although this is important, the therapist has to stop the diffusion to keep the family on one topic at a time.
MOM:	Yes, that's right. That is why it hurts me so much that things have gotten so ugly.	The negativity between JJ and Mom must be reduced in

THERAPIST: [*To JJ*] Do you also remember those good times with your mom when you were younger?

JJ: Yep! That is when she used to be nice to me.

THERAPIST: Let's make a deal that we are working to get those good times back, keeping in mind that JJ now is much older.

the course of the first session. For that reason, the therapist uses the rest of the first session to thematically deepen the reframes that were already introduced to the family about the meaning of hostility as connection and caring.

THERAPIST: Milton, how about you? How do you see all this?

For diagnostic and joining purposes, the therapist turns her attention to other members of the family.

MILTON: No ma'am. I not get involved with none of that. His momma don't want me interfering with her and JJ.

Milton is suggesting a triangle in which Mom and JJ are allied in keeping Milton out of their relationship.

THERAPIST: [*To the younger children*] Do any of you guys want to say something?

LILA: [*Answering for all*] We don't like them hollering all the time.

THERAPIST: I am not surprised that the younger children are upset by the fighting. But what the children missed is that behind this fighting, there is a lot of caring. Mom, you are very worried about the path that JJ's life is taking. That is why you get so upset. Please tell JJ, in your own words, what worries you about him.

The therapist highlights the children being upset, followed by a reframe about the caring between Mom and JJ.

The therapist tasks Mom to let JJ know that she is worried about him. These three steps— highlighting, reframing and tasking—constitute the restructuring sequence that directs Mom to communicate with JJ in a new and more positive way.

MOM:	I told him a million times that he is throwing his life away hanging out with those friends of his that are up to no good. But he won't listen.	In her usual negative way, Mom complains, although now the content is closer to a concern for JJ.
THERAPIST:	I can see that you want the best for JJ. You want to protect him from a life of trouble. He already got arrested a few times, and you don't want him to end up in prison.	Usually the task is not done the first time it is given. The therapist goes into "task-management" mode to break the task into parts to help Mom to carry it out. To achieve this, the therapist reframes again.
MOM:	Yeah, you are right. But he doesn't see that. He just thinks I want to boss him around.	
THERAPIST:	[*Softly*] Well, Mom, I want for you to tell JJ what your main worry is, but say it in a soft voice so that he knows that you're doing it because you care and not because you want to boss him around.	The therapist is much more specific when she retasks Mom to tell JJ "her main worry." The therapist models the caring tone and coaches Mom to say it softly, in a caring way.
MOM:	[*To JJ*] Like I said many times, if you keep doing what you're doing, one day you're going to end up in prison, and there goes your whole life.	
THERAPIST:	[*Leaning forward toward Mom*] Mom, let him know why you worry. You don't worry about the kids down the street. You worry about your son because he has a special place in your heart. Explain that to JJ.	The therapist is insistent, consistent, and persistent, critical qualities in a BSFT therapist.
MOM:	JJ, I don't want you to be in trouble with the law. I want you to do something with your life. To get a good job, to get married, and give me grandchildren.	
THERAPIST:	[*To Mom*] Because?	The therapist realizes that Mom has still not said that she cares, so she encourages Mom to do so.
MOM:	You are my son, and I care what happens to you.	

THERAPIST:	[*To Mom*] Well done. [*To JJ*] JJ, just for a moment put your guard down. Take a deep breath. And be honest. Tell her how it feels to hear what she just said to you—that she cares about what happens to you.	The therapist tasks JJ to listen to mom and be honest so that he can own Mom's feelings for him.
JJ:	She don't act like she cares. She act like I bug her.	
THERAPIST:	Mom, you need to say it again, and you need to say it with as many words as it takes so that he believes you and he hears your heart.	The therapist tasks Mom to do it again, with more depth and detail.
MOM:	You are my firstborn. I can still remember the first time I held you. I get real angry because you drive me crazy, but I love you just the same as I did then.	Mom completes the task given her: She communicates her caring without ambivalence.
	[*JJ smiles.*]	
THERAPIST:	JJ, are you ready to give your mother a hug? I know this is not fixed yet, but this is a good first step to stop all that ugly stuff that has been going on between the two of you.	To consolidate and reinforce the new interaction, the therapist moves to close the deal in which family members reinforce each other for the new interaction. In this case, the therapist does so by asking JJ to give a hug to his mom.
	[*JJ stands up and gives his Mom a hug.*]	
THERAPIST:	I am very proud of both of you. You rose above everyday ugliness. Mom, JJ, you are good people.	The therapist praises both of them and reinforces the frame that JJ is also a good person.

To sum up Session 1: We always want to close the deal in a session when there has been progress achieved as a way of leaving the family with a sense of accomplishment, a positive taste for the therapy, and a desire for more.

Diagnosis

This is a family that is strongly connected—with passion and intensity, although, more often than not, the connection is expressed with a negative quality. This overinvolvement and negativity are seen in the relationships between Mom and JJ, JJ and Milton, and Mom and Grandma, with Mom always playing a central role in each of these conflicts. The adult figures in the family are not in agreement, and thus, the adult "subsystem" is not working together. Grandmother supports JJ "against" Mom. JJ resents Milton, yet Milton is asked by Mom not to interact with JJ, which prevents Milton and JJ from developing a relationship. Thus, there are two triangles in the family.

Remember, we define a *triangle* as a conflict between two individuals (usually between two adult figures) in which a child (or another adult) is brought into the conflict in such a way that prevents the conflict from being resolved between the two individuals in conflict. One triangle is formed by Mom, Grandma, and JJ, in which Mom and Grandma disagree about JJ, with Grandma aligning with JJ and Mom being in conflict with both. The second triangle is formed by Mom, JJ, and Milton, with JJ aligning with Mom (in an enmeshed dyad) to not allow Milton to interact with JJ. Hence, Mom and JJ's alliance supports the disengagement between Milton and JJ. Interestingly, Milton and the rest of the family are not disengaged. As can be seen from both triangles and the role that Mom plays with the smaller children, Mom is central in this family.

Mom's parenting role is now ineffective. We might assume that this happened because developmental adjustments in the parent–child relationship did not occur as JJ entered adolescence. That is, she still tries to control JJ, a near-impossible task with an adolescent. In addition to the interactional patterns that are central to BSFT, we also heard from the younger children that they are negatively affected by the conflict in the family. Finally, we noted three instances of diffusion of conflict that, along with the triangles, prevent four dyads (Milton–Mom, Milton–JJ, Mom–Grandma, Mom–JJ) in the family from resolving their differences.

Several aspects of BSFT diagnosis are important to explain here. Perhaps most important is that in a short time, we can evaluate some of the essential interactional problems in the family that have to be corrected. This is key to the brevity of BSFT. The interactional patterns are quickly diagnosed, providing a road map to intervention. Although other patterns may surface later, in the first 15 minutes of the first session, there is much that we already know on which to build an effective treatment plan.

Early Treatment Steps

The first step in the treatment plan was to reduce the negativity between JJ and Mom. For that reason, throughout the first session, the therapist thematically deepened the reframes about the meaning of negativity as connection and caring. Research has shown that unless negativity is reduced in the first session, families drop out (Robbins, Alexander, Newell, & Turner, 1996; Robbins, Alexander, & Turner, 2000). This does not mean that we will get rid of all the negativity in the first session; rather, we start on the road to transforming the nature of the connection from negative to positive. In addition, the therapist targeted diffusion because it was impeding Mom and JJ from developing new and more positive interactions. Hence, the intervention to restructure diffusion this early was conducted in the service of reducing negativity.

SESSION 2

A focus on increasing positivity continues throughout all therapy. The plan for Session 2 is to restructure the Mom–Grandma–JJ triangle. To do so, the therapist will work in increasing the Mom–Grandma parenting alliance.

THERAPIST:	How is everybody? Lila, you had a soccer game. How did that go?	Every session starts with a short maintenance intervention, such as this one, to reestablish the therapeutic system.
MOM:	Oh, they always lose, but they have fun.	
THERAPIST:	How did your week go?	
GRANDMA:	Mom and JJ got at it again.	
MOM:	But it was only one time this week.	
THERAPIST:	Good, it is getting better already. What does the family want to work on this week?	This is the signal that work begins.
MOM:	JJ did not come home Tuesday and came home very late all week. He is taking drugs. When he came in a couple of nights, I hear it and got up. I saw his eyes when he came home—they were all red, and he smelled like he had been drinking too. And I got called from school that he did not show up to school Wednesday. Nothing's changed.	The therapist notes that except for the last phrase "nothing changed," Mom stated simple facts without the anger that she had the previous week. "Nothing changed" sounded more hopeless than angry.
THERAPIST:	Mom, tell JJ how you felt when you saw him in that condition.	This task is partly exploratory in that the therapist wants to explore the nature of interaction between Mom and JJ at this point. However, it also meant to move the session from behavior to emotions.
MOM:	I felt like choking him for doing this to me again.	

When families are so focused on behavior, it is helpful to move to affect to increase the family's repertoire beyond behaviors and thoughts. This is also a more constructive frame for family interactions.

THERAPIST: That is what you wanted to do because you felt angry. Besides angry, I want you to tell JJ how you felt seeing him in that condition.

MOM: I felt crushed.

THERAPIST: Tell JJ more about that feeling.

MOM: I felt it is hopeless. Afraid of what is going to happen to him. Where he is going to end up.

When the therapist asks the family to talk about feelings, it also places the therapist in a leadership role because feelings are not the language or experience of the family but of the therapist. The expression of feelings is an important area of therapist expertise.

THERAPIST: [*To JJ*] Let your mother know how it makes you feel when she talks like that.

[*JJ is quiet. He does not answer.*]

The therapist tracks by using Mom's statement as a springboard for asking JJ to share his feelings with Mom. This is an exploratory task to determine how JJ and Mom talk about feelings with each other.

THERAPIST: I know you have feelings. You are a human being, and all human beings like you and I have feelings. So, correct me if I am wrong, but I think that your silence says that it makes you sad when your mother talks like that. In your own words, tell your mother. It is very important that you tell your mother how you feel. How do you feel when your mother says she was crushed?

JJ: I don't want to hear that.

"I know you have feelings" is a way of highlighting that JJ is not being open. The reframe is that all humans have feelings. The therapist reframes the silence as sadness.

The task follows: "Tell your mother how you feel."

The therapist's affect has to demonstrate caring for JJ. Sometimes when a family member is not expressing affect, the therapist has to express affect that communicates that she cares.

This is a complete restructuring sequence: highlighting, reframing, and tasking.

THERAPIST:	Because when you hear that, it makes you feel . . .?	Therapist is insistent, consistent, and persistent.
JJ:	Bad.	This is JJ's first expression of feelings—he cares!
THERAPIST:	I am happy to see that you two care a lot about each other, even though the only way you have had to show that is by getting angry with each other. When I look at you when you say "bad" what I see is sad. So, let's try another way.	
	[The therapist moves Mom to the seat next to JJ.]	To facilitate direct communication between a dyad and further intensify the positive connection, the therapist brings the dyad close to each other and face to face.
THERAPIST:	Mom, take JJ's hand and look him in the eyes and tell him the truth, which is the only reason you get so angry is because you love him.	
MOM:	You know I get angry with you when you do something wrong.	
THERAPIST:	And you get angry when JJ does something wrong because . . .?	
MOM:	Because I worry about what's going to happen to you.	
THERAPIST:	And you worry because . . .?	
MOM:	Because you are my child.	
THERAPIST:	And what else?	
MOM:	Because I care for you.	

THERAPIST:	JJ, when you hear her say that, let her know how it makes you feel.	
JJ:	Good.	
THERAPIST:	"Good" is a 15-year-old way of telling your mom that you care for her too and you like hearing that. Is that right, JJ?	The therapist reframes that the scarcity of words is due to JJ being 15 and not that he does not care. Hence, the therapist gives a deeper meaning to JJ's "good."
JJ:	Yep!	
THERAPIST:	I want the two of you [*Mom and JJ*] to digest what just happened. You both said how much you care for each other. Seal it with a hug!	The therapist reinforces and, to close the deal, task JJ and mom to hug.
THERAPIST:	Lila, Grandma, anybody, let them know how you feel when you see this.	Now it is the moment to dissolve the JJ–Mom–Grandma triangle. The therapist opens to the rest of the family, expecting Grandma to attempt to reestablish her place in the triangle.
LILA:	[*With a big smile*] I like it. [*All children and Milton nod in approval.*]	
GRANDMA:	You see, I told you he was not such a bad kid. I wish it would last, but it probably won't.	
THERAPIST:	Mom, what do you want to say to that? Please talk with Grandma, not me. This is between the two of you.	
MOM:	This is what you always do. You always put me down, no matter what I do.	
GRANDMA:	I'm not putting you down. It's just that you have been fighting with JJ for 3 years.	
MOM:	You are probably right. He will find some new way to piss me off.	
GRANDMA:	You are too hard on him.	
THERAPIST:	There you go again, fighting instead of supporting each other. I can see you both love JJ, and what he needs is for the two of you to put your heads together and work together, instead of arguing. I need for the two of you	Highlighting conflict Reframing Highlighting "instead of arguing"

	to come up with a plan to have this wonderful thing that we just saw happen more often.	Tasking
GRANDMA:	Stop criticizing him all the time.	The task is diffused. The old pattern reemerges in an enactment that prevents Grandma and Mom from doing the task assigned by the therapist.
MOM:	Stop criticizing me all the time.	
THERAPIST:	There you go arguing again. Mom, I understand why you jump like that because your feelings are hurt. . . . Grandma, what you said to your daughter had a lot of truth in it, but the way you said it was hurtful to Mom. Can you give your daughter the same advice while showing the love you have for your daughter?	Highlight followed by reframe [*feelings are hurt*]. Reframe followed by a reconnection task
	[*Grandma is quiet, so that the therapist facilitates.*]	
THERAPIST:	Grandma, tell your daughter that you don't like to see her or JJ suffering and that is why you don't want to see them fighting. Please be more caring with your daughter when you talk with her about her handling of JJ. Show her that you love her and that is why you give her advice.	Reframe and task

The therapist lowers her voice and talks with Grandma with great sweetness to set the correct tone. |
| GRANDMA: | [*To Mom*] You know I love you; that is why I am always here trying to help you out. What I really meant is that we need to find a way to help JJ without hurting him. | The therapist adds specificity in an effort to prevent diffusion. |
| THERAPIST: | Grandma, that was very well said. Mom, you like it better that way, don't you? And JJ will too. I want to ask you to commit to each other that you will help each other without criticizing each other. Grandma, would you tell your daughter that you will do this? | Praise

Task |
| GRANDMA: | Yes, all I wanted to do is help her. | |

THERAPIST:	What do you want to say to your daughter about criticizing her?	Task management
GRANDMA:	I will try!	
THERAPIST:	I know you can do better than just try.	
GRANDMA:	Okay. I will do it. I will stop criticizing her, but she has to understand that when I tell her something it is for her own good.	
THERAPIST:	Good. But, for your daughter to understand that what you are saying is for her own good, you have to give her advice in a loving way. Let's try that now. Tell your daughter that when you tell her something it is for her own good, but say it in a very loving way.	Because that is "not good enough," the therapist continues to manage the task.
GRANDMA:	[*In a soft voice*] I only want the best for you and JJ. I will mind to give you advice in a loving way, like I am doing now.	
THERAPIST:	That is great, Grandma. Milton, Lila, kids, what do you think about your awesome grandma?	Praise followed by reframe
MILTON:	I like Grandma. I like this lady a lot. I'm happy they are getting 'long.	
	[*The kids laugh, and Lila gives Grandma a hug.*]	
THERAPIST:	Mom, what would you like to say to Grandma?	
MOM:	I like it! It feels good. I want my mother to be nice to me.	
THERAPIST:	Mom, Grandma, I want you to shake on it. [*They do.*] Good job, everyone.	The task is intended to close the deal, to have Mom praise Grandma's new behavior.
		The task is completed. The reversal of interactional patterns is completed. Deal closed!
		Praise of everyone

In Session 2, the relationship between JJ, Mom, and Grandma began with Grandma allied with JJ against Mom. With this triangle removed, Mom's ability to effectively parent increased. During Session 2, Grandma moved from attacking Mom on her parenting to cooperating with Mom on parenting JJ. The fact that Mom, rather than being undermined by Grandma, is now supported by her, begins to empower Mom.

SESSIONS 3 TO 5

For Sessions 3 to 5, the therapist continues to work on the positive communication between Mom and JJ and Mom and Grandma, to block diffusions, and to reinforce the cooperation between Mom and Grandma. This new alliance, Mom–Grandma, has become a more effective parenting subsystem. The focus of Sessions 3 to 5 is to continue to empower Mom as a parent by reinforcing the alliance with Grandma to effectively support Mom's role and to work on the Mom–JJ relationship to cooperatively negotiate a set of rules for his behavior. This builds a set of new interactions in which Mom and JJ collaborate in charting a new trajectory for him.

To portray Sessions 3 to 5, we present excerpts that are directly relevant to the major restructuring sequences discussed in this section. Milton was working out of town for 3 weeks, and we asked Mom whether she might have her sister babysit, which she did. Thus, we used these sessions to focus on Mom's parenting.

Session 3 began with Mom complaining that JJ arrived home at 3 a.m. the previous Tuesday, and he was obviously drunk and/or high. Mom, Grandma, and JJ were present.

MOM:	Last Tuesday, JJ came home at 3 a.m. drunk and drugged.	
THERAPIST:	JJ, talk to Mom about what happened.	Tracking for enactment
JJ:	[*To mom*] You think you know what I do. You had a big fit over nothing.	JJ diffuses by blaming Mom.
MOM:	You came at 3 a.m., and you were drunk. I know that. Of course, I have a fit. We've been over this all the time and you keep doing the same thing.	Mom is specific and direct.
THERAPIST:	Mom, I can see how powerless you felt. It seems that having a fit did not work for you again.	Reframe followed by highlight
MOM:	He keep doing the same thing.	
JJ:	Mom always having a fit.	

THERAPIST:	JJ, tell Mom if having a fit is going to change what you do.	Task
JJ:	No way. She's like a madwoman.	
THERAPIST:	Tell your mom what is like for you when she has a fit.	Task
JJ:	Don't bother me. I just ignore her.	
THERAPIST:	Mom, there it is. JJ is saying that he doesn't mind you when you have a fit. Grandma, in a very loving way, I want you to tell your daughter to stay calm and be in charge of herself, like the grown woman she is.	Highlight
		The therapist tasks Grandma to support Mom as an adult. If Grandma does so, it will continue to reinforce the Grandma–Mom alliance in which Grandma treats Mom as an adult by supporting her. It also continues to empower Mom as a parent.
GRANDMA:	Honey, stay cool and collected. You got do this right for JJ.	Grandma does the task and creates a motivational context for change by focusing on "doing this right for JJ."
THERAPIST:	Mom, you are the mom, and JJ needs to hear what you have to say. Mom, because you love JJ, I want you to tell him—like Grandma said—in a very calm and collected way so that we can be sure he is hearing you and not ignoring you what worries you when he comes home late and is drunk.	Reframe
		Task
		Note the specificity of the task directions.
	[*Mom does the task well. She tells JJ her worries and concerns and that she wants the best for him. The therapist praises Mom.*]	
THERAPIST:	JJ, tell your mother what you heard her say. Let's make sure you got her right because this is very important.	Task
		A frame that emphasizes that Mom is important
	[*JJ does a relatively good job of repeating in his short-of-words style.*]	

THERAPIST:	[*Praises JJ*] Hey, hey, high five. You got that right. . . . I always knew there was a very smart guy behind all this goofy stuff. Now JJ, tell Mom which of her concerns you think are valid and real. Tell her what she is right about.	The therapist praises JJ for his good job. Extra praise is given in an effort to elicit the best from JJ. The therapist will ask a lot from JJ [task], and this has to be preceded by strong praise and joining.
JJ:	[*Begrudgingly, to Mom*] Yeah, Mom. . . . I came late, and I know bad things happen out there in the street at night, but also anytime. I'll admit I been drinking and other stuff. But you never happy with me anyway.	
THERAPIST:	Mom, tell JJ how proud you are that he was honest.	Mom is tasked to praise JJ's honesty—a new behavior for JJ.
MOM:	It's not true I am never happy with you.	
THERAPIST:	Mom, please listen. I want you tell JJ that you are proud of him for telling you the truth. And don't say anything else.	Task management: The therapist has to be more specific with the task to avoid Mom saying something negative.
MOM:	Yeah, JJ. I'm proud of you. You telling me the truth.	This is a full reversal of a highly conflicted interactional pattern between Mom and JJ regarding his acting out behavior. JJ tells the truth, and Mom effectively praises him. She is now acting like an adult rather than ineffectively fighting like a peer.
THERAPIST:	I am very proud of all three of you.	The therapist praises all for a new set of interactions.

In Session 3, we exemplify an important belief underlying BSFT—that is, that the context of the family influences the child's behaviors. This means that when the child misbehaves, our treatment is to change the adults' behaviors to no longer enable the child's misbehavior. Enabling, in this case, occurs in a number of ways. For example, in the case of this family, it occurred first because Grandma undermined Mom as a parent and then later because

Mom's response to JJ's misbehaviors was ineffective. She was getting into fights with JJ that placed her at his level—as a teen, a mismanagement of JJ. Another way adults enable is by protecting the symptom by minimizing it (as Grandma did).

Moving Mom Into an Active Caretaker Role

Having accomplished a constructive interaction between Mom and JJ about her worries about his behavior, the therapist, with Grandma's support, empowers Mom to work collaboratively with JJ on setting rules and rewards to improve JJ's behavior. Although in the last session, Mom moved from peer to adult, in this session, she must grow into an adult caretaker for JJ.

MOM:	JJ came home late drunk again.	The therapist balanced Mom's negativity by eliciting the IP's positive accomplishments.
THERAPIST:	Anything good to report?	
MOM:	Yeah. He went to school every day.	
THERAPIST:	So, what are we going to work on today?	This is the work signal.
GRANDMA:	So, what are we going to do to stop all this nonsense?	
THERAPIST:	[*To Grandma.*] Good question. Ask Mom.	Joining followed by an exploratory task
GRANDMA:	Yes, honey. What are we going to do to stop all this stuff, once and for'll.	
MOM:	[*After a silence.*] I really don't know.	
THERAPIST:	I have a good idea that we can try, and it works for many families like yours. I want for you, JJ, to look inside your mind and your heart and, as honestly as you did last week, tell your mom what is going on that you drink and stay out to all hours and put yourself in danger.	The therapist places herself in the expert role and gives hope. Task ("I want for you, JJ"), reframe ("inside your mind and heart and, as honestly as you did last week"), highlight (put yourself in danger)
JJ:	Nothin'.	
THERAPIST:	JJ, how do you feel right now?	The therapist does some work with JJ to help him to move from "nothin'" to "something." This is
JJ:	Not so good.	
THERAPIST:	I can see that you look sad.	

JJ:	Don't know.	the kind of work we might do with an individual to enable him to behave in a new way within the family.
THERAPIST:	Tell me what makes you sad.	
JJ:	I never do nothing right at home. She's always picking on me. All kids drink and take drugs and come home late. Not only me.	
THERAPIST:	Mom, let him know why the other kids don't matter to you, that he is the only one that matters to you.	Task
MOM:	Yeah, JJ. You are my son. I don't care 'bout the others.	
THERAPIST:	Tell JJ why it is that you care for JJ and not the others.	
MOM:	Like I told him before, he's my first-born. And I love and I worry 'bout all my children.	
THERAPIST:	I want to ask the two of you to come up with a plan for JJ to feel that you are doing everything you can to make him feel good about himself. This plan needs to include house rules that protect him and reward him for when he does right. And I want you to do it together. And Grandma, you can chime in. Maybe you have some ideas too.	The therapist assigns a major task with specificity (do it together, include rules and rewards) about what Mom and JJ have to accomplish with Grandma's help.
MOM:	How do we do this?	
THERAPIST:	You are going to propose to JJ what you think are the important rules, one by one. For each rule, you and JJ are going to negotiate and come to an agreement on what you can both live with. The same thing goes with rewards. For rewards, JJ will propose what he wants and when, and then, you and him will negotiate what is possible and realistic.	In tasks that are this complex and difficult because of the give and take that is needed, all the previous interactional problems will surface again (e.g., negativity between Mom and JJ and Mom and Grandma, effort at diffusion). Thus, these tasks require a great deal of the therapist's attention so that she

		can be directive in managing these impediments to successful completion. The actual agreements will be left up to the family. The therapist's job is to facilitate constructive interactions while allowing the family to address the content as they deem appropriate.
JJ:	Yay. I propose that I get a Maserati. A white one, convertible.	JJ diffuses.
THERAPIST:	Back to the real world, back to Brooklyn.	Blocks diffusion
	[*All laugh*.]	Laughing is a good way to break the ice and to release tension.

The specifics of the plan of rules and rewards will be developed by Mom and JJ with Grandma's input. The therapist's job is not to get involved with the content of the plan but rather to facilitate the process of discussion and negotiation by preventing the family's previous maladaptive interactions from reoccurring, which would derail the family and thus prevent task completion.

Managing the Task of Family Rule-Setting

What the therapist does repeatedly is task management, a tedious therapeutic process in which a decentralized but directive therapist must be watchful of every move that will derail the process from the path to task completion. Examples of task management here include, in the first item that Mom raises, coming home late, Mom getting angry with JJ, the therapist reframing her anger as frustration, and tasking her to repeat her concern in a calm, collected voice. At another moment, Mom and Grandma speak at the same time, which occurs in enmeshed dyads. Talking over each other does not allow the members of the dyad to hear each other. Thus, the therapist has to intervene by asking them to speak one at a time, making sure they have listened to each other: "What you're both saying is very important [reframe], but you are not listening to each other [highlight]. Make it short and sweet [task]."

At the end of Session 4, the family has been able to agree on a reasonable curfew for a 15-year-old, with a longer curfew for Fridays and Saturdays, and the reward that JJ will receive for keeping curfew each week. The reward was set up in a progressive manner such that for each day that JJ comes home on time, he gets a reward, but when he comes home on time in consecutive days, the reward increases. Thus, for the second consecutive day, the reward would be larger than for a single day, and so on for each week, up to 7 consecutive days.

Rewards do not have to involve money. For example, they may involve having special time with someone they treasure, going on field trips, participating in team activities, having extra time on the computer or cell phone, getting a vacation from house chores, inviting friends for dinner, having a special meal, and so forth. Of course, for these rewards to be possible, entitlements such as cell phone and computer time must be limited, and the larger access to these become rewards for good behavior. Similarly, the rules setting has to ensure that JJ has house chores from which vacations can be awarded.

Session 5 continues to maintain all the gains of the previous sessions and to focus on the development of the plan of behaviors and rewards, including how the family will work together to help JJ eliminate his substance use. Kids who lack sufficient bonding with family and schools, who come from families in conflict, who have mental health challenges such as depression, and/or who come from families with poor parental leadership and monitoring and ineffective executive control are more likely to develop troublesome drug use. Before the youth can give up his substance use, the family conditions that create risk must be corrected, the youth will have to experience positive bonds with his family, and the parents will have to develop effective leadership skills. The central reframe that will permit this transformation of interactional patterns in the family will be, "Your mother loves you and is ready to do whatever it takes to help you be successful and happy."

SESSIONS 6 AND 7

As in other sessions, the therapist continues to work on previous gains to ensure their consolidation, including positive communication between Mom and JJ and Mom and Grandma. The therapist also plans to block diffusions and reinforce the cooperation between Mom and Grandma. This new alliance, Mom–Grandma, has become a new parenting subsystem. In addition, the therapist will continue to review progress in the maintenance of the plan for rules and rewards for JJ's behavior and reinforce the frame "that your mother is ready to help you, JJ, to make all the changes that will make you successful and happy."

The next major focus for restructuring in Sessions 6 and 7 will be dissolving the Mom–JJ–Milton triangle and, in its place, establishing a positive Milton–JJ relationship. The first step will be resolving the Mom–Milton conflict about his involvement with JJ. The second step, with Mom's support, will be to establish a positive relationship between JJ and Milton. We show next the critical restructuring excerpts for Sessions 6 to 7 regarding the dissolution of the Mom–Milton–JJ triangle. For these sessions, the therapist requested that the whole family come, but she especially wanted to ensure that Milton would be present. Thus, she reached out directly to Milton via phone to reconnect after he had been out of town for 3 weeks and to let him know how important it was for him to be present for the rest of the therapy.

JJ:	I got home by curfew every day this week except Friday. So, I got to spend Sunday with my favorite friend, my cousin from Long Island.	JJ feels a sense of progress. He is happier and accomplished.
THERAPIST:	Congratulations, JJ. That is wonderful. And congratulations to the whole family. You did a great job this week.	The therapist praises all for doing a good job.
	Milton, I am so happy you are back. Mom, do you mind if I ask Milton what he thinks about how well JJ is doing?	Joining ("happy you are back")
MOM:	Yeah, Milton, go ahead. Let him know.	The therapist remembers that Milton said that Mom did not want him interacting with JJ. Hence, the therapist respects the present structure.
MILTON:	Wow, JJ, you doing good. I know your mom is happy 'bout how well you're doin'.	The therapist is eliciting positive interactions between JJ and Milton where none existed before.
THERAPIST:	JJ, what do you want to say to Milton about that?	
JJ:	It's okay.	
THERAPIST:	What are we going to work on today?	Although the family has been working from the time they came into the session, the therapist acts as if JJ and Milton talking with each other is the most natural thing in the world and goes on to give the work signal, "What are we going to work on today?"
	[*Mom, JJ, and Grandma look at each other as if to say, "What do you think?"*]	
THERAPIST:	Well, I have an idea. Mom, now that we have Milton here, I want you to tell Milton what happened these last 3 weeks. Tell him what has changed.	The therapist tasks Mom to speak with Milton and provides task specificity that will have her treating Milton as someone in the family who has to
	[*Mom does so and tells Milton briefly about some of the rules and rewards that she likes.*]	

		be brought up to date and to discuss what has changed, some of which is changes in parenting.
THERAPIST:	Milton, what would you like to say to Mom about all the family has accomplished?	The therapist gives Milton a task that reinforces Milton's position as a member of the family rather than as just a romantic partner.
MILTON:	Good job. I guess you didn't need me after all.	
THERAPIST:	Mom, that cannot be true. You've told how much Milton does for this family. Tell him all the ways he is wrong about you not needing him. Tell him all the things he does that are helpful to you and to your kids.	Highlight ("that cannot be true"), reframe ("You've told me how much Milton does for this family"), task ("Tell him all the ways he is wrong about [that]")
	[*Mom begins to tell the therapist, and the therapist redirects her to speak directly to Milton.*]	Decentralizing
THERAPIST:	I would like the two of you to talk about how he could also help you in keeping JJ out of trouble.	Task This statement provides the opportunity to explore Mom's frame regarding Milton's role with regard to JJ.
MOM:	I don't know. Milton, don't fight with JJ. You and JJ can start getting along.	
MILTON:	I was not getting along because you told me not to interfere.	
GRANDMA:	Yeah, he is right.	Although this is a triangulation, it is harmless, and we do not want to deviate the direction of the work by attending to it.
THERAPIST:	JJ, we are talking about you, and you are saying nothin'. What do you have to say and to whom do you want to say it?	Highlight ("talking about you, and you are saying nothin'"), task ("What do you have to say?")
JJ:	I just don't need Milton bossing me around. I got enough with my mom.	

THERAPIST:	Having a good relationship with Milton doesn't mean that he is going to boss you around. Perhaps this is a good point for Mom and Milton to discuss. Mom, tell Milton how you see Milton and JJ getting along.	Reframe about the possible nature of the relationship between Milton and JJ in an effort to overcome JJ's fears, followed by task.
MOM:	[*To Milton*] JJ is a big boy; you're not his father, so I don't want you disciplining JJ.	
	[*The therapist worked with Mom and Milton to encourage Mom to clarify her expectations about the boundaries that she wants for Milton in regard to JJ: Mom wants to be the parent and wants Milton to support her in that role. If Milton agrees to not disciplining JJ, then Mom would allow Milton and JJ to have a nice relationship where they can share "guy" stuff. Once mother has expressed her wishes with clarity and Milton has agreed to her proposal, the dialogue continues.*]	
THERAPIST:	Good job, guys. I knew you could do this.	Praise
	[*In Session 7, the therapist asks Mom and Milton to remind JJ what Mom and Milton agreed to in the last session. After they finish, the therapist turns to JJ.*]	The therapist initiates a new set of interactions in which Mom and Milton collaborate in communicating to JJ their agreement.
THERAPIST:	What do you have to say about that?	
JJ:	What you want me to say?	
THERAPIST:	Say how you feel about it.	Tracking task
JJ:	About what?	
THERAPIST:	Mom and Milton, explain again to JJ what you would like to see happen between Milton and JJ.	Often when the client does not understand the task or know how to carry it out, the therapist has to break it down into smaller steps.
MOM:	So Milton can be like an uncle, but he's not going to be your father.	
JJ:	We'll see about that.	

Encouraging the Development of a New Family Relationship

It is important for Milton and JJ to have this conversation in front of Mom to ensure that the therapist can effectively block any of her attempts to reestablish the previous triangle. JJ has a lot of questions and reservations about how this could turn out. The therapist encourages JJ to ask all his questions of Milton to develop the dyadic relationship. The therapist tasks Milton to say to JJ, "I am not going to be disciplining you." To reassure Mom, the therapist also highlights that Milton is working within the framework that he and Mom agreed to. In spite of the therapist's efforts to reassure Mom, at one point, Mom tries to micromanage what Milton is saying to JJ. The therapist then gently says to Mom, "Let them work it out together. That is how good relationships are made." The therapist blocked Mom from becoming triangulated between Milton and JJ again. However, when Mom says, "But Milton doesn't understand," the therapist says, "Sorry, JJ, we are not quite ready for you yet. I would like to ask you to step outside for Mom and Milton to talk. And when they are finished, I will bring you back in."

Blocking Triangulation

When the therapist realizes that there is something with which Mom is not comfortable, rather than permitting a triangulation, she asks JJ to leave and goes back to facilitating a full resolution between Mom and Milton about the boundaries for the Milton–JJ relationship that are comfortable for Mom. The therapist is balancing the need for Mom to be sufficiently comfortable so that she does not have to interfere in Milton's conversation with JJ. The therapist wants Mom to say that she is entirely comfortable with the new Milton–JJ arrangement. In doing so, the therapist is taking every possible precaution to avoid Mom having an excuse for interfering again.

The therapist turns back to Mom and says, "Mom, I am sure that Milton wants you to be fully comfortable with how he is approaching JJ [reframe]." The therapist wants to check this out with Milton: "Right, Milton?" In this way, the therapist prevents her "mind reading" Milton. To Mom, she says, "If you still have some doubts in your mind, please ask Milton any and all questions that you need to be fully comfortable so that he understands exactly what it is you want [task with specificity]."

Once Mom clarifies her concerns, and Milton gives her further reassurance, the therapist asks Mom whether she has any other concerns. Once Mom says that she does not, the therapist is ready to call JJ back into the session to resume the building of the relationship between him and Milton.

SESSION 8

The overall plan for Session 8 is to continue to consolidate previous gains and to reinforce the budding Milton–JJ bond. The therapist requested that the whole family be present for this session. It was important to determine how the family would react to a newly formed JJ–Milton kinship. The therapist begins with some joining and maintenance, followed by the signal to work: "What does the family want to work on today?" As often happens, some of the old issues rear their head, and the therapist reestablishes the previous gains by preventing diffusion and triangulation. The therapist then states how proud she is of how far the family has come and goes on to invite the family to take the next steps.

Milton eagerly says, "I want to talk with JJ about how we are going to do things together," to which the therapist says, "Go ahead, Milton. That's a good idea. Talk with JJ." A similar process ensues as happened with Mom and Milton wherein JJ raised the many misgivings he had about a relationship with Milton. Again, concerns emerged about disciplining, setting boundaries, and making him do stuff he does not want to do. The therapist's primary job was to encourage JJ to be open and Milton to be reassuring. A couple of times, Mom chimed in, and the therapist gently turned the focus of the conversation back to JJ and Milton. The smaller children with whom Milton already had a relationship were concerned that this new relationship would compete with their relationships with Milton, and they too had to be reassured both by Milton and Mom.

At the end of the session, the therapist praised the family; in particular, she emphasized how well Mom, Milton, and JJ had worked together to begin to establish the relationship in a way that was comfortable for everyone. The therapist then asked each family member to praise each other for what had happened that day, at times prodding someone to give their praise. When Mom, Milton, and JJ praised each other for making this new relationship happen, it represented the closing of the deal.

SESSIONS 9 TO 12

Now that the major structural changes have been completed, the therapist turns her attention back to the presenting symptom. Before the therapist is able to address the issues that were the content of the most conflictive interactions, such as the presenting complaint, in this case, drug use, the therapist had to effectively reduce negativity, reestablish love bonds, and rewire the family in such a way that the adults in the family collaborated and/or supported each other (e.g., addressing alliances and triangles that undermine collaboration on parenting). Issues of hierarchy—Mom fighting with JJ as if she were another teen—had to be corrected before addressing the symptoms.

In the case of JJ's family, the better strategy was to reduce negativity and restructure maladaptive interactional patterns before addressing the presenting complaint. The anger regarding the symptoms did not make the symptoms amenable as contents with which to transform the many maladaptive interactional patterns in this family. Moreover, a youth such as JJ needs adults to care, validate, and love him. It might be said that there is anguish in JJ that arises from the hostility experienced at home, which is partially filled by his friends and medicated by his drug use.

Our general guidance is that in cases in which there is anger at the crux of the symptom, the therapist must first reestablish bonds of love and restructure maladaptive interactional patterns before the symptom can be addressed. However, in families in which the presentation is not anger but sadness, worry, or concern about the symptom, it is possible to organize the therapy immediately regarding the symptom as content.

Checking the Status of the Behavioral Contract

In Session 9, the therapist planned to explore how well the contract between Mom and JJ (with Grandma's support) was going.

MOM:	JJ comes home on time almost every day but never on Friday. His Friday curfew is 12, but he comes at 2 or 3 in the morning, and sometimes his eyes are red.	Mom, instead of being angry, as in early sessions, is factual in her description of the symptom, reflecting her growth as a parent and also that she did not feel as helpless as before.
THERAPIST:	Mom, please discuss with JJ what the two of you can do about that.	The therapist decentralizes herself by giving a task to redirect Mom to interact with JJ.
MOM:	What do you mean?	
THERAPIST:	It sounds like you have made a lot of progress, and yet I have a feeling that Mom doesn't know everything she needs to know about your life, but by now you know that you can trust her, that you know where she is coming from. Let's start with one thing at a time. Let's talk about the curfew first. So, start the discussion, JJ, by you telling Mom how come you are always late that one night.	Validation Highlight Reframe Task
MOM:	Yeah, JJ. How come you are coming late on Fridays?	
JJ:	Okay. This is how it goes: I am 16, and I have a girl. Her Friday curfew is later. I look bad if I can't stay with her until her curfew.	

THERAPIST:	Good job, JJ, for being so open with Mom. Mom, did you know about the girl?	Praise and validation
MOM:	No. He never tell me anything.	These statements show the new ability of the family to continue a conversation on their own, with Grandma supporting Mom and Milton reframing JJ's secrecy as it is "hard for guys to talk about this stuff."
GRANDMA:	He didn't tell me either.	
MILTON:	Sometimes it's hard for guys to talk about this stuff.	
THERAPIST:	JJ, let your mom know more about your girl.	Task. This kind of sharing is useful to set the context for a discussion on the curfew.
JJ:	She is in two of my classes, and she help me with homework.	
THERAPIST:	Mom, your turn to let JJ know what you think about that.	
MOM:	Doing homework is good.	Mom praises JJ's girlfriend.
THERAPIST:	In light of this new information, Mom, do you want to tell JJ what you want to do with the Friday curfew situation?	Task
MOM:	I don't know. He is coming with those red eyes.	
THERAPIST:	Yes, but we are going to discuss the red eyes in a minute. Now let's just fix the curfew problem. Tell JJ what you want to do about Fridays.	Task management by blocking diffusion Task
MOM:	Huh?	
THERAPIST:	Mom, do you want JJ to propose something? Ask him what he thinks would work to take care of your worries and help him with the girl.	The therapist proposes the give and take, in that Mom can ask JJ what he proposes. Task with direction (what will work).
JJ:	Yeah, that is a good idea. What about having a curfew of 1:30 on Fridays. I can stay with her till the end of her curfew at 1:00 and get home.	

THERAPIST:	Mom, does JJ's proposal work for you?	The therapist continues to facilitate the negotiation.
MOM:	Well, where does she live?	Most conflicts that emerge are not resolved because the parties do not know the concept of negotiation. It has always been who wins and who loses.
	[*JJ answers.*]	
MOM:	That is only 10 minutes away from here. I would agree to 1:15.	
THERAPIST:	Mom, that sounds good. JJ, I would take that deal if I were you.	
MILTON:	I would too. That's a good deal.	Milton supports Mom.
JJ:	Uh-huh.	
THERAPIST:	Mom, I know that we still have "red eyes" to deal with, and we will next time. Once again, you guys make me so proud. You did it again. What do the rest of you think?	The therapist reassures Mom that she has not forgotten her "red eyes" concern. Praise and validation.
	[*Family members congratulate JJ for his girlfriend and for agreeing with Mom about curfew without arguing about it.*]	The therapist asks other family members to praise Mom and JJ for a job well done.

Addressing Substance Use

Because of the focus on JJ's substance use planned for this session, the therapist requested that the smaller children not come. Grandma also did not come because she had to stay with them.

THERAPIST:	Last time you made terrific progress. How did the curfew go this week?	
MOM:	All right.	
THERAPIST:	Good. This week we said that we were going to work on the "red eyes" problem. Who wants to start?	This is the work signal.
JJ:	All my friends smoke pot.	
THERAPIST:	Mom, what do you want to ask JJ about that?	Task. The therapist asks the question in

a way that is likely to avoid a squelching response from Mom but to encourage dialogue that explores what is happening with JJ.

MOM: You also do pot?

JJ: Uh-huh!

MOM: And you also come home drunk?

Mom is able to ask JJ directly and calmly about his use of pot. This reflects the transformation in Mom–JJ interactions.

JJ: No, I'm never drunk. My girlfriend hates alcohol.

JJ's honesty with Mom also reflects this, as well as JJ's increased trust of Mom.

THERAPIST: Mom, it's great that you asked JJ straight out, and JJ, I am so proud of you being honest about your smoking pot.

Praise to Mom and JJ

MILTON: JJ, admitting it makes you a big man. I hope you're being honest about the drinking.

JJ: Sure I'm. I don't drink anymore. But pot is legal in this state.

MILTON: Not for 16-year-olds. You can get arrested, and any adult who knows you are smoking can also get arrested. Better let your girlfriend know.

MOM: Thanks, Milton. You mean I can get arrested because I know that JJ is smoking pot?

MILTON: I think so. And now, I also can get arrested because I also know. I am not going to jail for no teenager smoking pot.

Whereas Milton might have said this earlier with the effect of undermining Mom, he now waited until the therapist supported JJ's honesty before showing his own support, but he also challenges JJ on drinking.

THERAPIST: In the State of New York your children can be taken away if you are encouraging any of your children to use alcohol and drugs because they are illegal for a minor.

MOM:	[*Sounding desperate*] JJ, please don't get us into this kind of problem with the law. I don't want to have my children taken away from me. That would be too horrible!	
JJ:	I'm sorry I told you.	JJ tries to diffuse by changing the topic from his own use to whether or not he tells his mother he is using.
THERAPIST:	All of us who care about you are not sorry that you told your family. On the contrary. I know your family is glad that you did because now together you can put an end to this bad situation. Mom, work out with JJ what you are going to do.	Reframe

Task |
MILTON:	It is just a suggestion, but you could drug test him every weekend. Then you would know if he is using.	
MOM:	That is a good idea.	
JJ:	Hey, you are getting me in trouble with my girl. What'm I going to say to her when she's smoking and I am not?	
MOM:	I will talk with her mom.	
JJ:	Noooooo! Then she'll think I am a snitch.	
MOM:	How about you talk with her and let her know that I don't want to be arrested or lose my kids. And she got to do this for your family.	
JJ:	I can try, but she's not going to be happy.	
THERAPIST:	Every week I feel more and more proud about how well you all work on problems together. Soon you won't need me.	The therapist praises the family.

JJ's Family Masters Skills for Interacting Adaptively

As can be seen in the last couple of sessions, as families improve in their ability to communicate directly and specifically and resolve problems on their own, the therapist is less active because the interactional patterns in the family have improved, and thus, she does not have as much to do, beyond nudging them in the right direction. The next session continued the work on JJ's pot use. JJ spoke with his girlfriend. He said that he told her that smoking pot is illegal for 16-year-olds and that they were both less than the legal age for smoking pot. He said that now that he had told his mom, his mom could lose her children because she cannot allow a minor to use drugs. The girlfriend was shocked that little kids could be taken away. She also has a little sister. She agreed that she could do without it for JJ's mom and her mom. Mom and JJ agreed on drug testing once a week. The same rewards that were in the initial contract would be used for JJ's clean drug tests. At the end of the session, the therapist took Mom aside to tell her that the effects of JJ's last smoke could show up for up to a month in the urine drug tests. The rest of the therapy continued to review the gains made and goals achieved. Therapy was terminated at Session 12.

A therapist coming from other ways of working might wonder whether the family has to be prepared for termination. In BSFT, preparation for terminations begins in the first session. It takes the form of creating mastery of the skills the family needs to interact adaptively. Once the family is interacting adaptively, the therapist has successfully worked her way out of a job. The single most important job of the BSFT therapist is to work herself out of a job by always focusing the therapy on letting the family do the work.

KEY TAKEAWAYS

- The overall treatment strategy in BSFT is to steer the therapy to correct the maladaptive interactional patterns among family members.

- Maladaptive interactional patterns are first diagnosed in the first session. Occasionally, other interactional patterns emerge in the second session.

- To be able to diagnose the family correctly, the whole family must be present.

- BSFT Engagement assures that the whole family can be brought into treatment.

- The order in which maladaptive interactional patterns are addressed depends on the specific diagnosis, the urgency of the presenting symptom, and whether the symptom is surrounded by anger or sadness. Immediate attention is always given to reducing negativity through reframing (e.g., building bonds of trust and love) and restructuring the interactional patterns contributing to negativity as well as the interactional patterns that undermine parental leadership and effectiveness.

- In cases in which the anger is at the crux of the symptom, the therapist must first create bonds of love and restructure maladaptive interactional patterns before the symptom can be addressed. However, in families in which the presentation is not anger but sadness, worry, and concern about the symptom, it is possible to organize the therapy immediately around the symptom as content.

- The single most important job of the BSFT therapist is to work herself out of a job by always focusing the therapy on letting the family do the work.

Concluding Thoughts

We have a passion for our work. We hope that we have shared this passion with you, as well as our unshakable belief, built on 4 decades of clinical and research experience, that families are relatively easy to treat, with one caveat: We have to understand systems and patterns of interactions. We have to be able to join, lead, strategize, and change our old habits to enable us to change those of the family. Our work is infinitely hopeful. We firmly believe that when we are not making progress with a family, it is because "I," the therapist, must change my behavior. To the extent that I am willing and able to change my behavior in ways that will elicit love, bonding, constructive interactions, and dialogue, I believe that I can bring about the kinds of changes in patterns of interactions that will eliminate the family's pain. In Brief Strategic Family Therapy® (BSFT®), "the buck stops with the therapist."

This work requires a therapist who is mature and who does not need to seek nurturance from the family but rather is ready to generously allow the family to nurture itself. This work requires a therapist who can get close enough to the family to elicit the family's trust yet be able to maintain sufficient distance to permit her to see the family as a whole unit. This work requires a therapist with the ability to think abstractly to permit her to observe behaviors, organize them into patterns of interactions, and understand how several patterns of interactions are interlocked, resulting in one whole organism. The whole is not visible. Rather, she must be able to conceptualize it.

One aspect of BSFT about which we are passionate is its brevity, its ability to achieve its goals with swiftness and precision. Invariably, therapists who

http://dx.doi.org/10.1037/0000169-011
Brief Strategic Family Therapy, by J. Szapocznik and O. E. Hervis

watch our sessions are both amazed and puzzled by the speed of change. How do we create the swift pace that characterizes BSFT? First, the creation of the therapeutic system with the therapist as its leader places the therapist in a position to mobilize change quickly. Second, BSFT is a diagnostically driven therapy. That means that typically, in Session 1, we diagnose the interactional patterns that have to change, and this allows BSFT to be laser focused on making these changes happen. The diagnoses permit us to plan and strategize the overall treatment as well as each session so that not one minute of therapy is lost in trying to figure out what to do. We come into each session with a precise plan of what we must achieve and how to do it. Plans are always specific to each family's diagnosis and peculiar characteristics. Third, there are many contents to a family but few interactional patterns that have to be changed. The focus on process permits therapeutic gains to be generalizable to the family's many contents. Fourth, we capitalize on the family's relational energy (e.g., their fighting, their discontent, their struggle) to fuel therapeutic change, which we do with the ample use of reframes. Fifth, when we put all the BSFT elements together in defined sequences, they work seamlessly to transform maladaptive interactions into adaptive ones.

Finally, BSFT termination is not a separate element. Rather, we work on termination from Session 1 by placing the therapist in a decentralized position in which all the action and nurturance take place within the family, which incrementally increases the family's competence and mastery to manage its affairs. In the last session, termination consists of reminding the family of their outstanding achievements and validating the mastery they have already demonstrated. Hence, termination completes the work began in the first session to develop, validate, and consolidate the family's mastery and competence.

Another aspect of BSFT about which we are passionate is the ever-present strength orientation that is at the heart of every aspect of BSFT. We believe that love is abundant in families but is weighed down by conflict and distrust. Our job is to uncover the love that lies behind the relational pain in a family. We also believe that even in the case of what appears like meanness in a family member, we can uncover the humanity that hides within, leading thereby to a transformation of interactions.

We hope that by providing a variety of case examples with different family compositions and clinical dilemmas from different backgrounds and cultures, we have enabled you to reexamine scenarios you have encountered in your practice and reflect on how BSFT concepts and techniques could help, as they have with the thousands of families we have treated or supervised. We also hope that you have started to think about the next steps you should take to use BSFT in your practice.

To help you start thinking about how you will use BSFT in your practice, we invite you to reflect on your responses to the clinical scenarios provided in this book. Ask yourself, "Would BSFT help my clients? And if so, it is a good fit for me?"

What are the basic skills the therapist must learn to do BSFT? The first is being in the present. This is the kind of skill that is learned through meditation and mindfulness training. In BSFT training, we insist that clinicians attend solely to the here and now and teach them how to achieve this. This is needed because the other skill a therapist must learn is to attend to process. Attending to process means seeing the here and now interactions of the family as they emerge. Most often, families talk about the past and tell stories about past interactions. But our here and now comprises the interlocking sequences of behaviors among family members that occur in front of the therapist.

The therapist must also learn to be a leader and not a member of the family; to be like a choreographer and not a dancer (i.e., a leader who is directive but not intrusive); to be planful and not just flow with the emerging issues (i.e., set a path that changes interactions and stick with it); and to be persistent, insistent, and consistent and not let the family derail you from your planned strategy.

Finally, the therapist must learn the art of joining by developing a therapeutic system in which the family feels trusting, accepted, and safe. Once joined, she creates a motivational context for change that builds on two pillars: the art of highlighting what is occurring in the family in a way that is acceptable to the family and the art of reframing the behavior of family members in a positive way that opens new avenues for change. In this context, she can direct tasks that elicit these new behaviors, which form new and more adaptive interactions.

When we provide clinical training on BSFT, we prefer to train in teams of four therapists. To maximize the learning curve, a support system of therapists who work in the same manner is optimal. We often provide short overview training to acquaint therapists, program managers, and funders with the model. However, training in BSFT involves a long-term commitment that includes three workshops and ongoing supervised on-site work experience to achieve competence, followed by fidelity monitoring to ensure ongoing adherence. Ongoing monitoring is needed because research has shown that BSFT has an impact on youth and family only when it is done with good adherence (Robbins, Feaster, Horigian, Puccinelli, et al., 2011). We are thus committed to your outcomes: that you will continue to deliver BSFT with the quality required to positively impact the families that are your clients.

As in our work with families, in which therapy is often delivered in the family's natural environment, we prefer to teach BSFT in the therapist's or program's natural context. It is essential to have BSFT accommodate to your agency and specifically target your families. Consequently, training to competence and ongoing monitoring is conducted with a therapist's or agency's clients.

Beyond the purview of this book is the work we conduct with agencies to implement BSFT. This work includes aligning agency policies, organizational structure, service delivery to accommodate to the client population, referral patterns, intake processes, and funding support to sustain the BSFT program in the short and long term. Our implementation experience with community programs has shown that good family outcomes consistent with funder guidelines and goals are essential for ongoing funding.

More information on BSFT training and implementation can be found at http://www.bsft.org and http://www.bsft-av.com.

REFERENCES

Adalbjarnardottir, S., & Hafsteinsson, L. G. (2001). Adolescents' perceived parenting styles and their substance use: Concurrent and longitudinal analyses. *Journal of Research on Adolescence, 11*, 401–423. http://dx.doi.org/10.1111/1532-7795.00018

American Psychiatric Association. (2013). *Diagnostic and statistical manual of mental disorders* (5th ed.). Arlington, VA: Author.

Anderson, H., Goolishian, H. A., & Winderman, L. (1986). Problem determined systems: Towards transformation in family therapy. *Journal of Strategic & Systemic Therapies, 5*(4), 1–13. http://dx.doi.org/10.1521/jsst.1986.5.4.1

Baranowsky, A. B., Young, M., Johnson-Douglas, S., Williams-Keeler, L., & McCarrey, M. (1998). PTSD transmission: A review of secondary traumatization in holocaust survivor families. *Canadian Psychology/Psychologie canadienne, 39*, 247–256. http://dx.doi.org/10.1037/h0086816

Barber, J. P., Luborsky, L., Gallop, R., Crits-Christoph, P., Frank, A., Weiss, R. D., . . . Siqueland, L. (2001). Therapeutic alliance as a predictor of outcome and retention in the National Institute on Drug Abuse Collaborative Cocaine Treatment Study. *Journal of Consulting and Clinical Psychology, 69*, 119–124. http://dx.doi.org/10.1037/0022-006X.69.1.119

Barlow, D. H., Farchione, T. J., Sauer-Zavala, S., Latin, H. M., Ellard, K. K., Bullis, J. R., . . . Cassiello-Robbins, C. (2017). *Unified protocol for transdiagnostic treatment of emotional disorders: Workbook* (2nd ed.). New York, NY: Oxford University Press.

Barnes, G. M., Hoffman, J. H., Welte, J. W., Farrell, M. P., & Dintcheff, B. A. (2006). Effects of parental monitoring and peer deviance on substance use and delinquency. *Journal of Marriage and Family, 68*, 1084–1104. http://dx.doi.org/10.1111/j.1741-3737.2006.00315.x

Bava, S., & Tapert, S. F. (2010). Adolescent brain development and the risk for alcohol and other drug problems. *Neuropsychology Review, 20*, 398–413. http://dx.doi.org/10.1007/s11065-010-9146-6

Beck, J. S. (2011). *Cognitive therapy: Basics and beyond* (2nd ed.). New York, NY: Guilford Press.

Bengtson, V. L. (2001). Beyond the nuclear family: The increasing importance of multigenerational bonds. *Journal of Marriage and Family, 63*, 1–16. http://dx.doi.org/10.1111/j.1741-3737.2001.00001.x

Bögels, S. M., & Brechman-Toussaint, M. L. (2006). Family issues in child anxiety: Attachment, family functioning, parental rearing and beliefs. *Clinical Psychology Review, 26*, 834–856. http://dx.doi.org/10.1016/j.cpr.2005.08.001

Bowen, M. (1974). Alcoholism as viewed through family systems theory and family psychotherapy. *Annals of the New York Academy of Sciences, 233*, 115–122. http://dx.doi.org/10.1111/j.1749-6632.1974.tb40288.x

Boyd-Franklin, N. (2003). *Black families in therapy: Understanding the African American experience* (2nd ed.). New York, NY: Guilford Press.

Branje, S. J. T., van Doorn, M., van der Valk, I., & Meeus, W. (2009). Parent–adolescent conflicts, conflict resolution types, and adolescent adjustment. *Journal of Applied Developmental Psychology, 30*, 195–204. http://dx.doi.org/10.1016/j.appdev.2008.12.004

Broderick, C. B. (1993). *Understanding family process: Basics of family systems theory*. Thousand Oaks, CA: Sage.

Bronfenbrenner, U. (1996). *The ecology of human development experiments by nature and design*. Cambridge, MA: Harvard University Press.

Bronfenbrenner, U. (2005). *Making human beings human: Bioecological perspectives on human development*. Thousand Oaks, CA: SAGE.

Burkett, L. P. (1991). Parenting behaviors of women who were sexually abused as children in their families of origin. *Family Process, 30*, 421–434. http://dx.doi.org/10.1111/j.1545-5300.1991.00421.x

Campbell, B. K., Guydish, J., Le, T., Wells, E. A., & McCarty, D. (2015). The relationship of therapeutic alliance and treatment delivery fidelity with treatment retention in a multisite trial of twelve-step facilitation. *Psychology of Addictive Behaviors, 29*, 106–113. http://dx.doi.org/10.1037/adb0000008

Cano, M. Á., Schwartz, S. J., Castillo, L. G., Romero, A. J., Huang, S., Lorenzo-Blanco, E. I., . . . Szapocznik, J. (2015). Depressive symptoms and externalizing behaviors among Hispanic immigrant adolescents: Examining longitudinal effects of cultural stress. *Journal of Adolescence, 42*, 31–39. http://dx.doi.org/10.1016/j.adolescence.2015.03.017

Carlo, G., McGinley, M., Hayes, R., Batenhorst, C., & Wilkinson, J. (2007). Parenting styles or practices? Parenting, sympathy, and prosocial behaviors among adolescents. *The Journal of Genetic Psychology, 168*, 147–176. http://dx.doi.org/10.3200/GNTP.168.2.147-176

Casey, B. J., Jones, R. M., & Hare, T. A. (2008). The adolescent brain. *Annals of the New York Academy of Sciences, 1124*, 111–126. http://dx.doi.org/10.1196/annals.1440.010

Casey, B., Jones, R. M., & Somerville, L. H. (2011). Braking and accelerating of the adolescent brain. *Journal of Research on Adolescence, 21*, 21–33. http://dx.doi.org/10.1111/j.1532-7795.2010.00712.x

Casey Family Programs. (2017). *Implementing evidence-based child welfare: The New York City experience*. Retrieved from https://www.casey.org/evidence-based-child-welfare-nyc/

Center for Behavioral Health Statistics and Quality. (2016). *Key substance use and mental health indicators in the United States: Results from the 2015 National Survey on*

Drug Use and Health (HHS Publication No. SMA 16-4984, NSDUH Series H-51). Retrieved from https://www.samhsa.gov/data/sites/default/files/NSDUH-FFR1-2015/NSDUH-FFR1-2015/NSDUH-FFR1-2015.htm

Chen, X., Fu, R., & Zhao, S. (2015). Culture and socialization. In J. E. Grusec & P. D. Hastings (Eds.), *Handbook of socialization: Theory and research* (pp. 451–471). New York, NY: Guilford Press.

Chrousos, G. P., & Gold, P. W. (1992). The concepts of stress and stress system disorders. Overview of physical and behavioral homeostasis. *JAMA, 267,* 1244–1252. http://dx.doi.org/10.1001/jama.1992.03480090092034

Coatsworth, J. D., Pantin, H., McBride, C., Briones, E., Kurtines, W. K., & Szapocznik, J. (2002). Ecodevelopmental correlates of behavior problems in young Hispanic females. *Applied Developmental Science, 6,* 126–143. http://dx.doi.org/10.1207/S1532480XADS0603_3

Coatsworth, J. D., Santisteban, D. A., McBride, C. K., & Szapocznik, J. (2001). Brief Strategic Family Therapy versus community control: Engagement, retention, and an exploration of the moderating role of adolescent symptom severity. *Family Process, 40,* 313–332. http://dx.doi.org/10.1111/j.1545-5300.2001.4030100313.x

Crosby, R. A., DiClemente, R. J., Wingood, G. M., Harrington, K., Davies, S., Hook, E. W., III, & Oh, M. K. (2002). Low parental monitoring predicts subsequent pregnancy among African-American adolescent females. *Journal of Pediatric and Adolescent Gynecology, 15,* 43–46. http://dx.doi.org/10.1016/S1083-3188(01)00138-3

Dakof, G. A., Quille, T. J., Tejeda, M. J., Alberga, L. R., Bandstra, E., & Szapocznik, J. (2003). Enrolling and retaining mothers of substance-exposed infants in drug abuse treatment. *Journal of Consulting and Clinical Psychology, 71,* 764–772. http://dx.doi.org/10.1037/0022-006X.71.4.764

Dallos, R., & Smart, C. (2011). An exploration of family dynamics and attachment strategies in a family with ADHD/conduct problems. *Clinical Child Psychology and Psychiatry, 16,* 535–550. http://dx.doi.org/10.1177/1359104510387391

Dallos, R., & Vetere, A. (2012). Systems theory, family attachments and processes of triangulation: Does the concept of triangulation offer a useful bridge? *Journal of Family Therapy, 34,* 117–137. http://dx.doi.org/10.1111/j.1467-6427.2011.00554.x

D'Aniello, C., & Nguyen, H. N. (2017). Considerations for intentional use of self-disclosure for family therapists. *Journal of Family Psychotherapy, 28,* 23–37. http://dx.doi.org/10.1080/08975353.2017.1283147

Das Gupta, M., Zhenghua, J., Bohua, L., Zhenming, X., Chung, W., & Hwa-Ok, B. (2003). Why is son preference so persistent in East and South Asia? A cross-country study of China, India and the Republic of Korea. *The Journal of Development Studies, 40,* 153–187. http://dx.doi.org/10.1080/00220380412331293807

Diamond, G. M., Diamond, G. S., & Liddle, H. A. (2000). The therapist–parent alliance in family-based therapy for adolescents. *Journal of Clinical Psychology, 56,* 1037–1050. http://dx.doi.org/10.1002/1097-4679(200008)56:8<1037::AID-JCLP4>3.0.CO;2-4

Dishion, T. J., & Kavanagh, K. (2003). *Intervening in adolescent problem behavior: A family-centered approach.* New York, NY: Guilford Press.

Donovan, J. E. (2004). Adolescent alcohol initiation: A review of psychosocial risk factors. *Journal of Adolescent Health, 35,* 529.e7–529.e18. http://dx.doi.org/10.1016/j.jadohealth.2004.02.003

Donovan, J. E., & Jessor, R. (1985). Structure of problem behavior in adolescence and young adulthood. *Journal of Consulting and Clinical Psychology, 53,* 890–904. http://dx.doi.org/10.1037/0022-006X.53.6.890

Donovan, J. E., Jessor, R., & Costa, F. M. (1988). Syndrome of problem behavior in adolescence: A replication. *Journal of Consulting and Clinical Psychology, 56,* 762–765. http://dx.doi.org/10.1037/0022-006X.56.5.762

Donovan, J. E., Jessor, R., & Costa, F. M. (1991). Adolescent health behavior and conventionality–unconventionality: An extension of problem-behavior theory. *Health Psychology, 10,* 52–61. http://dx.doi.org/10.1037/0278-6133.10.1.52

Duncan, B. L., Parks, M. B., & Rusk, G. S. (1990). Eclectic strategic practice: A process constructive perspective. *Journal of Marital and Family Therapy, 16,* 165–178. http://dx.doi.org/10.1111/j.1752-0606.1990.tb00836.x

Duncan, T. E., Tildesley, E., Duncan, S. C., & Hops, H. (1995). The consistency of family and peer influences on the development of substance use in adolescence. *Addiction, 90,* 1647–1660.

Espelage, D. L., Bosworth, K., & Simon, T. R. (2000). Examining the social context of bullying behaviors in early adolescence. *Journal of Counseling & Development, 78,* 326–333. http://dx.doi.org/10.1002/j.1556-6676.2000.tb01914.x

Evans-Campbell, T. (2008). Historical trauma in American Indian/Native Alaska communities: A multilevel framework for exploring impacts on individuals, families, and communities. *Journal of Interpersonal Violence, 23,* 316–338. http://dx.doi.org/10.1177/0886260507312290

Fagan, R. (2006). Counseling and treating adolescents with alcohol and other substance use problems and their families. *The Family Journal, 14,* 326–333. http://dx.doi.org/10.1177/1066480706289651

Flückiger, C., Del Re, A. C., Wampold, B. E., & Horvath, A. O. (2018). The alliance in adult psychotherapy: A meta-analytic synthesis. *Psychotherapy, 55,* 316–340. http://dx.doi.org/10.1037/pst0000172

Flückiger, C., Del Re, A. C., Wampold, B. E., Symonds, D., & Horvath, A. O. (2012). How central is the alliance in psychotherapy? A multilevel longitudinal meta-analysis. *Journal of Counseling Psychology, 59,* 10–17. http://dx.doi.org/10.1037/a0025749

Fraga, M. F., Ballestar, E., Paz, M. F., Ropero, S., & Setien, F. (2005). Epigenetic differences arise during the lifetime of monozygotic twins. *Proceedings of the National Academy of Sciences of the United States of America, 102,* 10604–10609. http://dx.doi.org/10.1073/pnas.0500398102

Franck, K. L., & Buehler, C. (2007). A family process model of marital hostility, parental depressive affect, and early adolescent problem behavior: The roles of triangulation and parental warmth. *Journal of Family Psychology, 21,* 614–625. http://dx.doi.org/10.1037/0893-3200.21.4.614

Friedlander, M. L., Escudero, V., Welmers-van de Poll, M. J., & Heatherington, L. (2018). Meta-analysis of the alliance-outcome relation in couple and family therapy. *Psychotherapy, 55,* 356–371. http://dx.doi.org/10.1037/pst0000161

Galvin, K. M., Dickson, F. C., & Marrow, S. R. (2006). Systems theory: Patterns and (w)holes in family communication. In D. O. Braithwaite & L. A. Baxter (Eds.), *Engaging theories in family communication: Multiple perspectives* (pp. 309–324). Thousand Oaks, CA: Sage. http://dx.doi.org/10.4135/9781452204420.n20

Gaylord-Harden, N. K., Barbarin, O., Tolan, P. H., & Murry, V. M. (2018). Understanding development of African American boys and young men: Moving from risks to positive youth development. *American Psychologist, 73*, 753–767. http://dx.doi.org/10.1037/amp0000300

Gray, M. R., & Steinberg, L. (1999). Unpacking authoritative parenting: Reassessing a multidimensional construct. *Journal of Marriage and the Family, 61*, 574–587. http://dx.doi.org/10.2307/353561

Greenberg, L. S., & Safran, J. D. (1987). *Emotion in psychotherapy: Affect, cognition and the process of change.* New York, NY: Guilford Press.

Greenfield, H., & Sedaka, N. (1963). Breaking up is hard to do [Song]. On *Neil Sedaka sings his greatest hits.* RCA Victor. (Original work published 1962)

Haley, J. (1963). *Strategies of psychotherapy.* New York, NY: Grune & Stratton. http://dx.doi.org/10.1037/14324-000

Haley, J. (1971). *Changing families: A family therapy reader.* New York, NY: Grune & Stratton.

Halfon, N., Larson, K., Lew, M., Tullis, E., & Russ, S. (2014). Lifecourse health development: Past, present and future. *Maternal and Child Health Journal, 18*, 344–365. http://dx.doi.org/10.1007/s10995-013-1346-2

Halford, W. K., Sanders, M. R., & Behrens, B. C. (2000). Repeating the errors of our parents? Family-of-origin spouse violence and observed conflict management in engaged couples. *Family Process, 39*, 219–235. http://dx.doi.org/10.1111/j.1545-5300.2000.39206.x

Halik, V., Rosenthal, D. A., & Pattison, P. E. (1990). Intergenerational effects of the Holocaust: Patterns of engagement in the mother–daughter relationship. *Family Process, 29*, 325–339. http://dx.doi.org/10.1111/j.1545-5300.1990.00325.x

Hawkins, J. D., Catalano, R. F., & Miller, J. Y. (1992). Risk and protective factors for alcohol and other drug problems in adolescence and early adulthood: Implications for substance abuse prevention. *Psychological Bulletin, 112*, 64–105. http://dx.doi.org/10.1037/0033-2909.112.1.64

Held, B. S. (1986). The relationship between individual psychologies and strategic/systemic therapies reconsidered. In D. E. Efron (Ed.), *Journeys: Expansion of the strategic systemic therapies* (pp. 222–260). New York, NY: Brunner/Mazel.

Henneberger, A. K., Durkee, M. I., Truong, N., Atkins, A., & Tolan, P. H. (2013). The longitudinal relationship between peer violence and popularity and delinquency in adolescent boys: Examining effects by family functioning. *Journal of Youth and Adolescence, 42*, 1651–1660. http://dx.doi.org/10.1007/s10964-012-9859-3

Herz, L., & Gullone, E. (1999). The relationship between self-esteem and parenting style: A cross-cultural comparison of Australian and Vietnamese Australian adolescents. *Journal of Cross-Cultural Psychology, 30*, 742–761. http://dx.doi.org/10.1177/0022022199030006005

Hogue, A., Dauber, S., Stambaugh, L. F., Cecero, J. J., & Liddle, H. A. (2006). Early therapeutic alliance and treatment outcome in individual and family therapy for adolescent behavior problems. *Journal of Consulting and Clinical Psychology, 74*, 121–129. http://dx.doi.org/10.1037/0022-006X.74.1.121

Horigian, V. E., Feaster, D. J., Brincks, A., Robbins, M. S., Perez, M. A., & Szapocznik, J. (2015). The effect of Brief Strategic Family Therapy (BSFT) on parent substance use and the association between parent and adolescent substance use. *Addictive Behaviors, 42*, 44–50. http://dx.doi.org/10.1016/j.addbeh.2014.10.024

Institute of Medicine and National Research Council. (2015). *Harvesting the scientific investment in prevention science to promote children's cognitive, affective and behavioral health: Workshop summary.* Washington, DC: National Academies Press.

Jessor, R., & Jessor, S. L. (1977). *Problem behavior and psychosocial development: A longitudinal study of youth.* New York, NY: Academic Press.

Johnson, V., & Pandina, R. J. (1991). Effects of the family environment on adolescent substance use, delinquency, and coping styles. *The American Journal of Drug and Alcohol Abuse, 17,* 71–88. http://dx.doi.org/10.3109/00952999108992811

Kagitçibaşi, Ç. (1996). *Family and human development across cultures: A view from the other side.* Hillsdale, NJ: Erlbaum.

Karver, M. S., De Nadai, A. S., Monahan, M., & Shirk, S. R. (2018). Meta-analysis of the prospective relation between alliance and outcome in child and adolescent psychotherapy. *Psychotherapy, 55,* 341–355. http://dx.doi.org/10.1037/pst0000176

Kaslow, F. W. (Ed.). (1996). *Handbook of relational diagnosis and dysfunctional family patterns.* Oxford, England: Wiley.

Kazdin, A. E. (1992). Child and adolescent dysfunction and paths to maladjustment: Targets for intervention. *Clinical Psychology Review, 12,* 795–817. http://dx.doi.org/10.1016/0272-7358(92)90002-P

Knox, S., & Hill, C. E. (2003). Therapist self-disclosure: Research-based suggestions for practitioners. *Journal of Clinical Psychology, 59,* 529–539. http://dx.doi.org/10.1002/jclp.10157

Koerner, A. F., & Fitzpatrick, M. A. (2002). You never leave your family in a fight: The impact of family of origin on conflict-behavior in romantic relationships. *Communication Studies, 53,* 234–251. http://dx.doi.org/10.1080/10510970209388588

Krupnick, J. L., Sotsky, S. M., Simmens, S., Moyer, J., Elkin, I., Watkins, J., & Pilkonis, P. A. (1996). The role of the therapeutic alliance in psychotherapy and pharmacotherapy outcome: Findings in the National Institute of Mental Health Treatment of Depression Collaborative Research Program. *Journal of Consulting and Clinical Psychology, 64,* 532–539. http://dx.doi.org/10.1037/0022-006X.64.3.532

Laible, D., Thompson, R. A., & Froimson, J. (2015). Early socialization: The influence of close relationships. In J. E. Grusec & P. D. Hastings (Eds.), *Handbook of socialization: Theory and research* (pp. 35–59). New York, NY: Guilford Press.

Madanes, C. (1990). *Sex, love, and violence: Strategies for transformation.* New York, NY: Norton.

Madanes, C. (1991). Strategic family therapy. In A. S. Gurman & D. P. Kniskern (Eds.), *Handbook of family therapy* (Vol. 2, pp. 396–416). Philadelphia, PA: Brunner/Mazel.

Martin, D. J., Garske, J. P., & Davis, M. K. (2000). Relation of the therapeutic alliance with outcome and other variables: A meta-analytic review. *Journal of Consulting and Clinical Psychology, 68,* 438–450. http://dx.doi.org/10.1037/0022-006X.68.3.438

McComb, J. L., & Sabiston, C. M. (2010). Family influences on adolescent gambling behavior: A review of the literature. *Journal of Gambling Studies, 26,* 503–520. http://dx.doi.org/10.1007/s10899-010-9181-5

McEachern, A. G., & Kenny, M. C. (2002). A comparison of family environment characteristics among White (Non-Hispanic), Hispanic, and African Caribbean groups. *Journal of Multicultural Counseling and Development, 30,* 40–58. http://dx.doi.org/10.1002/j.2161-1912.2002.tb00476.x

McElhaney, K. B., Allen, J. P., Stephenson, J. C., & Hare, A. L. (2009). Attachment and autonomy during adolescence. In R. M. Lerner & L. Steinberg (Eds.), *Handbook of adolescent psychology: Individual bases of adolescent development* (pp. 358–403). Hoboken, NJ: John Wiley & Sons Inc. http://dx.doi.org/10.1002/9780470479193.adlpsy001012

Minuchin, S. (1974). *Families & family therapy.* Cambridge, MA: Harvard University Press.

Minuchin, S., Baker, L., Rosman, B. L., Liebman, R., Milman, L., & Todd, T. C. (1975). A conceptual model of psychosomatic illness in children. Family organization and family therapy. *Archives of General Psychiatry, 32,* 1031–1038.

Minuchin, S., & Fishman, H. C. (1981). *Family therapy techniques.* Cambridge, MA: Harvard University Press.

Minuchin, S., Rosman, B. L., & Baker, L. (1978). *Psychosomatic families: Anorexia nervosa in context.* Cambridge, MA: Harvard University Press. http://dx.doi.org/10.4159/harvard.9780674418233

Morris, A. S., Silk, J. S., Steinberg, L., Myers, S. S., & Robinson, L. R. (2007). The role of the family context in the development of emotion regulation. *Social Development, 16,* 361–388. http://dx.doi.org/10.1111/j.1467-9507.2007.00389.x

Muran, J. C., & Barber, J. P. (2010). *The therapeutic alliance: An evidence-based guide to practice.* New York, NY: Guilford Press.

Murphy, R., & Hutton, P. (2018). Practitioner review: Therapist variability, patient-reported therapeutic alliance, and clinical outcomes in adolescents undergoing mental health treatment—A systematic review and meta-analysis. *Journal of Child Psychology and Psychiatry, 59,* 5–19. http://dx.doi.org/10.1111/jcpp.12767

Nardone, G., & Watzlawick, P. (2005). *Brief strategic therapy: Philosophy, techniques, and research.* Lanham, MD: Jason Aronson.

National Academies of Sciences, Engineering, and Medicine. (2019). *The promise of adolescence: Realizing opportunity for all youth.* Washington, DC: National Academies Press. http://dx.doi.org/10.17226/25388

Noom, M. J., Deković, M., & Meeus, W. H. J. (1999). Autonomy, attachment and psychosocial adjustment during adolescence: A double-edged sword? *Journal of Adolescence, 22,* 771–783. http://dx.doi.org/10.1006/jado.1999.0269

Pantin, H., Schwartz, S. J., Sullivan, S., Coatsworth, J. D., & Szapocznik, J. (2003). Preventing substance abuse in Hispanic immigrant adolescents: An ecodevelopmental, parent-centered approach. *Hispanic Journal of Behavioral Sciences, 25,* 469–500. http://dx.doi.org/10.1177/0739986303259355

Patterson, G. R. (1982). *Coercive family process.* Eugene, OR: Castalia.

Patterson, G. R., Reid, J. B., & Dishion, T. J. (1992). *Antisocial boys.* Eugene, OR: Castalia.

Pequegnat, W., & Szapocznik, J. (Eds.). (2000). *Working with families in the era of HIV/AIDS.* Thousand Oaks, CA: Sage.

Perrino, T., González-Soldevilla, A., Pantin, H., & Szapocznik, J. (2000). The role of families in adolescent HIV prevention: A review. *Clinical Child and Family Psychology Review, 3,* 81–96. http://dx.doi.org/10.1023/A:1009571518900

Peterson, P. L., Hawkins, J. D., Abbott, R. D., & Catalano, R. F. (1994). Disentangling the effects of parental drinking, family management, and parental alcohol norms on current drinking by Black and White adolescents. *Journal of Research on Adolescence, 4*, 203–227. http://dx.doi.org/10.1207/s15327795jra0402_3

Pinquart, M. (2017). Associations of parenting dimensions and styles with externalizing problems of children and adolescents: An updated meta-analysis. *Developmental Psychology, 53*, 873–932. http://dx.doi.org/10.1037/dev0000295

Poasa, K. H., Mallinckrodt, B., & Suzuki, L. A. (2000). Causal attributions for problematic family interactions: A qualitative, cultural comparison of Western Samoa, American Samoa, and the United States. *The Counseling Psychologist, 28*, 32–60. http://dx.doi.org/10.1177/0011000000281003

Prochaska, J. O., & Norcross, J. C. (2014). *Systems of psychotherapy: A transtheoretical analysis* (8th ed.). New York, NY: Oxford University Press.

Rabkin, R. (1977). *Strategic psychotherapy: Brief and symptomatic treatment.* New York, NY: Basic Books.

Repetti, R. L., Taylor, S. E., & Seeman, T. E. (2002). Risky families: Family social environments and the mental and physical health of offspring. *Psychological Bulletin, 128*, 330–366. http://dx.doi.org/10.1037/0033-2909.128.2.330

Robbins, M. S., Alexander, J. F., Newell, R. M., & Turner, C. W. (1996). The immediate effect of reframing on client attitude on family therapy. *Journal of Family Psychology, 10*, 28–34. http://dx.doi.org/10.1037/0893-3200.10.1.28

Robbins, M. S., Alexander, J. F., & Turner, C. W. (2000). Disrupting defensive family interactions in family therapy with delinquent adolescents. *Journal of Family Psychology, 14*, 688–701. http://dx.doi.org/10.1037/0893-3200.14.4.688

Robbins, M. S., Feaster, D. J., Horigian, V. E., Puccinelli, M. J., Henderson, C., & Szapocznik, J. (2011). Therapist adherence in Brief Strategic Family Therapy for adolescent drug abusers. *Journal of Consulting and Clinical Psychology, 79*, 43–53. http://dx.doi.org/10.1037/a0022146

Robbins, M. S., Feaster, D. J., Horigian, V. E., Rohrbaugh, M., Shoham, V., Bachrach, K., . . . Szapocznik, J. (2011). Brief Strategic Family Therapy versus treatment as usual: Results of a multisite randomized trial for substance using adolescents. *Journal of Consulting and Clinical Psychology, 79*, 713–727. http://dx.doi.org/10.1037/a0025477

Robbins, M. S., Szapocznik, J., Alexander, J. F., & Miller, J. R. (1998). Family systems therapy with children and adolescents. In T. H. Ollendick (Ed.), *Comprehensive clinical psychology: Vol. 5. Children and adolescents: Clinical formulation and treatment* (pp. 149–183). Oxford, England: Pergamon. http://dx.doi.org/10.1016/B0080-4270(73)00123-1

Robbins, M. S., Szapocznik, J., Horigian, V. E., Feaster, D. J., Puccinelli, M., Jacobs, P., . . . Brigham, G. (2009). Brief Strategic Family Therapy™ for adolescent drug abusers: A multi-site effectiveness study. *Contemporary Clinical Trials, 30*, 269–278. http://dx.doi.org/10.1016/j.cct.2009.01.004

Roberts, J. (2005). Transparency and self-disclosure in family therapy: Dangers and possibilities. *Family Process, 44*, 45–63. http://dx.doi.org/10.1111/j.1545-5300.2005.00041.x

Robinson, B. E., & Post, P. (1995). Work addiction as a function of family of origin and its influence on current family functioning. *The Family Journal, 3*, 200–206. http://dx.doi.org/10.1177/1066480795033003

Robinson, C. C., Mandleco, B., Olsen, S. F., & Hart, C. H. (1995). Authoritative, authoritarian, and permissive parenting practices: Development of a new measure. *Psychological Reports, 77*, 819–830. http://dx.doi.org/10.2466/pr0.1995.77.3.819

Roche, K. M., Ensminger, M. E., & Cherlin, A. J. (2007). Variations in parenting and adolescent outcomes among African American and Latino families living in low-income, urban areas. *Journal of Family Issues, 28*, 882–909. http://dx.doi.org/10.1177/0192513X07299617

Rosman, B. L. (1978). *Family tasks and scoring.* Unpublished manuscript, Philadelphia Child Guidance Clinic.

Ruggles, S. (1994). The origins of African-American family structure. *American Sociological Review, 59*, 136–151. http://dx.doi.org/10.2307/2096137

Ryan, R. M. (1993). Agency and organization: Intrinsic motivation, autonomy, and the self in psychological development. In J. E. Jacobs (Ed.), *Developmental perspectives on motivation: Current theory and research in motivation* (pp. 1–56). Lincoln: University of Nebraska Press.

Sallis, J. F., Owen, N., & Fisher, E. B. (2008). Ecological models of health behavior. In K. Glanz, B. K. Rimer, & K. Viswanath (Eds.), *Health behavior and health education: Theory, research, and practice* (4th ed., pp. 465–485). San Francisco, CA: Jossey-Bass.

Santisteban, D. A., Coatsworth, J. D., Perez Vidal, A., Kurtines, W. M., Schwartz, S. J., LaPerriere, A., & Szapocznik, J. (2003). Efficacy of Brief Strategic Family Therapy in modifying Hispanic adolescent behavior problems and substance use. *Journal of Family Psychology, 17*, 121–133. http://dx.doi.org/10.1037/0893-3200.17.1.121

Santisteban, D. A., Szapocznik, J., Perez-Vidal, A., Kurtines, W. M., Murray, E. J., & LaPerriere, A. (1996). Efficacy of intervention for engaging youth and families into treatment and some variables that may contribute to differential effectiveness. *Journal of Family Psychology, 10*, 35–44. http://dx.doi.org/10.1037/0893-3200.10.1.35

Schwartz, O. S., Sheeber, L. B., Dudgeon, P., & Allen, N. B. (2012). Emotion socialization within the family environment and adolescent depression. *Clinical Psychology Review, 32*, 447–453. http://dx.doi.org/10.1016/j.cpr.2012.05.002

Schwartz, S. J., Unger, J. B., Baezconde-Garbanati, L., Benet-Martínez, V., Meca, A., Zamboanga, B. L., . . . Szapocznik, J. (2015). Longitudinal trajectories of bicultural identity integration in recently immigrated Hispanic adolescents: Links with mental health and family functioning. *International Journal of Psychology, 50*, 440–450. http://dx.doi.org/10.1002/ijop.12196

Schwartz, S. J., Unger, J. B., Baezconde-Garbanati, L., Zamboanga, B. L., Córdova, D., Lorenzo-Blanco, E. I., . . . Szapocznik, J. (2016). Testing the parent–adolescent acculturation discrepancy hypothesis: A five-wave longitudinal study. *Journal of Research on Adolescence, 26*, 567–586. http://dx.doi.org/10.1111/jora.12214

Sexton, T. L., & Lebow, J. (Eds.). (2016). *Handbook of family therapy.* New York, NY: Routledge.

Shearman, S. M., & Dumlao, R. (2008). A cross-cultural comparison of family communication patterns and conflict between young adults and parents. *Journal of Family Communication, 8*, 186–211. http://dx.doi.org/10.1080/15267430802182456

Shirk, S. R., & Karver, M. (2003). Prediction of treatment outcome from relationship variables in child and adolescent therapy: A meta-analytic review. *Journal of Consulting and Clinical Psychology, 71*, 452–464. http://dx.doi.org/10.1037/0022-006X.71.3.452

Stanger, C., & Budney, A. J. (2010). Contingency management approaches for adolescent substance use disorders. *Child and Adolescent Psychiatric Clinics of North America, 19*, 547–562. http://dx.doi.org/10.1016/j.chc.2010.03.007

Steinberg, L., & Morris, A. S. (2001). Adolescent development. *Annual Review of Psychology, 52*, 83–110. http://dx.doi.org/10.1146/annurev.psych.52.1.83

Stone, A. L., Becker, L. G., Huber, A. M., & Catalano, R. F. (2012). Review of risk and protective factors of substance use and problem use in emerging adulthood. *Addictive Behaviors, 37*, 747–775. http://dx.doi.org/10.1016/j.addbeh.2012.02.014

Strümpfel, U., & Goldman, R. (2002). Contacting Gestalt therapy. In D. Cain (Ed.), *Humanistic psychotherapies: Handbook of research and practice* (pp. 189–219). Washington, DC: American Psychological Association. http://dx.doi.org/10.1037/10439-006

Sullivan, S., Schwartz, S. J., Prado, G., Huang, S., Pantin, H., & Szapocznik, J. (2007). A bidimensional model of acculturation for examining differences in family functioning and behavior problems in Hispanic immigrant adolescents. *The Journal of Early Adolescence, 27*, 405–430. http://dx.doi.org/10.1177/0272431607302939

Szapocznik, J., & Coatsworth, J. D. (1999). An ecodevelopmental framework for organizing the influences on drug abuse: A developmental model of risk and protection. In M. Glantz & C. R. Hartel (Eds.), *Drug abuse: Origins and interventions* (pp. 331–366). Washington, DC: American Psychological Association. http://dx.doi.org/10.1037/10341-014

Szapocznik, J., Foote, F., Perez-Vidal, A., Hervis, O. E., & Kurtines, W. M. (1985). *One-person family therapy.* Miami, FL: Miami World Health Organization Collaborating Center for Research and Training in Mental Health, Alcohol and Drug Dependence, Department of Psychiatry, University of Miami School of Medicine.

Szapocznik, J., Hervis, O. E., & Schwartz, S. (2003). *Brief Strategic Family Therapy for adolescent drug abuse* (NIH Publication No. 03-4751). Rockville, MD: National Institute on Drug Abuse. http://dx.doi.org/10.1037/e598162007-001

Szapocznik, J., & Kurtines, W. M. (1989). *Breakthroughs in family therapy with drug abusing and problem youth.* New York, NY: Springer.

Szapocznik, J., & Kurtines, W. M. (1993). Family psychology and cultural diversity: Opportunities for theory, research and application. *American Psychologist, 48*, 400–407. http://dx.doi.org/10.1037/0003-066X.48.4.400

Szapocznik, J., Kurtines, W. M., & Fernandez, T. (1980). Bicultural involvement and adjustment in Hispanic American youths. *International Journal of Intercultural Relations, 4*, 353–365. http://dx.doi.org/10.1016/0147-1767(80)90010-3

Szapocznik, J., Kurtines, W. M., Foote, F., Perez-Vidal, A., & Hervis, O. (1986). Conjoint versus one-person family therapy: Further evidence for the effectiveness of conducting family therapy through one person with drug-abusing adolescents. *Journal of Consulting and Clinical Psychology, 54*, 395–397. http://dx.doi.org/10.1037/0022-006X.54.3.395

Szapocznik, J., Perez-Vidal, A., Brickman, A. L., Foote, F. H., Santisteban, D., Hervis, O., & Kurtines, W. M. (1988). Engaging adolescent drug abusers and their families in treatment: A strategic structural systems approach. *Journal of Consulting and Clinical Psychology, 56*, 552–557. http://dx.doi.org/10.1037/0022-006X.56.4.552

Szapocznik, J., Rio, A. T., Hervis, O., Mitrani, V. B., Kurtines, W., & Faraci, A. M. (1991). Assessing change in family functioning as a result of treatment: The Structural Family Systems Rating scale (SFSR). *Journal of Marital and Family Therapy, 17*, 295–310. http://dx.doi.org/10.1111/j.1752-0606.1991.tb00897.x

Szapocznik, J., Rio, A., Murray, E., Cohen, R., Scopetta, M., Rivas-Vasquez, A., . . . Kurtines, W. (1989). Structural family versus psychodynamic child therapy for problematic Hispanic boys. *Journal of Consulting and Clinical Psychology, 57,* 571–578. http://dx.doi.org/10.1037/0022-006X.57.5.571

Szapocznik, J., Rio, A., Perez-Vidal, A., Kurtines, W., Hervis, O., & Santisteban, D. (1986). Bicultural effectiveness training (BET): An experimental test of an intervention modality for families experiencing intergenerational/intercultural conflict. *Hispanic Journal of Behavioral Sciences, 8,* 303–330. http://dx.doi.org/10.1177/07399863860084001

Szapocznik, J., Santisteban, D., Rio, A., Perez-Vidal, A., Santisteban, D., & Kurtines, W. M. (1989). Family Effectiveness Training: An intervention to prevent drug abuse and problem behaviors in Hispanic adolescents. *Hispanic Journal of Behavioral Sciences, 11,* 4–27. http://dx.doi.org/10.1177/07399863890111002

Szapocznik, J., Scopetta, M. A., Aranalde, M. A., & Kurtines, W. M. (1978). Cuban value structure: Treatment implications. *Journal of Consulting and Clinical Psychology, 46,* 961–970. http://dx.doi.org/10.1037/0022-006X.46.5.961

Szapocznik, J., Scopetta, M. A., & King, O. E. (1978). Theory and practice in matching treatment to the special characteristics and problems of Cuban immigrants. *Journal of Community Psychology, 6,* 112–122. http://dx.doi.org/10.1002/1520-6629(197804)6:2%3C112::AID-JCOP2290060203%3E3.0.CO;2-R

Szapocznik, J., Scopetta, M. A., Kurtines, W. M., & Aranalde, M. A. (1978). Theory and measurement of acculturation. *Interamerican Journal of Psychology, 12,* 113–130.

Titelman, P. (2014). *Clinical applications of Bowen family systems theory.* New York, NY: Routledge. http://dx.doi.org/10.4324/9781315809717

Tononi, G., & Cirelli, C. (2006). Sleep function and synaptic homeostasis. *Sleep Medicine Reviews, 10,* 49–62. http://dx.doi.org/10.1016/j.smrv.2005.05.002

U.S. Census Bureau. (November 17, 2016). *The majority of children live with two parents* (Release No. CB16-192). Retrieved from https://www.census.gov/newsroom/press-releases/2016/cb16-192.html

Van Doorn, M. D., Branje, S. J. T., & Meeus, W. H. J. (2008). Conflict resolution in parent–adolescent relationships and adolescent delinquency. *The Journal of Early Adolescence, 28,* 503–527. http://dx.doi.org/10.1177/0272431608317608

Vostanis, P., Graves, A., Meltzer, H., Goodman, R., Jenkins, R., & Brugha, T. (2006). Relationship between parental psychopathology, parenting strategies and child mental health. *Social Psychiatry and Psychiatric Epidemiology, 41,* 509–514. http://dx.doi.org/10.1007/s00127-006-0061-3

Wagner, K. D., Ritt-Olson, A., Chou, C. P., Pokhrel, P., Duan, L., Baezconde-Garbanati, L., . . . Unger, J. B. (2010). Associations between family structure, family functioning, and substance use among Hispanic/Latino adolescents. *Psychology of Addictive Behaviors, 24,* 98–108. http://dx.doi.org/10.1037/a0018497

Wall, T. L., Garcia-Andrade, C., Wong, V., Lau, P., & Ehlers, C. L. (2000). Parental history of alcoholism and problem behaviors in Native-American children and adolescents. *Alcoholism: Clinical and Experimental Research, 24,* 30–34. http://dx.doi.org/10.1111/j.1530-0277.2000.tb04549.x

Walsh, F. (2012). Facilitating family resilience: Relational resources for positive youth development in conditions of adversity. In F. Walsh & M. Ungar (Eds.), *The social ecology of resilience: A handbook of theory and practice* (pp. 173–185). New York, NY: Springer. http://dx.doi.org/10.1007/978-1-4614-0586-3_15

Welmers-van de Poll, M. J., Roest, J. J., van der Stouwe, T., van den Akker, A. L., Stams, G. J. J. M., Escudero, V., . . . de Swart, J. J. W. (2018). Alliance and treatment outcome in family-involved treatment for youth problems: A three-level meta-analysis. *Clinical Child and Family Psychology Review, 21*, 146–170. http://dx.doi.org/10.1007/s10567-017-0249-y

Whitton, S. W., Waldinger, R. J., Schulz, M. S., Allen, J. P., Crowell, J. A., & Hauser, S. T. (2008). Prospective associations from family-of-origin interactions to adult marital interactions and relationship adjustment. *Journal of Family Psychology, 22*, 274–286. http://dx.doi.org/10.1037/0893-3200.22.2.274

Wiesel, E. (1986, October 27). One must not forget. *U.S. News & World Report*, p. 68.

Wight, D., Williamson, L., & Henderson, M. (2006). Parental influences on young people's sexual behaviour: A longitudinal analysis. *Journal of Adolescence, 29*, 473–494. http://dx.doi.org/10.1016/j.adolescence.2005.08.007

World Health Organization. (1992). *The ICD–10 classification of mental and behavioural disorders: Clinical descriptions and diagnostic guidelines*. Geneva, Switzerland: Author.

Wynn, T. A., Chawla, A., & Pollard, J. W. (2013). Macrophage biology in development, homeostasis and disease. *Nature, 496*, 445–455. http://dx.doi.org/10.1038/nature12034

Wynne, L. C. (1984). The epigenesis of relational systems: A model for understanding family development. *Family Process, 23*, 297–318. http://dx.doi.org/10.1111/j.1545-5300.1984.00297.x

Zeig, J. (Ed.). (1980). *A teaching seminar with Milton H. Erickson*. New York, NY: Brunner/Mazel.

INDEX

ABOUT THE AUTHORS

José Szapocznik, PhD, is the coauthor and codeveloper of Brief Strategic Family Therapy®. He is a professor of public health sciences, psychology, architecture and educational research, and counseling psychology at the University of Miami; director of the Brief Strategic Family Therapy Institute and the Center for Family Studies; codirector and multiple principal investigator of the Florida Node of the National Drug Abuse Treatment Clinical Trials Network funded by the National Institutes of Health (NIH); chair emeritus of Public Health Sciences; and founding and honorary director of the NIH-funded Miami Clinical and Translational Science Institute, all at the University of Miami Miller School of Medicine, and he is the founding chair of the NIH-funded National Hispanic Science Network on Drug Abuse. Dr. Szapocznik has held many policy roles, including membership in the NIH National Advisory Councils for the National Institute of Mental Health, the National Institute on Drug Abuse, the National Institute on Minority Health and Health Disparities, the AIDS Program Advisory Committee (now the NIH Office of AIDS Research), and the Substance Abuse and Mental Health Services Administration Center for Substance Abuse Prevention. His work has been recognized in awards and honors from the American Psychological Association, the American Family Therapy Academy, the American Association for Marriage and Family Therapy, the National Alliance for Hispanic Health, the Latino Behavioral Health Institute, and the Hispanic Health Professional Association, among others. He has received more than $125 million in NIH funding and has over 280 scholarly publications.

Olga E. Hervis, MSW, LCSW, is the coauthor and codeveloper of Brief Strategic Family Therapy® (BSFT®) and family effectiveness training. Since the 1970s, she has been developing family-focused models and designing and conducting training programs. In 2003, she founded the Family Therapy Training Institute of Miami (http://www.bsft-av.com) as a private effort to disseminate these models to behavioral and mental health professionals. She has extensively published in books and scientific journals and has been teaching family therapy for over 40 years. Ms. Hervis is an original founding member of the American Family Therapy Academy, a member of the American Association for Marriage and Family Therapy, and the International Family Therapy Association. She holds an MSW from Barry University and completed postgraduate training at the Ackerman Institute for the Family, the Philadelphia Child Guidance Clinic, the Gestalt Institute of New Orleans, the Gestalt Therapy Institute of Miami, and the Southern Institute of Neuro-Linguistic Programming. She has held academic positions at the University of Miami, Florida International University, and Barry University. Ms. Hervis has served on numerous national grant review committees for the National Institutes of Health and the Department of Justice and is a frequent consultant on scientific studies of family therapy. She has won numerous awards for BSFT, including the 2000 Exemplary Model in Substance Abuse Prevention Award presented to her and José Szapocznik, codeveloper of BSFT, by the Center for Substance Abuse Prevention in Washington, DC.